# CRITICAL ACCLAIM FOR
## *A WOMAN'S PASSION FOR TRAVEL*

"An enchanting collection that leaves one longing for more."

—Amazon.com

"*A Woman's Passion for Travel* is sometimes sexy, sometimes scary, some-times philosophical and always entertaining."

—*San Francisco Examiner*

"The threads that bind people to one another may be woven into dif-ferent patterns from one part of the word to the next, but they create the fabric of daily life, here examined in perceptive, often moving ways."

—*Trips*

"Exploration and discovery require an open mind and an open heart, and you'll find both in abundance in ⌐ collection of women's in-sights and tales of traveling around

—*Spa*

"This collection of essays mig⌐ ⌐t flight to someplace exotic."

'*king*

"Through stories of courage and confidence, ⌐ ⌐ro-spection, *A Woman's Passion for Travel* takes us clos⌐ of womankind. Each story will move you to get up an⌐

—*Palo Alto Daily News*

"*A Woman's Passion for Travel* is highly recommended for its significant and unique approach to the sharing of women's travels."

–*Library Journal*

"An exemplary collection of essays."

—*Kirkus Reviews*

"A diverse and gripping series of stories! These memorable vignettes of women's journeys around the planet will inspire readers to their own adventures."

—Arlene Blum, author of *Annapurna: A Woman's Place*

Travelers' Tales

# A WOMAN'S PASSION FOR TRAVEL

## True Stories of
## World Wanderlust

TRAVELERS' TALES

# A WOMAN'S PASSION FOR TRAVEL

## TRUE STORIES OF WORLD WANDERLUST

*Edited by*
MARYBETH BOND AND
PAMELA MICHAEL

*Series Editors*
*James O'Reilly and Larry Habegger*

TRAVELERS' TALES
SAN FRANCISCO

*Art Direction: Michele Wetherbee/Stefan Gutermuth*
*Interior design: Kathryn Heflin and Susan Bailey*
*Cover Photograph: © Frans Lemmens/Image Bank. Sand dunes of Temet.*
*Page layout: Patty Holden, using the fonts Bembo and Boulevard*

Distributed by: Publishers Group West, 1700 Fourth Street, Berkeley, California 94710.


Library of Congress Cataloging-in-Publication Data
A woman's passion for travel: true stories of world wanderlust/edited by Marybeth Bond and Pamela Michael.—1st ed.
     p. cm. — (Travelers' Tales)
  ISBN 1-932361-14-6 (pbk.)
 1. Travel—Anecdotes. 2. Women travelers—Anecdotes. I. Bond, Marybeth.
II. Michael, Pamela. III. Travelers' Tales guides.
  G465.W6452    2004
   910.4'082—dc22              2004018772

First Edition
Printed in the United States
10 9 8 7 6 5 4 3 2 1

*Do not follow where the path may lead.*
*Go instead where there is no path*
*and leave a trail.*

—MURIEL STRODE

# Table of Contents

## *Part Two*
## SOME THINGS TO DO

*Part Three*
GOING YOUR OWN WAY

*Part Four*
## IN THE SHADOWS

*Part Five*
THE LAST WORD

# Introduction

Only a few generations ago, women travelers were rare. Those who did venture out into the world almost always did so under the protection of a male relative, a father, husband, or son. Not a few solo women travelers—Alexandra David-Neel being perhaps the most famous—resorted to dressing as men in order to move about freely and with relative safety. Journeys were usually arduous and if they involved passion, an attitude toward travel celebrated in this volume, it was most likely in the archaic sense of the word: suffering.

For today's woman, though, travel evokes quite another kind of passion, defined as strength of feeling, boundless enthusiasm, eager desire, intensity, excitement, ardent love, lust. Perhaps the fervor with which women travel today is a response to our history of confinement and tethering, a joyous casting off of constraints. Whatever the reason—and who needs one?—more women are traveling than ever before. And quite a few of them are writing about their experiences.

As the growing body of women's travel literature suggests, women tend to make connections and build relationships on the road, seek contact with local people and cultures, and linger in one place. It has been said that women climb mountains not so much "because they are there," but for the journey itself—to see what's along the way as well as the reward of reaching the top.

Marybeth's first book of travel stories, *A Woman's World*, chronicled and celebrated the diverse and bold new ways women are exploring the planet. *A Woman's World* won the prestigious Lowell Thomas Award for Best Travel Book of the Year and elicited not only critical praise but thousands of letters from readers. Reactions were enthusiastic and—to invoke our current title—passionate.

"Sometimes in the frenetic pace of my everyday world, I lose that part of me that is so uniquely female. *A Woman's World* reawakened that wonderful place inside of me—and reminded me that I share it with every other woman out there. *A Woman's World* made me feel good about being a woman," wrote one reader.

Another letter read, "This was more than a book about travel for me—it was a book about living, about feeling, about learning, about loving. There are times in our lives when we all feel alone. I was at one of those places in my life when I read your book. What wonderful therapy! I came away still feeling alone, but feeling my strength in being a woman alone—and loving it."

A school librarian in Dyersburg, Tennessee lent the book to a friend who read one story a day to her dying mother. She wrote that her friend had found that the stories in *A Woman's World* were both healing and life-affirming. A high school English teacher used the book with her students to contrast with *Lord of the Flies*, in which there are no female characters. Ms. Halsey says "thank you for providing young women with confident, capable, adventurous role models as they move through such a period of upheaval in their lives, the teenage years."

Such heartfelt words inspired—almost compelled—us to begin work on a sequel to *A Woman's World*, which we've named *A Woman's Passion for Travel* to emphasize the zest, commitment, and tenacity of women travelers and travel writers alike. Once we began the search for stories, we were even more spoiled for choice than Marybeth had been the first time around. In considering stories for this collection, we were privileged to read a plethora of inspiring and remarkable tales. As women, our voices, our words, our stories are helping us understand and celebrate our collective experience and our individual strengths.

Through our travel we are able to act boldly and courageously, to see ourselves as the heroines of our own life stories. As the tales in *A Woman's Passion for Travel* attest, the richest vein of many women's life experience is mined on the road.

The stories we've collected come from women of all ages and all walks of life—college students, doctors, athletes, grandmothers, career women, and stay-at-home moms. Some, like Mary Morris, Frances Mayes, Anne Lamott, and Pam Houston, are well-known writers; a few will be familiar to Travelers' Tales readers; some are being published here for the first time.

The traveling women in these pages write about traveling alone, with a partner, a daughter, a lover, an entire reading group. They travel by train, plane, raft, dog sled, on horseback, on foot, on hope, and on adrenaline. They hail from diverse continents and cultures and bring a rich tapestry of insight and observations. In one story, Sekai Nzenza-Shand's "Following the Tracks Back," a woman's cultural background leads to self-discovery when she returns home to Zimbabwe with her new Australian husband to meet her family. In "An English Girl in Suez," Ann Mackintosh describes a tense visit to Egypt and her difficulty in adjusting to her daughter's adopted Islamic lifestyle.

As story after story here reveals, what makes a journey rich and memorable for most women is not so much the places we visit, but the people we meet. Indeed, developing or deepening a relationship can be the most important aspect of a journey; that relationship may be with ourselves, a travel companion, or someone met along the way.

Friendship is a common theme. In "A Russian Handshake," Barbara L. Baer recounts—and laments—a friendship with a mysterious Russian woman that began in India but could not survive decades of distance and Cold War. An impromptu outing in Barcelona with an older woman relieves exchange student Aleta Brown's loneliness in "Jump."

Another issue we as women face is our concern for our personal safety. Our very vulnerability can sometimes be an asset, however, for it often connects us with other women. We move more slowly through the world, perhaps because we are tuned in to the footsteps behind us.

Marybeth's story about a Mexican homestay with her two young daughters, "Guardians of the Dark," illustrates how women watch out for each other and how even when our backgrounds differ, we can nonetheless understand each other's fears and concerns. The night of terror in Paris described by Claire Tristram in "Why I Have Never Seen the Mona Lisa Smile" is a chilling reminder to all women about the special risks we face as women on the road.

As demonstrated throughout this collection, sometimes women use travel to discover themselves and to move forward in life, to make changes that would be harder to make at home. Pamela confronts Western consumption patterns and her own shortcomings on the banks of the Mekong in "The Boatman's Gift." Zoologist Rosiland Aveling is transformed by an encounter with a mountain gorilla in "Ndume." Laura Fraser seeks to heal the wounds of divorce in "Italian Affair."

Healing, adventure, romance, risk-taking, self-discovery, public service, scholarly explorations, escape, and pilgrimage—the variety of woman's travel pursuits provides a wealth of material and perspectives from which lives, literature, and legends are built. The stories women tell are an intimate record of culture and history. We invite you to walk with the women in these pages, to share their passion—not only for travel—but for life itself.

—MARYBETH BOND AND PAMELA MICHAEL

## PART ONE

# PASSION FOR TRAVEL

TANYA SHAFFER

# Looking for Abdelati

*An unexpected journey into the heart*
*of a family in Casablanca.*

HERE'S WHAT I LOVE ABOUT TRAVEL: STRANGERS GET A CHANCE TO amaze you. Sometimes a single day can bring a blooming surprise, a simple kindness that opens a chink in the brittle shell of your heart and makes you a different person when you go to sleep—more tender, less jaded—than you were when you woke up.

This particular day began when Miguel and I descended from a cramped, cold bus at 7 A.M. and walked the stinking, gray streets of Casablanca with our backpacks, looking for food. Six days earlier I had finished a stint on a volunteer project, creating a public park in Kenitra, an ugly industrial city on the Moroccan coast. This was my final day of travel before hopping a plane to sub-Saharan Africa and more volunteer work.

Miguel was one of five non-Moroccans on the work project, a twenty-one-year-old vision of flowing brown curls and buffed golden physique. Although having him as a traveling companion took care of any problems I might have encountered with Moroccan men, he was inordinately devoted to his girlfriend Eva, a wonderfully brassy, wiry, chain-smoking Older Woman of twenty-five with a husky Scotch-drinker's voice, whom he couldn't go more than half an hour without mentioning. Unfortunately, Eva

3

had to head back to Barcelona immediately after the three-week work camp ended, and Miguel wanted to explore Morocco. Since I was the only other person on the project who spoke Spanish, and Miguel spoke no French or Arabic, his tight orbit shifted onto me, and we became traveling companions. This involved posing as a married couple at hotels, which made Miguel so uncomfortable that the frequency of his references to Eva went from half-hour to fifteen-minute intervals, and then five as we got closer to bedtime. Finally one night, as we set up in our room in Fès, I took him by the shoulders and said, "Miguel, it's OK. You're a handsome man, but I'm over twenty-one. I can handle myself, I swear."

This morning we were going to visit Abdelati, a sweet, gentle young man we'd worked with on the project in Kenitra. He'd been expecting our arrival in Casablanca for a few days, and since he had no telephone, he'd written down his address and told us to just show up—his mother and sisters were always at home. Since my plane was leaving from Casablanca the following morning, we wanted to get an early start, so we could spend the whole day with him.

Eventually we scored some croissants and overly sugared *panaches* (a mix of banana, apple, and orange juice) at a roadside café, where the friendly proprietor advised us to take a taxi rather than a bus out to Abdelati's neighborhood. He said the taxi should cost twenty to twenty-five dirham—under three dollars—and the buses would take all day.

We hopped into a taxi, which took off with a screech of rubber before we'd agreed on a price.

"Forty or forty-five dirham!" the driver shouted over the roar of his engine. He was already careening around corners at top speed.

"Why isn't the counter on?" I asked.

"Broken!" he said.

Miguel rolled his eyes. "Eva would hate this," he whispered.

"If I had the counter, it would cost you fifty," the driver said.

Since the man in the café had told us twenty-five or thirty, I asked the driver to pull over and let us out. At first I put it politely: "We'd like to look at other options," but he simply said, "OK," and kept driving. After four such attempts, I said sharply, *"Nous voulons descendre"*—we want to get out.

Reluctantly he pulled over, saying we owed him ten dirham.

"Fine," I said. "Let me just get our bags down first—the money's in there." We yanked our backpacks off the overhead rack and took off, while the taxi driver shouted after us.

Miguel shook his head. "Eva would've killed that guy," he said.

It was an hour before we caught another taxi. Finally one pulled over, and a poker-faced man quoted us an estimate of eighteen to twenty dirham.

*"Très bien,"* I said with relief, and we jumped in. Apparently the address Abdelati had written down for us was somehow suspect, and when we got into the neighborhood, our driver started asking directions.

First he asked a cop, who scratched his head and asked our nationalities, looking at our grimy faces and scraggly attire with a kind of bemused fondness. After more small talk, he pointed vaguely to a park a few blocks away. There a group of barefoot seven- or eight-year-old boys were kicking a soccer ball. Our driver asked where Abdelati's house was, and one of the boys said Abdelati had moved, but he could take us to the new house. This seemed a bit odd to me, since Abdelati had just given me the address a week ago, but since a similar thing had happened in Fès, I chalked it up as another Moroccan mystery and didn't worry about it too much.

The little boy came with us in the cab, full of his own importance, squirming and twisting to wave at other children as we inched down the narrow, winding roads. Finally the little boy pointed to a house, and our driver went to the door and inquired. He came back to the cab saying Abdelati's sister was in this house visiting friends and would come along to show us where they lived.

Soon a beautiful girl of about sixteen emerged from the house. She was dressed in a Western skirt and blouse, which surprised me, since Abdelati's strong religious beliefs and upright demeanor had made me think he came from a more traditional family. Another thing that surprised me was her skin color. Whereas Abdelati looked very African, this young woman was an olive-skinned Arab.

Still, I'd seen other unusual familial combinations in Morocco's complex racial mosaic, so I didn't give it too much thought.

We waited in the yard while the sister went in and returned accompanied by her mother, sisters, and brother-in-law, all of whom greeted us with cautious warmth. Unlike the younger girl, the older sisters were wearing traditional robes, though their faces were not veiled. You see a range of orthodoxy in Moroccan cities, caught as they are between Europe and the Arab world. From the younger sister's skirt and blouse to the completely veiled women gliding through the streets with only their eyes in view, the women's outfits seem to embody the entire spectrum.

We paid our taxi driver, and I tipped and thanked him profusely, until he grew embarrassed and drove away.

We were ushered into a pristine, middle-class Moroccan home, with an intricately carved doorway and swirling multicolored tiles lining the walls. The mother told us in broken French that Abdelati was out, but would be home soon. We sat on low cushioned seats in the living room, drinking sweet, pungent mint tea poured at a suitable height from a tiny silver teapot and eating sugar cookies, while the family members took turns sitting with us and making shy, polite conversation that frequently lapsed into uncomfortable silence. Every time anything was said, Miguel would say "What?" with extreme eagerness, and I would translate the mundane fragment into Spanish for him: "Nice weather today. Tomorrow perhaps rain." At this he'd sink back into fidgety frustration, undoubtedly wishing Eva were there.

An hour passed, and as the guard kept changing, more family members emerged from inner rooms. I was again struck by the fact that they were all light-skinned Arabs. How did Abdelati fit into this picture? Was he adopted? I was very curious to find out.

After two hours had passed with no sign of Abdelati, the family insisted on serving us a meal of couscous and chicken.

"Soon," was the only response I got when I inquired as to what time he might arrive.

"You come to the *hammam*, the bath," the young sister said after we'd finished lunch. "When we finish, he is back."

"The bath?" I asked, looking around the apartment.

The sister laughed. "The women's bath!" she said. "Haven't you been yet?" She pointed at Miguel. "He can go to the men's; it's right next door."

"What?" said Miguel anxiously, sitting up.

"She wants to take us to the baths," I said.

A look of abject horror crossed his face. "The-the bath?" he stammered. "You and me?"

"Yes," I said, smiling widely. "Is there some problem?"

"Well…well…." I watched his agitation build for a moment, then sighed and put my hand over his.

"Separate baths, Miguel. You with the men, me with the women."

"Oh." He almost giggled with relief. "Of course."

The women's bath consisted of three large connecting rooms, each one hotter and steamier than the last, until you could barely see two feet in front of you. The floors were filled with naked women of all ages and body types, sitting directly on the slippery tiles, washing each other with mitts made of rough washcloths. Tiny girls and babies sat in plastic buckets filled with soapy water—their own pint-sized tubs. The women carried empty buckets, swinging like elephants' trunks, to and from the innermost room, where they filled them at a stone basin from a spigot of boiling water, mixing in a little cold from a neighboring spigot to temper it.

In a culture where the body is usually covered, I was surprised by the women's absolute lack of inhibition. They sat, mostly in pairs, pouring the water over their heads with small plastic pitchers, then scrubbing each other's backs—and I mean scrubbing. Over and over they attacked the same spot, as though they were trying to get out a particularly stubborn stain, leaving reddened flesh in their wake. They sprawled across each other's laps. They washed each other's fronts, backs, arms, legs. Some women washed themselves as though they were masturbating, hypnotically circling the same spot. Two tiny girls, about four-years-old, scrubbed their grandmother, who lay sprawled across the floor face down. A prepubescent girl lay in her mother's lap, belly up, eyes closed, as relaxed as a cat, while her mother applied a forceful up and down stroke across the entire length of her daughter's torso. I was struck by one young woman in particular, who reclined alone like a beauty queen in a tanning salon, back arched, head thrown back, right at the steamy heart of the baths, where the air was almost suffocating. When she began to wash, she soaped her breasts in sensual circles, proudly, her stomach held in, long chestnut hair rippling down her back, a goddess in her domain.

Abdelati's sister, whose name was Samara, went at my back with her mitt, which felt like steel wool.

"Ow!" I cried out. "Careful!"

This sent her into gales of laughter that drew the attention of the surrounding women, who saw what was happening and joined her in appreciative giggles as she continued to sandblast my skin.

"You must wash more often," she said, pointing to the refuse of her work—little gray scrolls of dead skin that clung to my arms like lint on a sweater.

When it came time to switch roles, I tried to return the favor, but after a few moments Samara became impatient with my wimpiness and grabbed the washcloth herself, still laughing. After washing the front of her body she called over a friend to wash her back, while she giggled and sang.

"What was it like in there?" asked Miguel when we met again outside. He looked pink and damp as a newborn after his visit to the men's baths, and I wondered whether his experience was anything like mine.

"I'd like to tell you all about it," I said eagerly, "but…" I paused for emphasis, then leaned in and whispered, "I don't think Eva would approve."

When we got back to the house, the mother, older sister, and uncle greeted us at the door.

"Please," said the mother. "Abdelati is here."

"Oh, good," I said, and for a moment, before I walked into the living room, his face danced in my mind—the warm brown eyes, the smile so shy and gentle and filled with radiant life.

We entered the lovely tiled room we'd sat in before, and a handsome young Arab man in nicely pressed Western pants and shirt came forward to shake our hands with an uncertain expression on his face.

"*Bonjour, mes amis,*" he said cautiously.

"*Bonjour,*" I smiled, slightly confused. "*Abdelati—est-ce qu'il est ici?*" Is Abdelati here?

"*Je suis Abdelati.*"

"But...but..." I looked from him to the family and then began to giggle tremulously. "I—I'm sorry. I'm afraid we've made a bit of a mistake. I—I'm so embarrassed."

"What? What?" Miguel asked urgently. "I don't understand. Where is he?"

"We've got the wrong Abdelati," I told him, then looked around at the assembled family who'd spent the better part of a day entertaining us. "I'm afraid we don't actually know your son."

For a split second no one said anything, and I wondered whether I might implode right then and there and blow away like a pile of ash.

Then the uncle exclaimed heartily, "*Ce n'est pas grave!*"

"Yes," the mother joined in. "It doesn't matter at all. Won't you stay for dinner, please?"

I was so overwhelmed by their kindness that tears rushed to my eyes. For all they knew we were con artists, thieves, anything. Would such a thing ever happen in the U.S.?

Still, with my plane leaving the next morning, I felt the moments I could share with the first Abdelati and his family slipping farther and farther away.

"Thank you so much," I said fervently. "It's been a beautiful, beautiful day, but please...could you help me find this address?"

I took out the piece of paper Abdelati had given me back in Kenitra, and the new Abdelati, his uncle, and his brother-in-law came forward to decipher it.

"This is Baalal Abdelati!" said the second Abdelati with surprise. "We went to school together! He lives less than a kilometer from here. I will bring you to his house."

And that is how it happened, that after taking photos and

exchanging addresses and hugs and promises to write, Miguel and I left our newfound family and arrived at the home of our friend Abdelati as the last orange streak of the sunset was fading into the indigo night. There I threw myself into the arms of that dear and lovely young man, exclaiming, "I thought we'd never find you!"

After greetings had been offered all around, and the two Abdelatis had shared stories and laughter, we waved good-bye to our new friend Abdelati and entered a low, narrow hallway, lit by kerosene lamps.

"This is my mother," said Abdelati.

And suddenly I found myself caught up in a crush of fabric and spice, gripped in the tight embrace of a completely veiled woman, who held me and cried over me and wouldn't let me go, just as though I were her own daughter, and not a stranger she'd never before laid eyes on in her life.

*Tanya Shaffer is an actress and writer based in San Francisco who has toured nationally with several solo shows. She has written for the Tony Award-winning San Francisco Mime Troupe, and she is the author of* Somebody's Heart is Burning: A Woman Wanderer in Africa.

# The Spanish Church

*A modern-day pilgrim stops*
*along the path.*

THE TOWN WITH THE FORTRESS CHURCH WAS NAMED PORTOMARIN, which sounded vaguely like "portal," but it didn't have to be a gateway to please me; I arrived happy. I had come to it the day before, late in the afternoon, walking down a very long hill through gold and green countryside.

My hiking companions went on, but I stopped just where the hillside started down and sat for a while on a lichen-painted wall of gray stone—not so much because I was footsore, but because I felt good and happy, and I wanted to sit on the wall in the Spanish sun and prolong the feeling. It was one of the best moments of the trip.

I remember that a couple of the hotshot Italian bikers zipped past me while I sat on the wall, their gears set for maximum speed as they began the downward coast. It was a perfect hill for bikers as well as walkers, but nothing in northern Spain—or maybe anywhere else—can really be counted on, especially if you're going too fast. I encountered them again at the bottom of the hill, one helping the other with a newly ruptured tire. He'd hit a rock at the bottom, where the road turned suddenly.

In another place, on another journey, I might have thought

smugly that they got what they deserved: the Camino de Santiago is a sacred way, even if it does make for good biking, and they certainly weren't going at it reverently or humbly. But I was trying to, and some of the lessons of that ancient pilgrim path were sinking in. I felt sorry for the time the two bikers were going to have to spend, prying the tire off, gluing a patch on the punctured inner tube, reassembling the thing, pumping air back in, and hoping the patch would hold. It was better to be on foot, I thought, as I swung across the bridge and up the bank beyond, where the red-roofed houses clustered.

That night, I stayed with my friends in a modern, white posada, sleeping well in clean sheets. We were on our way to the great shrine of Saint James in the city of Santiago de Compostela, which made all of us pilgrims of some sort. But none of us were religious ones; blisters and stiff muscles aside, we saw no merit in suffering.

Portomarin stands near the end of the Camino. It's a moved town, a reconstruction: a ruined medieval bridge and the skeleton of the original village lie beneath—just beneath—the waters of a dammed-up river. It was mid-September, and the water was low; stubs of abutments and outlines of walls broke the surface. If we hadn't known, the flooded buildings would have made us wonder what had happened there.

Before the dam was finished and the village drowned, the government managed to move—stone by historic stone—a small but high-walled chapel, boxy-looking and all but windowless because in the Middle Ages it had doubled as a fortress, protecting pilgrims. It now stood in the central plaza of the new village, lending authenticity.

In the morning, while my comrades downed bread and milky Nescafé in a tiny restaurant under the arcade of the plaza, I headed for the shiny green doors of the church.

I wanted the place to myself—and would have had it, the hour was so early. But a boy in a red windbreaker came in when I did. I passed him on the steps, just as he dismounted and leaned his bike against the church wall. The bike had saddlebags, so he was another long-distance traveler, another pilgrim. But he wasn't with the Italians; he was riding alone.

His presence in the church made me feel a little self-conscious. He must have felt the same way: as if by agreement, we walked in opposite directions, or as opposite as you can get in a place the size of a living room. I headed left; he went to the right.

What struck me was his youth. He might have been twenty-two, though I'd just as readily have believed thirty-one or seventeen. He had a plain, pleasant face, slightly freckled, with a wide mouth and sandy hair.

The chapel's high walls were plastered smooth and white, and there was a paucity of windows. The few it had were small and high up, so marauders couldn't get in. The windows were also too high to shoot arrows out of, but there is a profoundly spiritual difference between protection and defense, between a fort and a refuge. You could feel it here.

The light came from an opening high above the altar. It was morning light, at the right angle, and it flooded the place, so even the shadows were soft and pale.

After a few minutes, I sat down near the front and closed my eyes and prayed. Though I don't qualify as devout, I am drawn to spiritual places, so sitting in foreign churches was not new to me. But I was doing it more often than usual on this trip. It seemed to be part of the path. "Behave as if," a psychologist once advised, in a context I no longer remember. On the Camino, behaving "as if" means praying; simply because so many others have done so

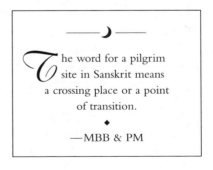

*The* word for a pilgrim site in Sanskrit means a crossing place or a point of transition.

♦

—MBB & PM

before you—millions, most likely, over nearly a thousand years.

I wasn't praying for anything. Requests didn't feel right on this trip, and besides, my habitual cravings had evaporated. I was just saying thanks—for the good afternoon the day before, for the repose of the current moment, for the rhythm of the days: the alternation of rest and walking, of food and hunger, of solitude and conversation.

Then I sat still. There was peace in that place, and I let it seep into me, basking in it a little, storing it up. I felt my heart relax.

When I stood to leave, I saw that the boy in the red jacket was also sitting down, farther to the front on his side of the aisle. He didn't see me rise or notice that I paused to watch him. He was staring upward at the window above the altar, as if the answer to life lay in it. Maybe for him, it did.

The light seemed liquid, like a purifying bath, a *mikvah* for the soul. It was transforming him, and maybe me as well. I felt a rush of inexplicable tenderness for the boy—the man, the child, all the ages he had been and would be. It was as if I'd known him all his life, as if I'd been his mother, sister, lover, friend, and they were all the same.

I stood there frozen by the thought, cradling him in my mind, sharing a lifetime with him in that moment. And then, like a bubble, the moment broke. The holy light was still shining in, the clean space still felt pure, but time had snapped back to normal.

The boy stood up then, his body moving into the aisle before he pulled his gaze away from the high window. As he turned, his eyes met mine, and his face broke into a smile—a wonderful, open, whole-hearted smile, as pure as the light. He had been lonely, I saw, and now he wasn't anymore. He'd gotten what he needed in that chapel. We both had, in different ways.

He would be all right now, I thought. I watched him walk back along the aisle and out the door. When I walked out, he was already gone, his red jacket disappearing on the far side of the cobblestones. I never saw him again.

My friends were still drinking coffee when I found them. I ordered a cup too, dropped three small white bricks of sugar into it, and stirred to cool it down. "How was the church?" they wanted to know.

"It was nice," I said, telling the truth. "Very nice."

*Catherine Watson took her first trip at the age of five, by train, from Minneapolis, Minnesota, to Grand Forks, North Dakota, in a blue suit her* mother had sewn and a new white straw hat. She has been fascinated ever since by the relationship between "home" and "away." She is the award-winning travel editor of the Minneapolis Star Tribune and the author of Travel Basics.

✳

# Special Delivery

*Hand delivering a postcard from the
Galapagos to Italy begins a string
of delightful surprises.*

I CERTAINLY DIDN'T VOLUNTEER TO DELIVER THE POSTCARD because I wanted to make new friends in exotic foreign lands. *Au contraire*, I'm a person whose travels are motivated by nature, architecture, and food—in other words, all the attractions Barbra Streisand isn't referring to when she sings about "peeeeeeople who need people." But there I was on Floreana Island, at the butt end of the Galapagos, 600 miles off the coast of Ecuador, and I wanted to send a postcard home to my partner Pamela in Miami. If I expected hand delivery of my own mail, *mano a mano*, it seemed only sporting to pick up somebody else's.

The Floreana post office is really just a raffish wooden barrel plunked down in the middle of the sand, a descendant of one installed in the eighteenth century by whaling crews. In those days it was an optimally efficient system: sailors who were passing through checked the mailbox for letters addressed to their ships' ports of call. Today the barrel is stuffed with postcards from tourists of all nations. You could schlep them home and stamp them, obviously, but the true spirit of ye olde mail barrel, according to our guidebook, demands the personal touch.

The day my daughter Miranda and I were in Floreana, most of

the mail was addressed to Norwegians and Argentines. But there was one postcard with frolicking sea lions on one side and *Saluti* scrawled on the other, intended for someone named Gina at an *erboristeria*, or herbal pharmacy, in Bassano del Grappa, Italy. I knew this was the home of grappa, the firewater liqueur. I had even been through it once on a train, so I also knew it was located at the foot of the Alps, in the Veneto region, about 120 miles from Venice. Pamela and I had frequent flier tickets to go to Venice in a few months. I pocketed the card.

Still, I wasn't prepared just to show up cold. When I got back home, I decided to write Gina a letter. I speak a little Italian—that is, I know a lot of hotel and menu words, which I sometimes say in Spanish by mistake. But with the help of a dictionary, I managed to explain all about the mailbox tradition. I assured Gina that there was no social obligation that went along with her receipt of the post-card—although I'd be glad to buy her a beer.

"Mom, you can't send this to strangers," warned Miranda, who majored in Italian. "They'll understand you, but they'll think you're a serial killer."

She rehabilitated my felo-

> *W*hile on a three-month European backpacking trip, I sent a postcard home to myself from every new city I visited. I detailed one special memory about the city or the people and sent it off. My trip continued long after I arrived home. One postcard I'd sent didn't show up until six weeks after my homecoming. I was warmed by the memories that flooded back to me when I held the postcard in my hands. I had traveled far and even though I was now home, I knew my travels would always be with me.
>
> ◆
>
> —Lisa Bach,
> "A Path of One's Own"

nious grammar. Off went a letter to Bassano del Grappa. A month later I got an E-mail from someone named Luca. There was a note in Italian, plus a serial killer English translation that read:

"Dear Sirs VAN GELDER, let off ourself for the postpone what we replay at your letter, but we were outside for a travel. We are very happy to meet yuo in Veneto for make a friendship. If yuo send to as the date of yuor travel we can organize ourself for meeting. Reverence, Gina"

It was around this time that Pamela, who speaks no Italian at all, began asking me pointed questions about exactly how much of our time in Venice was going to be devoted to this project. But I had made a commitment to the spirit of the mailbox, damn it. I sent the dates. Gina/Luca E-mailed back phone numbers and said we should call when we get to Venice.

A woman answered the phone.

*"Buon giorno,"* I burbled, *"e Gina chi parla?"*

No, it wasn't Gina. It was Edda. Whoever Edda was, she knew exactly who I was—"You're coming on Monday, yes?"—and we managed, despite my rotten Italian, to communicate some particulars about the railway schedules. "Just go to the counter in the station," she instructed.

When I got off the phone, I realized that I had no clue about which counter she meant. The ticket booth? The postcard had been addressed to a pharmacy. Could it be in the train station? Did it have a counter? A few hours later I called again, and this time a male voice answered. No, Gina wasn't there. Neither was Edda. The male voice belonged to Luca, my E-mail buddy, who explained to me in halting English that the train station was not very big and I shouldn't worry. Then he added: "You perhaps don't know that Gina really doesn't speak any English? As you will see when you meet her on Monday."

I was beginning to doubt her existence altogether. Was Gina actually a dog, the mascot of the pharmacy? Was I the butt of a joke that had already traveled 7,000 miles?

"You really don't have to come if you don't want to," I told Pamela. No, no, she'd come. But we just wouldn't stay any longer than we had to.

Our doubts began to melt the second we got off the train. There, carrying a single red rose and a big sign that said, "WELCOME LINDSY TO BASSANO DEL GRAPPA," were a college-aged

guy and two grinning 60ish ladies. One of them—an Italian lep-
rechaun—immediately grabbed me in a bear hug. The more bash-
ful of the two, dressed in brown and wearing eyeglasses, turned out
to be Gina. My new best friend was her sister Edda, dolled up in
bright red and wearing major eye makeup. The guy was Luca, their
younger sister's son, an engineering student who, alone among
the group, had once studied English. He had his dictionary out. So
did I.

Before I could proffer the small piece of cardboard that had gathered us together in this spot, Pamela and I were whisked off to a
restaurant for lunch. It was like being plopped down on the set of
*Amarcord*: We were joined by Luca's mother, who tooled in on a
bicycle, and briefly by his father, as well as a parade of cooks and
waiters to whom we were introduced as the Girls from America
Who Brought the Postcard. Mounds of antipasto arrived at the
table, followed by enormous platters of pasta with lobster and heaps
of delicate baby greens. Prosecco, the champagne of the Veneto,
flowed like the Adriatic. And a good thing, too, since most of the
conversation that we could all muster had to do with the cuisine of
the region. Someone would proclaim *sarde en saor*, and the rest of
the group would mmmm and ahhhh, and then someone else would
chime in with *spaghetti vongole* or *radicchio al griglia*, followed by
more orgasmic choruses. From time to time one of us would raise
a glass and toast, "From the Galapagos to Bassano del Grappa!"
and we would all whoop. I noticed that Pamela was not looking at
her watch.

The family's *erboristeria* was currently closed for renovations, we
learned, and perhaps they all had some time on their hands. But that
alone didn't really explain the brass-band welcome. Nor did the
famous postcard, which I finally presented to Gina over sorbet laced
with a lethal dollop of grappa. She glanced at it, remarked that it was
from a customer and packed it away in her purse, not to be referred
to again. The postcard was merely the message. Making friendship
was the medium.

And what was a little translation technicality among friends? By
the time the check was paid—the family refused to take our crum-

pled lire notes—we were all feeling punchily pleased with our ability to leapfrog over the language barrier. A tour of the town was proposed. Bassano is actually a gem of a place, with a spectacular Palladian wooden bridge spanning the Brenta River and a sinister castle on its banks—the home, Luca explained, of Ezzolino da Roma, a bloodthirsty tyrant so infamous that he was cited in Dante's "Inferno." Then we strolled on a bluff above the river past a row of lollipop-like trees. Bassano was notoriously active in the Resistance, Gina told us, and in 1944 the German army hanged thirty-one of the town's young men in retaliation—one for each tree. "I wrote a poem about it once," Gina added shyly. How nice, I thought with the genteel condescension of the professional journalist, a pharmacist who expresses herself in poetry. We tramped around to churches, Roman ruins, even the Museum of Grappa, where Gina insisted on buying us not one but three bottles of the stuff—regular, honey, and blueberry—as souvenirs.

Certainly we would also like to see a little of the region? *Si, si, certo.* Into the family station wagon we piled, Luca trying to drive and riffle through the dictionary at the same time. By then, we more or less had our shtick down. The Italians spoke slowly, with infinite patience and maximum hand-jive. Dictionary pages flipped like decks of cards. Somehow we managed to progress beyond cuisine to pets, gambling, art, birth order, the weather in Miami, the allure of Venice, Edda's arthritis, my bad knee, our feelings about spirituality vs. organized religion, even politics and politicians (for that one we all used the international sign of stuffing one's finger down one's throat). We took pictures of each other in the main square of Marostica, where the residents dress up as bishops and queens every fall and enact a days-long chess game. We climbed to the fort above the town. By then it was getting dark, and, alas, we had a train to catch.

But it was decided that we would meet the family cats and dogs. At Gina and Edda's house we got another surprise. Gina had written poetry, all right—she brought us out copies of all her books, as well as a CD on which several of her verses had been set to modern classical music and sung by the soprano Isabella Frati. These, she insisted, were gifts: one set for us, and one for Miranda.

By now we were sagging under the weight of three bottles of grappa and a small library of books, plus the CDs and a multilingual guidebook to Marostica that Gina had impulsively bought after Luca and I had exhausted our dueling dictionaries in the search for words to describe chess pieces and military architecture—all in exchange for one lousy postcard. Nor would the sisters dream of letting us take the train back to Venice. They drove us all the way to Piazzale Roma, the last niblet of mainland before one has to switch to a water bus or gondola. We kissed, cried, offered our respective spare rooms any time, promised to be fluent in each other's language the next time we met.

And indeed, with the help of my dog-eared dictionary, I am slowly reading Gina's poetry. The one about the thirty-one martyrs is a favorite, but there are also sexy, smoldering love poems. Pamela has been stockpiling South Florida culinary goodies to send the ladies. Luca and I have become E-mail pen pals. I correct his English, he corrects my Italian and tells me what the family is up to. Edda was recently in Australia. Somehow I feel certain she made herself understood.

Meanwhile, the postcard I mailed home to Pamela from Floreana hasn't turned up yet. I find myself getting oddly excited at the idea of meeting whichever stranger, speaking whatever language, eventually shows up with it. I may have been the one who went to the Galapagos. But it was Gina and her family who taught me about real adventure travel.

*Lindsy van Gelder is coauthor of* The Girls Next Door.

PAMELA MICHAEL

✱ ✱ ✱

# The Boatman's Gift

*A riverside encounter changes
a traveler's way of seeing.*

WHOEVER SAID "GETTING THERE IS HALF THE FUN" SURELY HAD never tried to get to Luang Prabang. Landlocked Laos is a mountainous country with no railroad, few roads, and a domestic airline that is off-limits to most foreign aid workers for safety reasons. Despite the obstacles—or maybe because of the challenge they presented—Luang Prabang beckoned.

I'd heard tantalizing tales from travelers in Bangkok and Vientiane about the old royal capital, said to be Southeast Asia's last Eden. The two weeks I had just spent in neighboring Thailand had me yearning to see a bit of Old Asia; new Asia being something of a neon nightmare. I wanted to lose myself in a place where the distinction between past and present was hazy, a place where golden arches offered sanctuary, not fast food. But time travel in Laos proved easier than actual travel: the Laotians may have reopened their country to tourists after years of war and revolution in 1989, but many years later they still hadn't marshaled the resources to move people from one place to another reliably.

To get from Vientiane to Luang Prabang, 215 miles north, I had three choices: first, up the Mekong by cargo boat—a five- or six-day trip if nothing broke down. Reportedly, bandits had been stopping boats with foreigners aboard, making this option almost as unappealing as Choice Number Two, overland through the mountains on the notorious Route 13. Everyone I'd met (with the exception of two stir-fried Australian junkies who clearly were oblivious to danger and just about everything else) had warned against taking this barely completed and very rough road. Antigovernment rebels and thugs were said to ambush about 1 out of every 300 vehicles at a particularly vulnerable spot in the jungle, odds that seemed too risky. Lastly, there were the aging Russian and Chinese prop planes, seventeen-seaters and such, flown by Lao Aviation, a company considered by some to be one of the world's most dangerous airlines.

I weighed forty white-knuckle minutes in the air versus several days of anxious land or river travel and decided to fly. Peering out the dirty window of the creaky twin prop at the rugged mountains below, I realized that I'd made the right decision. Even as thick clouds of white vapor began billowing out of the cabin's overhead compartments and condensing into "rain" that drenched the startled passengers, causing the flock of holiday-spirited retired Irish engineers on board to sing louder and faster—even then I was glad I wasn't down below, snaking along the side of a cliff in the back of a truck, scanning the shadows for gunmen.

The Laotian highlands from the air are a breathtaking solid mass of lush, trackless green. I spotted few villages and could see no roads leading to any of them, nor any glint of metal. Dwellings seemed to be constructed entirely from natural materials—wood, bamboo, and palm fronds—surprising, even in one of the poorest countries on earth. Looking down at the tiny villages, I had a hard time imagining what they had endured during the 1970s. Attempting to obliterate the Ho Chi Minh Trail—the supply line to North Vietnam—the United States secretly dropped more bombs on Laos than were used in all of World War II, the equivalent of a sortie every eight minutes, twenty-four hours a day, for nine years, making Laos the most-bombed country in history. I was to meet quite a few people who had spent their childhoods in limestone caves, where entire communities concealed themselves for years to escape the relentless rain of munitions.

And yet, just as they have doggedly prevailed for hundreds of years despite invasions by virtually all of their neighbors and the not-so-neighborly French, Laotians seem to bear little ill-will toward anyone. Centuries of animist and Buddhist tradition have honed a national temperament of tolerance, forgiveness, and compassion summed up in the oft-heard verbal shrug, *baw pen nyang.* Rough translation: no problem, never mind, it doesn't matter. My few days in languid Vientiane had already warmed me to this approach to life, and to these seemingly imperturbable people and their quick smiles. But nothing—or perhaps everything in my life up till then—had prepared me for Luang Prabang.

It appeared, dreamlike, nestled in a high valley surrounded by mist-shrouded peaks, golden temple spires rising from dense tropical foliage, glinting in the sun. Even the Irishmen fell silent as we all craned to see through the tiny windows of the plane. Below was a slender finger of land at the junction of two rivers: the mighty Mekong, Southeast Asia's longest river, the "Mother of Waters," and her more placid tributary, the Nam Khan. Arranged on this narrow peninsula, in ceremonial splendor only hinted at through the palm trees as we made our descent, stood thirty-two magnificent Buddhist temples, some several hundred years old. I was scrambling for my camera before my feet even touched the tarmac.

Luang Prabang, the oldest Laotian town still in existence, proved to be a vibrant mélange of color, texture, and architectural styles: the ornate gilt and mosaic-covered temples, called *wats*, with their soaring eaves in the Cambodian style; the traditional teak, bamboo, and thatch Lao houses built high off the ground; pastel Vietnamese-style arcaded shops with faded signs over arched doorways and shuttered living quarters above; crumbling stuccoed and half-timbered villas, a legacy of the French, who also left the Laotians with a taste for baguettes.

Wandering the streets my first day in town, camera in hand, I was giddy with pleasure. The town was beautiful, palpably sacred, and curiously familiar. I don't think I have ever felt so safe or so immediately comfortable anywhere ever before. *Sabadee!* passersby sang out to me, good day! *Sabadee!* I called back.

Glittering temple after temple lined the broad, dusty main street, formerly the royal boulevard, now promenaded by soft-gaited women in traditional handwoven Lao skirts and schoolchildren in crisp white blouses, or ancient Hmong tribeswomen down from the hills to sell their intricately embroidered textiles. Occasionally a bicycle or *tuk-tuk* glided by. But the ubiquitous fluttering clusters of orange-robed monks—the whimsical hallmark of Luang Prabang street life—caught the eye most of all. The majority of these engaging and high-spirited young monks are novices, boys sent by families from all over Laos for religious training. Most will return to their old lives and villages after a few months to study, marry, or continue their schooling. Despite a rigorous schedule of instruction and temple maintenance, they seem to spend many hours going from one *wat* to another, often in animated groups, dressed in every shade of orange imaginable, their shaved heads shaded from the tropical sun under huge black umbrellas.

The monks, who greatly outnumber the "civilians" in Luang Prabang, are not an isolated fringe or curiosity, however; they are the very foundation of the town, and of Laotian Buddhism and history. The monasteries they occupy are not mere monuments or historic artifacts, but still-vibrant religious and cultural centers where giant drums and gongs are played daily, like church bells; where ornate ceremonial dragon boats are lovingly maintained for annual boating regattas; where courtyards are swept daily and flower offerings left on shrines. Every turn of my head brought an exquisite new image into view—my camera lens felt like a giant straw, sucking in great gulps of color and magic. The pageantry of the town's regal past was almost visible—ghost images of royal parades, religious processions, and elephant marches lingered in the dazzling light and verdant shadows. I wanted to drink them all in, capture them all.

Meandering off the main street onto a narrow, mud-paved lane, I found myself, after a block or two, at the quiet banks of the Mekong. Houses, some once grand, some forever humble, looked out across a small dirt road to the café au lait river. Almost every house had a little riverside annex of some sort, a huddle of chairs, a hammock, or even a small hut—places to gather by the water with friends.

Laundry and fishing nets hung from tree branches at the river's edge, bamboo racks of sun-drying golden rice cakes sat propped up here and there, a sad-eyed monkey languished at the end of a tether, next to a stall selling sundries. There were several ramshackle open-air restaurants on stilts above the water. Fish, rice, and an enormous variety of fresh vegetables, cooked on charcoal braziers, seemed to be the standard fare. The air was spiced with a piquant fragrance. On both sides of the river, the broad, steep banks were a patchwork of kitchen gardens filled with tomatoes, beans, squash, and more exotic vegetables. Resourceful and prodigious gardeners, the Laotians seemed to find a way to cultivate even the most difficult terrain.

I was reminded of an ugly vacant lot near my home in California that was transformed into a veritable small farm by an extended family of Laotians who moved in several doors away. The abandoned lot had been a neighborhood eyesore for years, filled with trash and debris. The waste of arable land must have seemed incomprehensible to people so accustomed to farming every square foot of usable soil in their home country, which is mostly forest and mountains. So they cleaned up the lot, tilled and planted, then shared their harvest with the whole neighborhood.

Here, by the Mekong, the same tightly structured web of family, nature, and ceremony that I had seen among my immigrant neighbors, struggling just to get by, appeared to nurture a way of life that was full of rich relationships with each other and the natural world. The word *graceful* came to mind as I framed one beautiful shot after another of scenes along the river, clicking away. From the grace of giggling young girls brushing each other's glossy black hair by the roadside, to the sleek lines of the delicate, pencil-thin boats plying the water, to the slow-motion cast of glistening nets, or the low-slung sweep of a temple roof—the images were so beautiful I could feel my heart racing as I photographed them. Another American shooting at Laotians, I thought guiltily.

The act of taking a photograph, particularly in a foreign place—particularly in a poor foreign place—is at times hard to justify. For years I have mollified my apprehensions by telling myself that I am a sensitive archivist, a respectful documentarian who seeks to capture the moment, to record the illusory and transitory, to give meaning to shadow and light, to bear witness, to celebrate, to remember. Still, I couldn't deny that my passion for taking photographs when traveling was akin to greed, though my motives were a bit more complicated: I wanted to share what I saw on my journeys with others. Like Goethe, I knew that an experience shared is joy doubled. And yet, I was consuming beauty and time, in a sense, and driven by a covetous desire to take home what I saw, to own it. Even the language of photography exposes its darker purpose: we *take* photos, not make them.

So there I was, looting yet another culture, wandering the riverbank with a thousand-dollar shield of metal and ground glass between me and whatever I encountered. I spied a broad ceremonial stairway up ahead, leading from the entrance of an ancient monastery all the way down to the water. The stairway was guarded by two huge, white tiger statues whose mouths and penises had been painted bright red. Several

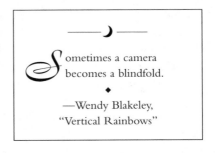

Sometimes a camera becomes a blindfold.

—Wendy Blakeley,
"Vertical Rainbows"

intricately decorated longtail boats were tied up at the bottom of the stairs, and a group of boatmen were gathered at the top, where a low, whitewashed wall ran alongside the road. One of the men, a wiry fellow in flip-flops, approached me as I sat down on the wall to change film in my camera, eager to "capture" the grotesque tigers.

"Caves, Madam? I have good boat. Buddha caves, two hours. Beautiful." He had a sweet, gap-toothed smile and a sparkle in his eye, but I was "loading for tiger" and didn't want to be bothered.

"No, thank you," I replied distractedly, struggling with my camera, which wasn't advancing the film properly. He prattled on in broken English and French, extolling the wonders of the Pak Ou Caves, which I had read much about and, indeed, planned to visit.

The caves, perhaps the most sacred site in Laos, were located high up a sheer limestone cliff face in a picturesque gorge upriver, at the confluence of the Mekong and Nam Ou. The only way to reach them was to dock at a floating bamboo platform, as Lao kings had done for centuries every Lao New Year, then climb a set of rough-hewn stone steps to the swallow-filled caves above. Inside were thousands of Buddha statues of all sizes and materials—wood, resin, horn, and stone—placed there by pilgrims over the last 600 years.

While the boatman continued his entreaty, my frustration with the camera was reaching near panic as I concluded that the batteries—surely not replaceable in this remote spot—were dead. I had just bought new ones a few days before in Bangkok; perhaps they had been on the shelf too long. This was catastrophe! I remember thinking, "What am I going to *do* for two weeks in this place with no camera?" I'd have to go back early, I concluded, despondently.

The boatman was clearly disturbed by my rising distress. Laotians consider overt displays of emotion, particularly anger or irritation, very impolite, and I was having a barely contained fit. "Madam! What's wrong?" he implored with alarm and genuine concern.

"There's something wrong with my camera," I snapped.

"*Baw pen nyang.* Don't worry."

"I think my batteries are dead," I whined, still fiddling with the film. He said nothing for several seconds. Then he touched my hand gently and sought my gaze. "But, Madam," he said soothingly, "your eyes are not dead."

*Pamela Michael is a freelance writer, radio producer, and education consultant. She is the editor of* The Gift of Rivers, *co-editor of* A Mother's World, A Woman's Passion for Travel, *and* Wild Writing Women: Stories of World Travel, *as well as the author of* The Whole World is Watching. *Currently, she is the director of The River of Words Project, which she co-founded with former U.S. Poet Laureate Robert Hass. She lives in Clayton, California.*

# Mysteries of Life

*How her boy was saved by the seals.*

I WAS WONDERING IF MAYBE YOU WERE HAVING A HARD DAY, AND might need a story about the presence of alchemy in the world. Because I have one: So there we were, my boy and I, an hour from shore on the Sea of Cortez. We were on a snorkeling expedition to Seal Island, where we and twenty other people were going to get to swim with the seals. Sam was the only kid, and there was only one child's wet suit, and it was just a crummy, pretend wet suit. First of all, it had no arms or legs, just a torso, and second of all, it was very thin. Also, it was bright pink, which I told Sam was considered an extremely manly color in Mexico. But when we anchored off Seal Rock, and everyone else got in the water and began bobbing along in their thick intensely buoyant wet suits, I got a sinking sensation.

But I am old and tough, and I said a little prayer and climbed off the little tailgate of the cruise boat into the frigid water. By then almost everyone else was already in the little cove where the seals were lounging around on the rocks, barking like clownish guard dogs. Sam was more excited than I can remember him being in a long time. He stood there on the boat in his snorkeling mask and his manly bright-pink wet suit, with his skinny little arms and legs, looking a little like a cross between Jacques Cousteau and Pee Wee Herman. And then he slid into the water beside me.

God, it was cold. And the current was stronger than I had imagined, and I felt really afraid. But courage is fear that has said its prayers, and so I prayed and we bobbed in place for a moment. He is a very strong swimmer, for a six-year-old, and finally we began swimming to the cove. The seals barked from the rocks, and we headed toward them, toward the other people who were in the water right near them. But after we'd gotten 20 feet away from the boat, Sam cried out in despair that one of his flippers had come off, and I peered through the bottomless water and could see it way below us, and I also had the sudden conviction that there were giant clams down there, just like in the movies of my childhood, which would open up their monstrous shells, grab your leg, and never let you go. It didn't make sense to leave Sam at the surface, in his crappy, pink, nonbuoyant wet suit, while I went after it, and so I watched the flipper sink.

We bobbed together for a moment, I and my boy, and the tide was pushing us along, not toward shore but toward the sea, and by then I was hearing the sound track of *Jaws* beginning to play, and I had to decide whether to make a break for the cove or to head back to the boat.

We headed back. And I hoped that someone would show up, a big, manly man-type guy, who was so big and such a strong swimmer that he could accompany Sam to the cove.

We got out of the water and sat at the tailgate of the cruise ship, and pretty soon the snorkeling guide said he'd take Sam with him in a moment and that I could head off alone. So I did.

I went on ahead to where everyone else was, and the seals swam up quite close and barked and were properly silly, as they are paid to be, and it was sort of goofy and sweet, and I bobbed along with the other people for awhile, and then tried to locate Sam in the water. I scanned the sea, looking for the bright-pink wet suit, but I couldn't find him anywhere.

To make a long story short, a story involving the zone that parents find themselves in when their children are missing, I finally realized that this tiny blue bundle back on the tailgate of the boat was my little boy. And I knew it hadn't worked, that he hadn't been big enough.

I swam back and my mask got all fogged up. I climbed back on board and sat down beside him. He was wrapped in a towel, and someone had brought him a Coke and some tortilla chips, and it turned out that he had started getting hypothermic less than a minute after getting in the water. He was in fact grievously disappointed, but was being very brave and manly, in his little pink wet suit. I was desperate to fix him, fix the situation, make everything happy again in my geisha-like way, and then I remembered this basic religious principle that God isn't there to take away our suffering or our pain, but to fill it with God's presence, and so I figured that I could enter into Sam's disappointment and at least keep him company in it; maybe have a little Coke-and-chip communion.

And it was about one moment later that the seals started swimming up to us. "Ahhh!" Sam cried, as a seal bobbed a few feet away, and this time it was a cry of total amazement, and then another seal emerged a few feet away, right next to the first one, and they bobbed near each of them and called out, "Hey—what d'ya think you are, a couple of comedians?" Five or six of them came up to us in the next fifteen minutes. Then, after awhile, all the adults swam back to the boat, from the cove, and the seals went under the waves, and soon we were on our way back home.

When we were in our room, I said, "Honey, you need to write this down, so that we never forget." He sat down and wrote for awhile. He is a very slow writer, and he misspelled every other word— "seals" was spelled "sels," and "came" was spelled "kam," but this is the story he wrote: "We went to swim with the seals, but I could not make it to the shore. And so the seals came to me and it was magic."

See what I mean? Alchemy: dross to gold.

*Anne Lamott is the author of several books, including the novels* Rosie *and* Crooked Little Heart, *and the nonfiction works* Operating Instructions, Bird by Bird, *and* Traveling Mercies: Some Thoughts on Faith. *This story originally appeared on Salon.com. She lives in Northern California with her son.*

MARILYN McFARLANE

# L'Air du Temps

*Scents and sensibilities.*

IN THE PICTURE, THE ONE MY EX-HUSBAND'S GIRLFRIEND RIPPED in half, I am wearing a white blouse and yellow gathered skirt that billows over full petticoats like an open parasol. I am sitting on the edge of a fountain, and I'm laughing—laughing because I've had a summer of freedom, I'm seventeen, and I'm in love with the boy taking the picture. And we're in Paris.

All the tears and pain destined to divide us lie ahead, but the girl in the snapshot doesn't see those. She's dazzled by a future that shimmers bright as the fountain spraying behind her.

I wonder about the petticoats. I don't remember packing them into that heavy brown leather suitcase I lugged all summer, but the picture says I did. Surely I didn't starch and iron them, as fashion required in 1955, to make the pastel skirts appear to float. Where would I have found the starch, and the iron? Yet there I am, fluffy as a peony.

With every step the boy and I took, wandering the streets of Paris, drenched in romance and innocence, we sealed our fate. I had my first taste of champagne and watched a dancer swathed in leopard skin slither across the stage of the Moulin Rouge. That evening I wore the pink linen dress my mother had made with loving care before she sent me off to a summer in Europe, thinking I would be protected because I was part of such a trustworthy, well-escorted group of students. The dress was so tight around the waist (stitched so at my insistence) that I could take only shallow breaths, and I never wore it again.

I had arrived in Paris on a train of World War II vintage, crouching in the dust under the compartment's wooden seat. Sheltered by my friends' legs and blankets, I rode there all night, cramped and drowsy, as the wheels clickety-clacked over the rails of western Europe. I was hiding from the conductor; I had lost both my passport and my train ticket from Copenhagen. As the train rolled into the old, echoey, smoky station and my friends whispered that the coast was clear, I crawled out and stretched, giggling. Anybody got a comb?

One girl rummaged in her purse and pulled out a handful of papers. "Look at this! Your passport and tickets! I had them all along."

I laughed. What did I care about inconvenience? This was adventure, and Paris.

On the Champs Elysées, the boy and I walked for miles, dodging traffic as if we were citywise, rather than small-town kids who'd never been anywhere. We climbed the Eiffel Tower, gazed at the Seine, watched the torch lighting at the Arc de Triomphe tomb, ate *jambon* and *fromage* and ice cream at sidewalk cafés. We tossed coins in every fountain we saw, always with a wish to return.

With the last of my money, I bought a minuscule bottle of perfume, L'Air du Temps. By dabbing my wrist sparingly, and only on special occasions, I made it last for months.

> ———)———
>
> The olfactory sense is, from the viewpoint of evolution, our oldest sense. It is precise, swift, and powerful, and it bores into our memory with persistent tenacity, hence the efficacy of perfumes. The secret is to always wear the same scent, until it becomes a personal, untransferable trademark, something that identifies us.
>
> ◆
>
> —Isabel Allende, *Aphrodite*

We went to the Louvre, and the boy sang, *Venus de Milo was noted for her charms, but strictly between us, you're cuter than Venus, and what's more you've got arms....* I thought it was charming. He saved the champagne bottle from the Moulin Rouge, and when we were aboard the ship sailing home, far out to sea, he wrote our names on a paper and put it in the bottle and corked it. Then he tossed it overboard—and kissed me. We were goners. I blamed Paris for a long, long time.

Twenty-five years later, long after the girlfriend had ripped the picture (I can imagine her frustration; how do you compete with triumphal seventeen, drunk on joy and life?), I returned to Paris, again arriving by train. This time my passport and tickets were tucked securely in a proper travel bag, one with shoulder straps and four zippered pockets. I stood by the train window watching the Parisian suburbs whiz by, feeling a trifle wistful, thinking twenty-five-years-have-gone-by thoughts.

Beside me, poking his head out the window, was my lover. I didn't know what he was thinking and didn't care; we'd had a rip-roaring argument the night before and a chill hung between us.

The train seemed dirty and too loud, the station a sad relic of the past. The hotel had tripled its rates since we'd booked a room. We refused to take it and went stumbling through the *arrondisement*, luggage in hand, searching for reasonably priced lodgings. The streets looked gray and grimy. A hundred tourists trampled the grass by the Eiffel Tower, which now seemed an awkward structure, out of place against the narrow buildings with their quaint chimney pots. Lines were long at the entrance to the Louvre, and once we were in, the guards eyed us suspiciously.

Paris has lost its romance, I thought bitterly. Another illusion destroyed.

But Paris knows me. She was biding her time.

A dismal, muddy rain was falling when we left the hotel, the two of us huddled under one umbrella and hurried down the darkening street in quest of dinner. The umbrella dripped annoyingly on my shoulder.

As if by chance, we ducked into the Polidor. Too crowded, too noisy, I muttered. But the warm, convivial Polidor, smelling of garlic and wine, drew us in. We were welcomed by a tableful of regulars who recommended the *boeuf Bourguignon* and the house Beaujolais. We feasted. We laughed. By the time we left, the rain had turned to a delicate spring mist. We strolled to the river and paused on the bridge, and my lover said, I'm sorry, and I love you, and as we watched the lights on the water he sang what he could remember of a Judy Collins's song: *My father always promised us that we would live in France; we'd go boating on the Seine, and I would learn to dance...*

Hand in hand, we walked back to the hotel in the mist, smiling. Paris was beginning to look a lot better.

Red geraniums bloomed outside our fifth-floor window and guitar music drifted up from the youth hostel across the street. My lover presented me with a nosegay of violets. I bought a piece of Limoges for my mother, discovered a fine, flinty Chablis. In a cooking class we listened to a mustachioed chef toss off *bons mots* while his knife flashed like a guillotine. Americans always want Cuisinart. No, no, he scolded, waggling his fingers and scattering bits of julienned leeks at us. Use your hands, a sharp knife. Sharp!

Our last night in Paris. Huge sausages, reflected in mirrored walls, hung from the archways of the restaurant. The *blanquette de veau* was smooth as butter; the wild strawberries were sweet gems. We sent our compliments to the chef. Moments later the waiter brought us a bottle in a holder of knitted wool, zippered: a bottle sweater. A gift from *zee keetchen*, he said with a grin. We unzipped the sweater. In the bottle was a clear liquid, and in the liquid a snake lay neatly coiled, its head rising into the neck of the bottle. I gasped; the waiter and the diners around us laughed merrily. We sipped the fiery liquor, and when we left we presented our surprised and grateful neighbors with the scarcely touched bottle.

"What an evening," my lover said, entwining his fingers with mine. "I'm savoring this." We were walking on a street of shops with well-lighted windows. A display caught my eye: a pyramid of perfume bottles, all of them L'Air du Temps. I stopped, overwhelmed by the sudden memory of a fragrance. There was plenty of time to return the next day, if I wanted to buy a bottle. "Do you want some of that perfume?" my lover, soon to be my husband, asked.

I turned away from the window and squeezed his hand. "No," I said. "I haven't worn that scent in years. And I've got all the gifts I need from Paris. Let's go home."

And so we did.

*Marilyn McFarlane is the author of several guidebooks, including* Best Places to Stay in the Pacific Northwest, *and a children's book,* Sacred Myths: Stories of World Religions. *She lives in Portland, Oregon.*

* ⭑ *

# Light on a
# Moonless Night

*A traveler returns to an island to rekindle
her dreams of paradise.*

I LIKE TO REMEMBER THE NIGHT OF MY RETURN TO THE REMOTE
Fijian island called Taveuni. Remembering it makes me smile.
Warm winds dried off the saltwater slapped in my face during their
earlier tantrum as I beached myself ashore after a thirty-six-hour
boat ride on high South Pacific seas. My balance was off as a tone-
deaf minstrel after a night of medieval merriment. I didn't care. I
was back in Taveuni.

TAV-EE-UUN-EE. I loved the feel of the word in my mouth,
full and rich and ripe like the island itself, about to burst with
ancient lava and laughter and secrets from the past. It made me
think of jumping from a place up high, like a rock, a tree, or a cliff,
into someplace unfamiliar and alive. The mere speaking of the
island's name carried its own magic for me, was a way of entering
and leaving the world. When spoken during the day, Taveuni was
an expansive name for a place containing mirth and light and possibly mischief, but at night the name held its own dark sort of
grace. And if whispered at night, or, even worse, whispered in just
the right tone, the name caused shivers. Taveuni whispered. Think
of it.

Eight months had fallen from the earth since I'd left Taveuni.

Eight months of exploring other places: New Zealand, Australia, Malaysia, Thailand, Indonesia. It didn't feel real, standing on that old Fiji dock again in the hot night, everything familiar in a dreamy kind of way. Even the taxi drivers came on like old friends. They sauntered toward us boat escapees looking as if they'd just heard the world's best joke. Or seen it. Our faces had to be green. One man was puking his boiled-fish dinner into the sea while his wife patted his back. That's true love. New visitors aren't hassled here as in parts of the world where a traveler can be swarmed by a sea of faceless strangers speaking the few words of English they know to conjure up business: "Room, room, taxi, hotel cheap, Miss, Miss, good food, cheap, speak English, please, Miss, come, cheap."

Life's gentler on Taveuni.

Like salty, fermenting pickles crammed in a jar, six of us shared a taxi ride along Taveuni's one road. The driver sang us a ditty. He was a happy man. As the taxi jerked its way along the bumpy road over hills and too fast around curves into the blackness of the night, I could imagine exactly where we were, what we'd see if it were daylight. Memories spilled over each other like ocean waves: of the two months I'd spent here, of the Fijians and their children I'd taught at the school, of the village that clings to the tropical mountainside, of the other travelers I'd met at the campground by the sea. And Laudi. Of course Laudi. I wondered if anyone would be awake at this hour. Would the quiet Fijian men and their children with immense eyes still be on the beach, circled around the kava bowl singing South Pacific harmonies? They'd be surprised to see me, of that I was sure.

I was surprised myself. Rarely do travelers return to such remote destinations even

> *Security is mostly a superstition. It does not exist in nature, nor do the children of men as a whole experience it. Avoiding danger is no safer in the long run than outright exposure. Life is either a daring adventure or nothing.*
>
> ◆
>
> —Helen Keller

if they had the best of intentions when leaving them. I was seventeen when I visited the island of Madeira on a school-sponsored holiday, and I vowed to return one day. Over ten years have passed, many of them spent traveling, and my list of secret spots on Earth to come back to is ever growing, with Madeira so far recessed that I don't know when I'll find my way back there.

But Taveuni called me back and I'd listened. I had daydreamed of this countless times over the past sweltering months, lost and bone-weary on noisy, diesel-hazed streets, caught in crushes of human traffic in jammed Asian markets, or waiting for trains, buses or cars with only a series of mangled strawhats between me and the unkind blaze of the equatorial sun. Ideas of returning to Taveuni—hidden so far and so secretly from the rest of the world that I often wondered if it really was of this world—had been growing steadily in my scorched mind.

I asked the taxi driver to stop half a mile or so before arriving where I thought, in the dark, Buvu Beach Campground lay. I wanted to walk the last part of the road as I imagined it. In my daydreams it had always been broad daylight, but I wasn't fussy. The driver didn't even question dumping me in the middle of nowhere at two o'clock in the morning. The other passengers eyed my tent skeptically. They were off to Taveuni's resort. An elderly Englishwoman warned me, oblivious to our native driver, "They were cannibals here, dear, right in this jungle. Whatever are you thinking?"

"That you shouldn't knock eating people until you try it yourself."

Okay, I said that after the taxi roared off and left me standing in the mud. I set off with my backpack through the darkness, hoping I wouldn't veer off the dirt road into the bush. I suppose it was possible that ghosts of cannibals might still be hanging around, suspended in the confusion of trees. Or perhaps underneath the tender ground lay mute bones of half-eaten men carved up for special occasions. If I stepped in the wrong place, the bones would crumble into powder and release terrible secrets. So I looked up instead, into the soft center of the universe. The sky is ancient and the ghosts there don't remember cannibals. The storm had passed back out to sea and a great white sweep of Pacific stars poured down. I tried to find the Southern Cross but couldn't see it. As usual. Instead I spotted Orion directly over me, and its familiarity reassured me that I was doing the right thing to return here. It's a consistent constellation.

No light of the moon floated down into the world that night. Into an awkward blackness I walked for what seemed like hours, gradually losing confidence that I knew where I was. Not only disoriented, I was dizzy. Landsickness. I wavered back and forth along the dirt road, giddy and excited. No lights shone anywhere since Taveuni (only 25 miles long and 6 miles wide) has no electricity except for the occasional house with a generator. Most people use oil lamps, all that is needed by islanders who live naturally with the sun, sea, and land.

I finally came to a hill so I knew I'd passed Buvu Beach just behind me. Exhilaration lifted my load of clothes, books, and gifts as I found my way back to the campground's entrance. I walked barefoot—the only way to walk on a muddy road. The earth is softer in Taveuni than in other places, and darker. It's how the earth must have been millions of years ago, in the world's warm beginnings. My hands remembered their way up a giant tree marking the pathway leading into the wooded beach. I'd arrived.

Heaven owns real estate on Buvu Beach. An extended Fijian family owns it also. They live up a hill across the road. The campground is shaded by towering and twisted trees which drop down leaves large enough to hide overfed cats. Coconut palms, mango trees, ferns, and bamboo shoots jump up everywhere to join the lush green picnic of it all. But it's the flower blossoms that lure people inside. The smells they emit refuse to be shunned. Scent-drenched, the blossoms fill your nostrils, swarm the cracks of your memory until you're inhaling more than flowers. You're inhaling echoes of how the world once was. Three or four little bamboo huts, known in Fiji as *bures*, lie hidden among the voluptuous vegetation. A few tents are always edged away somewhere too. I like to believe that travelers are blown this way by ancient sea winds. We fall inside the soft air and sleep to the pounding waves of the ocean's heart which beats in time to our own. Only the occasional annoying rooster or thud of a wayward coconut interrupts one's sleep.

Pitch-black. The hand extended in front of my face was invisible. This was the kind of utter darkness that falls only in remote places, inconceivable to city dwellers. Nothing but an eight-month-old memory of the place could get me over the preposterous tree roots erupting out of the sand. They were like mutant flora. Last time here I'd broken a toe, twice, on one of these roots. The Fijians made such a big deal about it and laughed at me so much that if I did it again I'd be forced to hop back out to the boat unseen. There's only so much jocularity about my feet I'll tolerate.

I walked in slow motion toward the grass-roofed hut and heard it creaking in the wind. The little hut always reminded me of *Gilligan's Island*, being so makeshift, crafted out of whatever grew on the beach. The hut was our refuge, our hangout, our sheltering haven. Here campers and Fijians would cook, talk, and laugh for hours into the night. It had a sand floor and no walls, a stove and cupboards, a few benches and a little table that mangoes, coconuts, and pineapples always lay on. We called the little hut our kitchen. Sometimes when the moon was full, the tide was high enough that the sea would slip right up and wet our kitchen floor. We didn't mind.

Beside the kitchen, we would gather on the beach at the end of each day and watch the sun setting over the Pacific. It would spread over us like a mauve shadow. When it grew dark, we would sit around a fire, drinking the Fijian elixir of life, kava, out of coconut bowls. Kava isn't alcoholic, but it's something. It slows down time. The Fijian men would sit with us and sing and play their guitars. After a while we'd all be singing. Then we'd tell stories. We'd tell travel stories mainly, since we were all travelers of some sort. The Fijians would tell stories too, stories of their lives growing up on Taveuni. Storytelling is important in television-free places like Taveuni. It's important anywhere. I remembered all the stories told around those campfires. And now I stood in the kitchen again, remembering these things as if I'd never left.

But I had left. I left because I couldn't stop moving. I couldn't stop searching for the perfect place. That's the thing about travelers. We always have to see what's over the next hill. But someone once wrote that to leave is to die a little. So I came back to the place I left. And immediately I found my heart beating alive inside this strange island's quiet grace, stirred to see into the life of things here. I stood still and listened as moist night air invaded my hair like seaweed. What I heard was a kind of song coming out of the sea, like a drum banging in the waves, but singing too. All that time over in Asia, I'd only remembered the adventures I'd had here — the hiking, the snorkeling, the music, the family, the kids in the school. But now I understood it was the waves that had pulled me back. They'd been here all along like a steady pulse, patiently keeping time for the world. Waves like this never stop rolling inside a person, just beneath one's awareness. The sea has a way of slipping us back to our beginnings, soothing a rusty place inside us, to remind us of something. Like a secret trance, a forgotten calling.

I stood in water as warm as my blood and exhaled a tremendous unconditional breath like a wind itself. The sea washed something out of me, freed me in its imperceptible way of what lay smoldering within: eight months of traveling alone on a road full of startling faces and unfamiliar tongues. I'd been traipsing through too many days and nights of dog-ridden streets and climbing over shaky mountaintops, not always liking what I found on the other side. But traveling is a journey to the center of the soul, a crazy Irishman once shouted at me. One forges through dark mountains and unnamed streets until there's nothing left to see but chiseled pieces of light.

As I walked along the shoreline, I thought about how nature overwhelms everything with the sea's pastel-painted fish and purple coral, the island's extravagant trees of sweet unrecognizable fruit growing amidst waterfalls and volcanic mountains, rugged and wet. It would be difficult not to be delirious in such a place, a place where nature overpowers people, where people give themselves over to the land and sea. Little bits of phosphorescence, colored dots of fluorescent green, washed up at my feet. Laughter came in on the waves. I was home, as close to home as a traveler can get, and I felt like staying for good.

Eventually I turned and felt my way back in the dark to the woods and the little wooden shower house behind the kitchen. Two days on a dirty boat had left me with a film of dust and salt I didn't want to experience Taveuni through. Showering in blackness isn't as bad as it sounds. The cold water jolted me awake. The familiarity of the shower and the same old creaking of the bamboo door latch made me think of Laudi. Laudi was part of the Fijian family who owned the campground and lived across the road. The first time we met he'd just returned from university in Suva, Fiji's capital on the main island. He'd missed Taveuni and wanted to take care of his family campground. Laudi was raised on this island, under a canopy of enchanted trees and the enormous breasts of his aunts. When we saw each other the first time, we flashed identical sideswiping grins, the truest kind. It made us laugh that he and I were the same age exactly but had led such different lives. We'd written letters back and forth while I'd been away. Gushy love letters.

Laudi and his cousins would come down to the beach after sunset every night to sing and play their guitars for the campers. Almost always, as astonishing little group of travelers from around the world would collect, none knowing each other initially, stay for days sliding into weeks, and become lifelong friends. I was easy here. The music brought us together. The high-voiced harmonies of such big men singing Fijian love songs touched a chord in us that could reverberate anywhere in the world if listened for under the stars or beside the ocean. It was the unexpectedness of it all.

At this hour, though, no guitars strummed, no fires burned, no kava slid down throats and lulled minds, and no stories were born into the night. I couldn't possibly sleep. I'd look for Laudi, or his teasing cousin, Kalisi. I knew if I waited until morning to see the family, they'd ask me why I hadn't woken them immediately. But it was so late. Maybe I'd just find Laudi.

I walked back out to the road again, still dizzy and wavering, needing a flashlight. The rain had muddied the hill up to the family houses, and I now slipped as well as staggered. Anyone who saw me would have wondered who the drunken white person was and where she would be going at this hour. Fortunately only a dog saw me.

A dim light shone in Laudi's old room. Fijians often sleep with their lanterns dimmed low so it didn't mean he'd be awake. I felt like a kid as I stood on a stump beneath the window, looked in and whispered, "Laudi, Laudi." I could barely make out someone sleeping on the bed. "Laudi, it's me, Laurie." A head jolted up. Then another body on the floor rustled and mumbled something in Fijian. I tried to remember what Fijian I knew and whispered, "*Bula, keri keri, Laudi e vei?*" hoping that meant "Hi, please, where's Laudi?" Clearly, neither of these two people was turning out to be Laudi and being awoken in the middle of a dark night by a foreign stranger in your window who's screwing up the language would confuse anybody. The boy who had been asleep on the floor turned the oil lamp up bright and held it toward my face. All I could see was a set of perfect piano-key teeth. I was surprised I didn't recognize the boy or the man on the bed.

"*Bula*, please who are you?" the boy asked in his lovely polite mix of a Fijian English accent.

"I'm Laurie, Laudi's friend, Laurie from Canada."

"Oh, Laurie! *Bula, bula*, Laurie! I'm Pita, Laudi's cousin."

"*Bula*, Laurie, I'm Salote," spoke up the man on the bed. "Laudi sleeps down the beach tonight in his tent. I'm his uncle."

While never taking their eyes off me, they whispered to each other in Fijian. I felt silly standing there. I said thank you, apologized for waking them, and accepted a lantern. By now it was probably close to four in the morning. I was still wandering around, still not in straight lines, but at least I knew where Laudi was and with the lamp I wouldn't crash into anything.

Back on the beach I began my search of tents. How many could there be? I whispered outside four different tents and disturbed at least six mere strangers that night before I spotted a tent with a broken zipper. It didn't look like the other tents. It wasn't igloo-shaped nor was it the fancy multicolored variety. It was more like a gypsy tent, a large canvas triangle with several tarps cleverly tied to trees to keep out rain. No dangerous coconut trees hovered above this tent. I figured only a Fijian could be staying there. The tent was cradled inside the massive crawling roots of a gnarled tree that drooped white blossoms.

I set the lantern down on the sand outside the tent. A guitar, a flashlight, and a mosquito coil lay in the tent's corner. I looked inside and saw Laudi sleeping. It was one of those moments that catch a person off guard, that come from a place unknown and rarely suspected. A moment that, if frozen and preserved for future generations to thaw out and contemplate, would make them think life had ripped them off because happiness doesn't come like that anymore. I started to call Laudi but hesitated. Everything would change after this. Here and now, as I crouched on the sand in the warm dark night, were all the things I wanted to feel or see or hear, and I didn't want it to end. In the precious space of time just before drinking water in a desert, before a child opens a present, before calling out Laudi's name, the world tells us a secret. It's a quiet message that whispers life can be what we want it to be. Any sudden movement could destroy it—a voice, a shudder of wind, a dog barking in the distance.

A fruit bat whooshed its wings just over my head. "Laudi," I finally called out. "Laudi, it's me. Laurie." Laudi jumped up and yelled—Fijians are very superstitious.

"What? Laurie! Is it really you? I thought you were a ghost! Is it you? Am I dreaming?"

"I think we are," I said. He held out his arms to me as the day's first light was just breaking. We hadn't seen each other in eight months. I'd been traveling alone a long time and had almost forgotten what human touch felt like. When his sleepy warm skin pressed against mine, I nearly melted into dark eternity.

Somewhere there exists on the horizon an invisible line between dream and reality. That night I think I crossed over that line and found that all of us, all of life, in love and beauty, can if we choose, lie out there in the hazy glow of the pink dawn where no lines exist. For a little while anyway. We must cherish the little whiles. They're all that really matter in the end.

*Laurie Gough is the author of* Kite Strings of the Southern Cross, *which won a silver medal for ForeWord Magazine's Best Travel Book of the Year, and was short-listed for the Thomas Cook/Daily Telegraph Travel Book of the*

*Year award in the U.K. She has also written for Salon.com,* Outpost, *and the* Toronto Globe and Mail. *Her work appears in several travel anthologies, including* Travelers' Tales Greece, A Woman's World, The Adventure
of Food, Her Fork in the Road, Sand in My Bra and Other Misadventures, *and* Hyenas Laughed at Me and Now I Know Why. *She lives in Ontario, Canada.*

MARY MORRIS

* * *

# On Italian Time

*Trains, of course, leave on*
*schedule. Trust me.*

RECENTLY MY FAMILY AND I TRAVELED BY TRAIN FROM ZURICH
to Milan. Having just spent the night on a plane, we collapsed into
the train compartment intending to sleep during the six-hour ride.
Shortly after we left Zurich, a Swiss conductor told us the train
separated at the border. We would have to move into one of the
front cars, but the half-hour stop in Chiesa would give us ample
time to make the shift.

Somewhere, as we dozed through Switzerland, our conductor
left the train. Another one, who was younger, Italian, and seemingly wiser, woke us, shouting that we'd be in Lugano in ten minutes.
The train would separate there, but it was a short stop. "You'd better hurry." At Lugano my husband and I dragged our luggage, sleeping daughter, and assorted paraphernalia onto the platform and
dashed toward the front. As we approached another trainman, I said
to him in Italian, "Excuse us, sir, but which cars go to Italy?" He
looked at me with slight disdain as he uttered in a resonant baritone, *"Signora, tutto il treno va in Italia."* He said it three times to
make sure I understood. The whole train goes to Italy.

It was a difficult moment. We had given up our secluded little
compartment for what looked like a long section of second-class

47

smoking cars. Too tired to return, we climbed on. A high school soccer team was celebrating, but our daughter had fallen back asleep, and we didn't have the heart to move her again. In Chiesa, when I got off to change money, I watched the part of the train we had originally been sitting in divide off and head for Austria.

I am not a cynic and I love Italy. But I have discovered that time and space are relative notions there. I have followed signs to the Palazzo Grassi that led directly into a wall, and floated the wrong way down a one-way canal, the gondolier shouting all the way. I've read timetables that had no relation to actual departure times, and followed a sign to Verona that in fifteen minutes brought me back full circle to the place on Lake Garda where I had begun.

No one maliciously puts you on the wrong part of the train or sends you in the wrong direction. It's just that arrivals and departures matter much less than wines and sauces, the state of your frescoes, and lovemaking. Italy, like Mexico, is fundamentally a pagan land that has embraced Christianity out of necessity, guilt, and belief. Scratch the surface and you'll find heathens, and heathens don't really care what day it is, let alone what time. What matters is seeing, smelling, tasting. Who cares if you turn left, when right is just as beautiful and the wine is just as good.

In Verona we rented a small green Fiat from a disgruntled Eurocar representative named Gemania who had dyed red hair. When I stopped by to extend our rental, she asked for the contract. "I'm sorry," I said, "I can't seem to locate it."

"But you must find it," she insisted. "If you do not have the contract, we cannot give you the weekly rate." The message was clear: without the rental agreement we were essentially buying the car. That night my husband and I went through every bag and every shred of paper, but we found no contract. I decided to call Gemania. I would plead, bribe, do anything. But when I explained the situation she said, "Oh, don't worry. No problem. It's fine."

What had happened to Gemania since the previous day? Had she eaten a wonderful meal, had a troublesome tooth pulled, received a letter from a long-lost love? Sheer whimsy seems to be a national trait. Terra firma becomes quicksand. For some reason I find this charming.

Later, on the train to Venice, the conductor kindly suggested we would save time if we got off in Venice and waited for the direct train to Venice on Binario 3 (Track 3). He held up three fingers. "Numero tre," he said emphatically. We sat contentedly with our luggage at Binario 3, thinking how lucky we were to be the only people going to Venice that day. Look at the poor people stuffing themselves into that overcrowded train on Binario 2.

As we watched the train for Venice depart from Binario 2, I was left once again to ponder the Italian character. Our conductor could not have been more self-assured. After all, we are helpless tourists and he has this one job: to collect our money and tell us where to go. Perhaps we tourists are victims of intentional misinformation— a plot whose purpose is to drive us away.

However, the natives suffer similar fates. When we visited Manuela, a friend who lives in Vicenza, she served us lunch on her patio. Afterward she came with us to spend an afternoon touring Vicenza. We returned to her house to find her sons and husband missing and messages on her answering machine from people concerned about her well-being.

It turned out that a local doctor, a family friend, had noticed that a woman with a name similar to Manuela's had been admitted to the hospital. She had been bitten by a tiger mosquito, an aggressive insect, and had swollen up like a balloon. Coincidentally, she resembled Manuela, if Manuela were blown up like a balloon.

The doctor phoned his wife who phoned her sister who phoned Manuela's sister who phoned the sons and so on. Several families rushed to the hospital to stand at the swollen woman's bedside, debating whether or not this was Manuela (who, at the time, was having gelato with us in the piazza).

Manuela insisted we drive with her to her friend Marina's house. That was where everyone had assembled to await word on whether the woman in the hospital was Manuela. The sun was setting as we arrived at a beautiful villa in the countryside surrounded by cypresses and Roman pines. There under the trees sat all the friends and family. *"Manuela vive!"* they cheered as Manuela got out of the car. Champagne corks popped and a celebration began

I was thinking we should get going, but my husband was drinking wine from unmarked bottles that had been brought out of the cellar. I decided to stroll through the vineyards. When I returned, Marina had set a long table outside with a red-checked cloth. She had a salami, someone else had olives. Pepino, Marina's husband, went to pick tomatoes. One of Manuela's sons fetched some mozzarella from my car. Marina asked me to light the candles, and I replied, in my best Italian, *"Dov'e il semaforo?"* Everyone laughed because I'd asked for the traffic lights.

The table was spread with cheese and tomatoes and Tuscan bread and salami. Though we had reservations elsewhere and other places to be, we all sat and drank wine under the stars until it was time for bed.

*Mary Morris is the author of twelve books, including five novels, three collections of short stories, and a trilogy of travel memoirs, including* Angels & Aliens: A Journey West, Wall to Wall: From Beijing to Berlin by Rail, *and* Nothing to Declare: Memoirs of a Woman Traveling Alone. *She has also co-edited with her husband, Larry O'Connor,* Maiden Voyages, *an anthology of the travel literature of women. Her numerous short stories and essays have appeared in such places as* The Paris Review, The New York Times, Travel & Leisure, *and* Vogue. *The recipient of the Rome Prize in Literature from the American Academy of Arts & Letters, Morris teaches writing at Sarah Lawrence College and lives in Brooklyn with her husband and daughter.*

VIRGINIA  BARTON  BROWNBACK

# Unpaved Roads

*A grandmother trades the nanny
track for a fanny pack.*

NOTHING ZAPS UP THE ADRENALINE LIKE UNCERTAINTY. IT WAS
morning, and I was in Bacalar on the southeastern Yucatán peninsula. I prepared to leave my pretty lakeside hotel, stuffing my thief-
proof purse down my bosom and trying to memorize some phrase-
book Spanish. Then I sat on the curb of the road and waited for the
bus. After fifteen minutes a Mexican woman asked where I was
going. "Chetumal." She signaled me to follow her to the main road.
I had been so overanxious I'd been sitting in the hotel driveway.

For the solo traveler off the beaten track, false starts are as normal as missed meals and lumpy beds. My miscue en route to
Chetumal was one of the many acceptable bumps on the road I was
traveling along the coast of the Mexican state of Quintana Roo into
neighboring Belize and onward, I hoped, to Tikal, the great ceremonial center of ancient Mayan civilization.

Everything I had read about Tikal made me want to go there.
And not by the tiny plane most visitors take to the excavated ruins
in the jungles of northeastern Guatemala, but by the only road that
connects it with the outside world.

The essence of my journey was to be self-discovery. The last
thing I wanted was the quick and easy.

I'd been in limbo for a year, derailed on the nanny track, fulfilling the prescribed role of one who has just celebrated her 70th birthday. My wake-up call came as I lifted my grandson up to blow out the candles. As our breathing dovetailed, I felt my life sliding out from under me. It was a glorious party: flowers, toasts—my life story in rhyme and song, beginning to blur into myth. But in some cobwebby corner I was previewing my own funeral; I knew this was not all I wanted in the final life plan.

I had to get my hands out of the diaper bag and into the backpack again. I had to get back to the particular kind of moving around the Third World I had done for fifteen years—what I considered Real Travel. This invited disturbances and the reshuffling of one's assurances. It was the open classroom. It was breathing *out*, not in; it meant thinking bigger, wider, seeing the strand farthest away as part of the rug we're sitting on.

Now, after bus hops to Chetumal and Belize City, I was aboard my dream bus on the long road to Tikal. I had heard rumors—false I was sure—that this was the "Bandito Road."

The way was disarmingly straight, the people along the way a mix of African and Caribbean, speaking English. On board, the bus was scattered with European backpackers discussing where we would be at nightfall. My guidebook advised: "Cross early in the morning—best chance of catching buses onward." I opted to get off at San Ignacio, the last town in Belize with a choice of hotels.

The next morning I rose early and found a bus stop on a back road where horses ran free in a field. A school bus soon picked me up and dropped me off at the Guatemalan border. There I shared a taxi and found myself headed west to Flores and on to Tikal. I was thoroughly enjoying myself, talking photography with a biologist from Berlin, when—flashing past me on the side of the road—a poster of a comic-strip bandit appeared. He had a face mask, a twirling mustache, and two pistols pointing down the road. Above him, the warning: *"Peligroso! Bandidos!"* We *were* on the Bandito Road! No turning back now.

"I'm wearing my Guatemalan shirt," I said. "If they come on board, they won't attack *me*."

"Shhhh!" said the Berliner in my ear, as if the masked men were lurking nearby. But the land was flat, treeless, and empty. There weren't even any bushes for them to hide in.

The taxi dropped us off at the main parking lot of Tikal National Park. "Home free!" I thought, flushed with the sense of accomplishment that only the small-time risk taker knows. I would stay for two, maybe three nights. Here I could walk into the jungle at any hour—really see this wonderful place. By now I was ready for a few amenities. Which hotel? There were three. I picked the simplest with the most rooms, the Jungle Lodge.

"We're full," the hotel clerk said.

"Full? I thought this was the slow season." I suspected they didn't want to bother with me. I wasn't part of a Conspicuous Consumption Group—buyers, eaters, drinkers, with dollar signs on their foreheads.

"Okay, I'll go to The Jaguar Inn."

"That's full too."

"The Tikal Inn?"

"They have no rooms; I just called over there." No one to blame but myself. I was furious; I knew better. Everyone comes to see the great Tikal.

"Okay. What are my options?"

"I'm sure you can find a room in Flores. There's a shuttle bus leaving at two, or you can see the ruins this afternoon and go back later."

"But I just *came* from Flores," I moaned. "That's not where I want to be. I want to be at Tikal. That's why I've spent two days traveling to get here." ("Real travelers never go back," I murmured sotto voce.)

Then I remembered something from my guidebook. "Isn't there a campground that rents hammocks?"

Now it was her turn to be surprised. "Yes!" She gave me directions.

The campground had about twenty concrete platforms spaced far apart on a wide green lawn. A guard stood outside the nearby johns. I knew about hammocks. I had stayed in one on a beach five days ago.

I was shown to a platform already occupied by two young women: Marcella, a dark-eyed Costa Rican, wispy in a long, graceful shirt, and Lili, a sleek Danish blonde in denim shorts. They had sleeping bags and a camp stove, and all the young men who worked on the grounds were hovering around offering assistance. "Matches?" "Wood?" "Blankets?"

After I introduced myself, the two women announced they would be celebrating Lili's eighteenth birthday that night inside their favorite ruin, El Mundo Perdido (The Lost World). There would be candles and cake at six. Did I want to come along?

After stepping off the graveled parking lot and paying the guard $6, I entered the vast ruins set in the 575-square-kilometer preserve and found myself suddenly enveloped by jungle. The path was narrow and rough with exposed roots crawling underfoot. As I walked in, it got darker and denser; the birds began to screech and howler monkeys swung through the branches overhead. I worried about birds eyeing my white hair for nesting material (an oyster-catcher had done that in the Hebrides years ago); I wondered if vipers could be up among the monkeys. I'd watched *Nova*.

At last I came around a corner and emerged into the Great Plaza, a breathtaking compound surrounded by dozens of temple-pyramids, palaces, altars, and shrines. As I stood still before one particularly immense pyramid, I found myself standing tall, looking up at this "being," eye to eye. Just for a second, I thought I felt something touch my shoulder. "Straighten up!" the spirit seemed to whisper—a no one from the deep past, desperate to win the approval of an all-powerful master.

As the afternoon waned, I wandered several miles, discovering more landmarks, sometimes following my guidebook, sometimes my nose—and getting gloriously lost. I encountered a British group, studying birds. They had their scopes trained on an orange-breasted falcon, the sun full on its brilliant vest. As I came across others, I noticed I was asking "What?" a lot.

It was the birds. They had taken over the ruins. They were all you could hear. I caught flashes of their bright, long tail-feathers. They were courting, arguing, pulling down vines, I was losing my light. I wouldn't be able to get myself back to camp if I stopped for the birthday party. So walking faster and faster, bird eyes, monkey eyes, and snake eyes following me, I retraced my steps through the jungle as best I could in the dark.

When I reached the campground, I realized I had no idea which concrete slab was mine. The grassy terrain was wet and pockmarked with holes. There were a few scattered lights, but I didn't want to barge into someone else's bedroom. My beauties—and their admirers—were nowhere to be seen or heard. I assumed they were still in the jungle, eating cake. I noticed one light, set lower than the others, and headed for it. Closer, I spotted my hammock and suitcase. My newfound friends had thought ahead. They had set a tiny candle out for our way home. What a relief! Home free.

Well, almost. The night air in Mexico and Belize had been so warm I had not foreseen the cold that suddenly descended over the Tikal jungle. As the night crept onward, I had to dip into my suitcase time and time again to put on new layers until I'd emptied it. The last item I plucked was a towel that I wrapped around my head so only my breath leaked out. I was too cold to cross the grass to ask the staff for a blanket, and when I heard Lili and Marcella return after midnight, I was too chagrined at my lack of preparedness to ask them for help.

I was getting what I asked for: no frills, spontaneous, be-your-own-leader stuff. Disturbances were daily and the agony/ecstasy factor was high. But, the next morning I decided I'd had enough of hammocks; it was time to see more of Guatemala.

I returned to Flores and hopped a plane to Guatemala City. As the small aircraft lifted over the densely covered terrain, I wondered how much of the jungle below hid other temple-pyramids. Inside the cockpit, two pilots peered at a torn map taped above their control panel. An hour later we landed on the Bank-Air airstrip of the capital, a sprawling asphalt jungle of more than two million and the takeoff hub to the Guatemalan highlands.

The most appealing venture seemed to be to explore the

unpaved roads north of Quiché. I was halfway along in a taxi when my English-speaking driver asked cautiously, "Why do you want to go there?"

"To get off the tourist track," I said. "I hear it's beautiful and unspoiled."

"The guerrilla fighters live in these hills," he said quietly. "Sometimes they stay away… and sometimes they come down."

I didn't like the odds, turned around, and got back on the popular route: Antigua and Lake Atitlán.

Visitors orient themselves to the small colonial city of Antigua, once the capital of Guatemala, by its three volcanoes; Volcán Agua, Volcán Fuego, and Volcán Acatenango rise from the ends of the cobblestone streets. But what I remember most, now that I'm back on drabber streets, are the colors: orange walls, mustard-yellow walls, turquoise walls, subdued by the late-afternoon light.

On my first day I rode by bus up to Chichicastenango (6,800 feet) for the market. It was midday when I arrived at this huge-scale photo-op. Tourists from all over the world aimed their cameras and camcorders at the Indians, mostly women and children. The Guatemalans tried to hide their faces, but they couldn't leave the scene; they needed to go home that day with money in their pockets.

---

*A* delightful side effect of developing a shock of white hair is that other travelers often feel a need to help an "older" woman. Never mind that I'm on my way to shoot the rapids of a wild New Zealand river, or explore an ancient shipwreck with a scuba partner. When I patiently listen to a teenager giving directions to a place from which I've just come, it creates a bond that invites further interaction. I've made friendships, uncovered new places, sampled exotic fare, just because for a moment I traded my need to assert self-assurance for the exhilaration of discovery.

◆

—Judy Wade, *Gutsy Women: Travel Tips & Wisdom for the Road*

All steps led to the church of Santo Tomás where the pungent incense was knock-you-over strong. The white towers of the Roman Catholic church rose behind a foreground jammed with calla lilies, iris, fruit, and native women wrapped in vibrant fabrics. Outside the church doors, in front of lighted candles and offerings of flowers, several Indian men and women swung incense pots across the threshold so energetically that they appeared and disappeared in the clouds of smoke. I instantly knew I was in the presence of what the Spanish call *lo maravilloso* ("the marvelous").

I found out later that the ritual we watched appeases the spirits who guard the entryway; it asks permission to step across their territory. The intensity on the faces of the swinging cloud makers hinted that they were not alone on the steps.

Next I bounced by motorboat across the waters of Lake Atitlán to the village of Santiago Atitlán where Tzutuhil Mayan women invite you into their courtyards to buy embroidery. For economic survival trade goes on, but the highlanders kept to themselves and their rural ways. They spoke a mishmash of languages I'd not heard before, and some Spanish.

Sometimes it was possible to decode the babble, to get the drift of the bird-talk, but without the details contained in the language, most encounters were a series of frustrations.

As with the frosty night that fell down on me at Tikal, I was caught unaware. This was different from Asia, where the lasting imprint of the British had left English as the language of commerce and of the educated. Here the visitor was cut out of a vastly rich and complex tangle of threads, a great ball whose core was embedded in the history and literature and art of Spain blended with the culture of its indigenous people.

I was stuck on the other side of a t-shirt I had seen in Guatemala City: "*English* is spoken here, but not understood." If I managed to ask a question in Spanish correctly, I couldn't understand the answer. And most questions were too hard. I could only ask ones that began with "What?" "Where?" and "Who?" I wanted to ask "How?" and "Why?"

The reflections in the lake—the pink dawn outlining the cones of volcanoes—were distant postcards. But their shallowness mimicked the thinness my Real Travel had become. I still had two weeks before my return flight. I decided the best thing I could do with the time left was stop moving and deep-dive into one of Antigua's renowned Spanish-language schools.

My days from then on began and ended with Juan Castillo's face. I can still hear his pure voice, his dark eyes holding mine fixedly as he repeated the words. I tried to block my linear thinking and just hear the cadence. That way I could *sometimes* imitate what he had said. I loved the one-to-one format of total immersion. Exiled just days ago from the language, now language was all there was.

My days were complete with lessons, homework, and new friends. After a week I tried extending my plane ticket and could not. I felt cheated. By now I was relieved not to be going anywhere. I was conjugating *"voy, vas, va, vamos, van"* in my sleep—even the interior advice I gave myself was sprinkled with Spanish.

On my last day in Antigua, I took off for school with my bag packed so I could fit in a morning break with Juan, who wanted to show me his favorite church, the Iglesia de San Francisco. A lovely place, the interior walls were lined with messages of *"gracias"* (thanks for getting someone a job, thanks for making someone well, etc.). Pedro founded a hospital there in the 1600s and is now up for sainthood. The oldest messages were engraved in marble, the newest were scrawled on file cards.

I told Juan I did not believe in miracles, and he said, resignedly, his brown eyes looking sad: "I know."

On my flight home I realized that although I'd often been in the dark, lost—and wrong—I had been there, someplace else, and had never once longed to be there any other way. I'm not young and don't feel young, but swaying on the overhead straps, sometimes the only outsider on a bus, looking out different windows every day, I felt ageless—a work still in progress—with more discoveries awaiting me over the horizon.

I'm not sure how to name what I brought back from Guatemala's many roads and sights and faces. But in the land where the marvelous, without ceremony, gets kneaded into the corn-flour, all the lumps cleared customs and came home with me.

*Virginia Barton Brownback has made more than thirty trips on unpaved roads since 1977. She is the author of* Daredevil Twilight.

# Following the
# Tracks Back

*An African homecoming provides*
*unexpected enlightenment.*

THE ROAD HOME WAS AS DIFFICULT AS I REMEMBERED IT, A ROUGH, three-hour drive over the corrugations, not helped by the fact that we were travelling in one of Charles's huge old BMWs which could not have been less well adapted to this journey.

Adam was used to driving on rough roads back home in Australia, but I could tell from his expression that he had never seen anything like this before. The road was really only intended for the village buses that plied this route twice a day. It began as a neat, two-lane strip of tar, but that was short-lived; a single-lane, tarred stretch continued uncertainly for a while, until abruptly the dusty road took over. You could always tell when you had left the commercial farms owned by the whites because the tarred road and electricity poles would end. After that, you were in the Tribal Trust Lands, now known by the more politically correct title of Communal Lands. The change of name had meant little to the people: it had really just been a case of changing masters.

The BMW did not like the dirt road and neither did my husband. He did not see the magnificent blue of the Wedza mountains, the picture-postcard villages, and the little children running out to greet the car. He only saw the potholes, the jagged rocks, and the deep culverts where the rains had turned road into riverbed. This was not the honeymoon drive he had in mind. Travelling at 30 kilometres an hour produced vibrations that drowned out the stereo and when, after half an hour, the dashboard fell away in our laps, we had to forget about music altogether. We stopped frequently to clear away rocks or to survey the road ahead, which at every turn potentially concealed axle-snapping obstacles.

Still, we were getting closer to home all the time. Soon we were in sight of the mountain, Dengedza, that overlooked my village; familiar faces appeared on the roadside. The road had become smooth and my husband was clearly enjoying himself now — he was even smiling and commenting on the scenery. I didn't have the heart to tell him about our driveway.

On reflection, it was less a driveway than the result of a rockslide. Not that we stopped to reflect too much when the rock struck the bottom of the car: a big rock all right, but hardly big enough to stand out against the hundreds of others that were scattered across the final 200-metre stretch to the homestead.

Our homecoming was rapturous. I hadn't been back for a while, and my mother ran out from the kitchen to greet us, ululating and dancing, raising dust as she came. My brother Sydney, his wife, Mai Shuvai, and their children heard the commotion and came running up from their huts to see what it was all about. Bathed in the purple light of late afternoon, it was a perfect scene, and I felt a peace and happiness that only being home can bring.

Then somebody saw the oil pouring into the red dust underneath our car.

"*Maiweeeeee!*" (My mother!) screeched Mai Shuvai irrelevantly, as she tried to stem the flow of hot oil from the sump with cotton wool. The cotton wool was replaced by a tin mug, which quickly overflowed and was replaced with a pot, and then a still bigger one. Soon just about every kitchen utensil was filled with the steaming oil.

To me, this scene had a familiarity about it that, if anything, made me feel more at home. Life in the village was an ongoing cycle of crisis and resolution. Nothing, except sickness and death, could disturb the overall pattern. As time was rarely an issue, wasting it meant virtually nothing at all; therefore, there was no urgency to find a solution to our problem. This was the art of life in the village.

But for my husband, being 150 kilometres from civilization with a broken car, no tools, and no hope of a passing BMW mechanic, was nothing short of a major crisis, an absolute showstopper. After he finished yelling and kicking the dust, he just sat down and stared into the distance, trying to resign himself to the prospect of an indefinite stay in the village. Here was a person who had never experienced the feeling of being abandoned by twentieth-century technology.

The people in the village did not understand what all the fuss was about. Tomorrow at four in the morning, the bus back to Harare would come by the village, waking everybody with its three-note horn blaring out "Strangers in the Night." If the car could not be fixed, the white man could simply get on the bus for the six-hour journey back to town.

Uncle Chakwanda, who had arrived from the main village, appointed himself mechanic to our stricken automobile. He had never fixed anything more complex than a windlass or a paraffin lamp but he led Adam away in search of "parts" to fix the oil sump. Adam followed him, his shoulders drooping, all his power as a civilized Westerner visibly ebbing away. An hour later, the two of them returned with a half tube of two-part epoxy cement, with which Uncle Chakwanda intended to restore the damage to the pride of German engineering the following morning.

"It will never work. This old man must be bloody crazy," said Adam, laughing without an ounce of mirth. "Has anybody else got a car around here? Maybe there's a farmhouse somewhere that has a phone."

Everybody laughed at the sight of the white man covered in oil and dust, looking wildly around for some sign of hope—an electric light in the distance, an airplane flying overhead, some ingenious technology to help him out of his predicament.

Two or three beers and a bath in the warm water from the borehole lifted Adam's spirits enormously. He and I sat with our backs against the whitewashed wall of my mother's house, watching a huge white moon rise behind the hill, casting long, flat shadows on our little homestead.

Years before, we young girls longed for these full-moon nights, when we would meet in the forest, down in the valley far from the kitchen fires, to dance and talk of romance and the future. There were leopards in the forest back then, hidden amongst huge, dark trees which stretched out to the horizon. It was wartime and sometimes we would hear the guerrillas passing quietly in the scrub, heading into the village to get food, supplies, and perhaps the warmth of the older women. We would hold our breath until they passed, and then our songs and laughter would slowly start up again, lilting through the trees back to the huts. In that half-light, the faces of my friends had been innocent of the hardships that were to come: teenage motherhood, the decades of drought, long years of war, and a revolution that meant very little to rural people.

It would seem that I was among the last children to share the secrets of the forest, the last generation to hope for better things. The forest was virtually gone now. Even the big trees that did remain seemed somehow smaller, twisted and gnarled, their limbs distorted by the yearly harvest of firewood. Where there was once forest there was now just naked earth, cut with erosion gullies which increased with each rainy season. The songs of the village girls had been replaced by the mournful chanting of the white-clad followers of the Apostolic Faith. Times were hard, and many people were seeking consolation in this Old Testament-based religion. Perhaps they were looking for the spirits that had disappeared with the forest.

That night, we were to attend an all-night ceremony honoring the spirit of a long-dead ancestor. The *bira* was to be held in the main village, a line of huts towards the river. Walking there with Adam and Sydney, I noticed that the drought winds had seared the chalky soil and that there were no crops in the fields, as there should have been at this time.

As we drew near, we could hear the sound of drums and voices coming from the kitchen hut, naturally amplified by the mud bricks and thatch. Groups of men sat outside by fires, drinking *doro*, village beer, a sweet and heady seven-day brew. The drinking of beer has always been a part of Shona life, creating a fellowship between people that cannot be erased by the hardships of life in the village.

People were coming in from all parts for the ceremony, as *biras* were the central social activity in the village—apart from funerals, which seemed to dominate the calendar these days.

Faces of half-forgotten relatives, classmates, neighbors, domestic workers, teachers came out of the darkness to meet me. Greeting upon greeting was exchanged for more than ten minutes as we moved towards the kitchen hut, where a ragged choir of over thirty married women were singing up a storm by candlelight, in celebration of the ancestor's *mudzimu* or spirit. Three male drummers were pounding out solemn rhythms which from time to time would spontaneously spill into an upbeat tune led by one of the stronger singers.

The air in the small hut was heavy and sensuous—a pervasive smell of body odor and wood smoke enveloped me. Herd boys and schoolgirls drifted past the open door, sneaking looks at the singers. Every so often, noted village dancers, both male and female, would bound into the centre of the hut to perform; the rest of us watched them, laughing and singing. Two short planks were passed from hand to hand as clap sticks, to fill out the band....

In Shona culture, someone will dress in the style of a dead person and imitate the mannerisms of this ancestor while dancing, in a ritual that is calculated to awaken the spirit of the dead person in his fellow celebrants. The ceremonies usually last all through the night and are a key element in maintaining village harmony, good seasons, and fertility.

The belief in ancestral spirits is woven into village law. Families can demand compensation for wrongs committed long ago to an ancestor by another family; the descendants of people who failed to stop someone being killed in their village are considered guilty of a crime against the ancestors; and a man who insults his mother will face continual bad luck, even after her death, until he puts things right. You ignore the ancestral spirits here at your peril, whatever the white missionary might tell you on Sundays about worshipping idols. People who observe the customs find that the ancestors look after them, as many freedom fighters reported during the war for independence....

The beer was still flowing when we began our walk back to the homestead. Sydney was reluctant to leave while the pot was being passed around, but he came with us all the same. As we crossed the fields, he recited a list of developments at his school that Adam and I were to organize by the time of our next visit.

The sky was full of stars, more than my husband had ever seen in the city. "There's a satellite," he said, with great satisfaction.

*Sekai Nzenza-Shand was born and lives in Zimbabwe. She trained as a registered nurse in England before moving to Australia, where she completed a Ph.D. in international relations. Her books include* Zimbabwean Woman: My Own Story *and* Songs to an African Sunset: A Zimbabwean Story, *from which this story was excerpted.*

# Guardians of the Dark

*A mother and her daughters learn more than*
*Spanish on a trip to Mexico.*

"ARE YOU SCARED, MOMMY?" MY SEVEN-YEAR-OLD DAUGHTER whispered in the backseat of the battered Mexican taxi. The driver accelerated, swerving into the left lane to pass a farm truck full of cows. The pale, hazy sun slipped behind the mountains. It would be dark before we arrived. Night descended quickly as we roared through the desert toward San Miguel de Allende.

My queasy stomach, more than the forced smile on my face, spoke the truth. I was very nervous about our maniac driver, the lack of seatbelts, and how long it was taking us to get to our destination. Annalyse, the seven-year-old, squeezed my hand, snuggling her head into my shoulder. She thinks I am invincible, I thought with a sense of irony. Her mom, the author of a book called *Gutsy Women*, felt like an un-gutsy wimp. I could be so brave when I was alone, but add the responsibility of traveling with my daughters and I was going into an attack of insecurity.

I avoided an honest answer and calmly, if not confidently, responded, "Sweetie, whenever I travel somewhere I've never been before, I'm both excited and uncomfortable." I explained, "I am just wondering what our host family will be like. During meals together will we be able to communicate? We don't know very much

Spanish do we? I bet they don't know much English either. I hope our teachers at the Language Institute will be as nice as your first-grade teacher this past year."

In the silence that filled the dark cab, I realized for the first time this trip wouldn't be easy. I wished there was another grown-up along to help me keep an eye on my exuberant, wandering blonde daughters. Why was I so insecure about going to Mexico alone with my kids? Before marriage and motherhood, I had traveled alone around the world for two years. I used to be a confident traveler. Motherhood seemed to have taken the "piss and vinegar" out of my wanderlust. It had made me wary and cautious.

I could blame it on traveler's fatigue. We were exhausted, having survived three flights to Mexico City. Of course, the flight was "direct" but that didn't mean it was nonstop. News programs in the U.S. had warned us about the violent crime in and outside the Mexico City Airport. We held hands to stay together in the crowded terminals. Julieclaire and I wore our backpacks over our chests, instead of on our backs, to thwart pickpockets and thieves. Outside the terminal there were no benches for weary travelers at the curbside bus stop, so we stood waiting for over an hour for the bus to Quaretaro. I was exhausted from watching our luggage, protecting my children, and keeping them entertained.

Aboard the Primera Plus deluxe bus while Julieclaire and Annalyse napped, I nervously thumbed guidebooks during the four-hour trip. At the bus stop we hailed a cab for the hour journey to our final destination, a Mexican home in San Miguel de Allende.

The scrubby countryside of the highlands of central Mexico ended abruptly as we drove into town. We passed shops and bars with men spilling onto the unpaved streets. Where were the traffic lights, the neon signs, and fast-food establishments I saw in other Mexican towns? Where were the narrow cobbled-stone streets and the charming colonial villas described in the guidebooks? Our cabbie stopped twice to ask for directions. When we careened around a corner into a dirt alley, I was sure we were lost or being taken for a ride. Our decrepit cab lurched to a stop as the grizzled driver pointed with pleasure at a messy hand-written sign on a whitewashed wall, "Jaimi Nuno." That was the street address I had given him. I slumped back in stunned silence. This neighborhood had no reassuring streetlights, no pedestrians, no trees, and not even a stray barking dog. It was deserted and dirty. When he found the house address, my stomach churned. I didn't want to get out of the taxi. The darkness, silence, and poverty of the scene were intimidating.

The cabbie wanted no part of my hesitation or insecurities. He dumped our luggage on the street, grabbed his pesos, and sped off. We pounded on the wooden door and hoped for the best. Annalyse's tiny warm hand found its way into my clammy cold fist. Julieclaire impatiently scuffed her foot in the dirt.

A short woman with charcoal-colored hair threw open the door, grabbed my free hand, and pumped it in an energetic greeting. She was wearing a starched white apron over a somber black dress. Her unlined face made me guess she was in her thirties. She introduced herself as "Lourdes," and wasted no time welcoming Annalyse and Julieclaire with hugs.

Julieclaire, at ten years old, was almost as tall as Lourdes, who took charge, leading us through an empty garage and into the main house chattering nonstop in staccato Spanish. Her monologue, of which we

---

At home I'm a fascist about seat belts. Here I have no choice other than to cling to my girl in the backseat and hope the driver's dashboard saints are on duty protecting us. The playgrounds we've found have rough cement under the teeter-totters, rusty swing sets, and worn monkey bars peeling lead paint. Mexico, it turns out, has not been childproofed.

And yet, isn't this what we came for? I have to learn from Mexican parents how to be less paranoid. Of course, I don't want Annalena to get hurt, but I do want her to experience the kind of security Mexican children get from the assumption that they are protected because the community as a whole has their best interests at heart.

◆

—Gina Hyams, "Escape Artists"

didn't understand one word, cheered us up as we stacked our heavy luggage in a corner of what was to be our new home for the next fifteen days.

My children were hungry and I wanted to be taken care of. Lourdes knew intuitively what we needed. She led us into a large, empty dining room and seated us at the only piece of furniture, a lace-covered table. She brought in bowls of cornflakes and cold milk. Ah—reassuring cornflakes! I remembered another time, when I had been on the road for over nine months, alone. I discovered cornflakes on a restaurant menu in southern India and relished every bite as I was transported back to Ohio and my childhood breakfasts. Cornflakes had been my emotional link with home. And now, lifetimes later, my daughters also found a bowl of familiar cereal reassuring. Removing her apron, Lourdes smoothed down her glossy hair, smiled and sat down at the table with us. Little Patrick, her cheerful five-year-old son, climbed onto her lap and furtively glanced at the girls. He made funny faces to get their attention. Julieclaire made goofy faces in return, and our laughter echoed through the bare rooms.

After our snack, Annalyse and Julieclaire argued over who would get the bigger drawer in the dresser for their clothes and who had to sleep with mom on which bed. As we unpacked our suitcases in our tiny dark bedroom, Patrick peeked through the half-open door. He was fascinated by these two foreign girls who were squabbling as they pulled hair bows and games out of their bags.

Meanwhile, Lourdes gave me a tour of her three-bedroom, one-dining room, cement-block home, showing me what I would need to know—how to use the key to lock the front door, where to find purified water to refill our water bottles for drinking and brushing teeth. We climbed up a narrow set of chipped cement stairs to the flat roof that served as the laundry. Lourdes showed me the clotheslines where we should hang our damp towels. A big enamel washtub, with a wooden washboard and bars of soap stood in the corner. This is where I would hand wash our clothes and hang them up to dry.

Wooden clothespins held sheets and underwear on the clotheslines. They crisply flapped in the balmy summer breeze. A crescent moon was pasted against the black-velvet sky. A myriad of stars competed with each other for space in the heavens. I was awed by this nocturnal beauty but pleasure lay shrouded beneath fatigue and sobering maternal responsibility.

Lourdes held back the corner of a drying sheet and motioned for me to follow her through the laundry to the other side of the open roof. I was unprepared for the sight that awaited me. Dominating the city's panorama was a pink Gothic cathedral with ornate steeples aglow with tiny lights. We could hear the children below, giggling together in the bedroom. They were playing peek-a-boo. I let out a sigh of relief.

Lourdes spoke to me in slow sentences. My knowledge of French helped me to piece together her Spanish words. Lourdes was divorced, living alone with her children. She supported them by taking in language students as boarders. In addition to Patrick, she had a twenty-year-old son who worked the night shift in a dry cleaning factory and an eighteen-year-old daughter who was still in school and spent most of her time with her *novio*, boyfriend. With a shrug and resigned, laugh she explained that her teens were rarely at home.

Lourdes attended elementary school for four years and could read and write "a little." She considered herself fortunate, because after her divorce, she kept the house (but little else). Now I understood why the rooms were sparsely furnished. Julieclaire noticed there were no pictures on the walls and not a book to be seen in the home.

When Lourdes finished speaking I wanted to tell her about my family, my life. Many times in my travels I have confided in other women, often relative strangers. I have told them secrets about my loves, my losses, my insecurities. Under the regal moon, Lourdes and I stood for a while in silent female communion. Then I tried to explain my fear.

I pointed to the dark empty streets below and asked her in my schoolbook Spanish: "I am with my daughters. My husband, their Papa, is not with us. No other adult is with us. Is it possible to walk in the streets at night?" We wanted to go after dinner to the main square, to sit on the wrought-iron park benches near the bandstand to watch people or hear the mariachis play, to see the peddlers offering candy and the old men get their shoes shined. But there are no lights here. I motioned to the dark and deserted street below and asked, "No one is in the streets. I am afraid. Is it a problem? Is my purse safe? Are my girls safe?"

Lourdes reached out and looped her arm through mine. She was small but solid and smelled as fresh as the hand-scrubbed washing that hung around us. As we stood arm in arm, amid the fluttering laundry, I knew she understood my distress. She pointed to a nearby rooftop. I saw two women rocking in chairs, quietly conversing as they watched the streets below. They were partially hidden by their own drying laundry. I was surprised, for I hadn't noticed any other life in the neighborhood. She motioned to other rooftops and open windows where women sat, witnesses to the dark and silent night.

"No problem, Señora. Many women watch out for you. No problem to walk in the streets at night with no man," she assured me.

I had traveled to San Miguel to experience the customs and the language but the lasting legacy of our journey was this female kinship, we confide in and support each other. My daughters and I learned some Spanish, shared in another family's life, walked confidently in the dark, laughed at ourselves, and ate too much ice cream. Most importantly, we returned home, forever changed, surer of ourselves, strengthened, stretched, and having touched other women with our spirits.

*Marybeth Bond is the editor of this book, as well as* A Woman's World, A Mother's World, A Woman's Passion for Travel, *and the author of* Gutsy Women *and* Gutsy Mamas.

LETTY COTTIN POGREBIN

⋆ ⋆ ⋆

# And Miles to Go

*How the years simply fall away.*

THE OLDER I GET, THE MORE I LOVE TO TRAVEL. I'VE ALWAYS WANTED to see the world, but never so urgently as since I turned fifty and faced up to the mathematical discrepancy between the years I have left to live and the places I have left to see.

Middle-aged travel just may well be as developmentally predictable as hearing loss, bifocals, and midriff bulge. For those who can afford it, traveling for pleasure can become a detour from the downhill jitters, an antidote to existential angst, and the best revenge against aging since collagen.

Vacations give us something to look forward to as a counterweight to the apprehension of our incredible shrinking future. I have spent the last few years obsessing about time and behaving as if my days were numbered, which, of course, they are. I would gladly pay for more time if it were for sale, like air rights, but failing that I prefer to pay for experience. Thankfully, my husband and I have considerably more discretionary income now than we did twenty years ago (one of the few perks of age). Yet the more we indulge our travel appetites, the hungrier I am for the next trip.

Does this mean I'm hopelessly sybaritic? Is midlife pleasure-seeking politically incorrect? Is travel lust a sign of terminal self-indulgence? Am I wrong to want to coast a bit after so many years at full throttle? Right or wrong, getting away from it all offers some compensation for the physical deterioration and mental slippage that threatens my dignity on a daily basis.

Travel allows one to feel new when it is no longer possible to feel young. Every day, just by being alive, kids have experiences from which they grow and learn, while the rest of us have to pursue the new, struggle against inertia, and push ourselves to keep growing, a task that gets more difficult as we become more set in our ways. But when we take a trip and enter unfamiliar settings, we reconnect with our childish sense of wonder and discovery, and we discover an unexpected bonus: the clock slows down and life seems to expand.

Time is a slippery toad—elusive, malleable, and prone to trickery. In youth, it took a year to get from January to June and summer lasted forever. Anyone who has survived a car accident will tell you that while it was happening, time stood still. A millisecond felt like a minute or an hour. At one level, things seemed to be unfolding in slow motion; at another, life flashed before our eyes and yet we saw it all with utter clarity and calm.

Something similar, though rather more pleasant, happens on vacation. Travel is the ultimate time extender. In a strange, new country, the world slows down because we are paying attention, trying to figure things out. Exotic locales elicit the same sharpened focus and intense concentration as did all of life when we first encountered it. We look long and hard at people, art, and architecture; we sit in outdoor cafés and study the cobblestones; we smell the flower market a block away; we perch at the edge of a fountain watching the spray; we look up, down, and around instead of straight ahead to our destination.

Because we are more mindful, each day is long and lazy, its contents memorable, separable, and distinct. This is why a week spent in a new place always seems to have many more days than a week at home. On our return, we are astounded when our friends say: "Are you back already? Gee, that was fast." For them, time has whizzed by in a blur of routines. For us, time was too full to fly.

Another characteristic of my revitalized passion for midlife travel is the comfort factor. Once upon a time, a cot, an outhouse, or a shared bath would suit me fine. Now I want my privacy and indoor plumbing. No more roughing it, thanks. My husband and I slept in tents and did the cookout-and-latrines bit for years, sometimes with our three children lined up on air mattresses beside us. Now, I want a hotel room with thick towels in the bathroom and a chocolate on my pillow at bedtime.

This, mind you, is not what I come from. I grew up in Queens, where travel meant a subway ride to "the city"—an outing deemed worthy of nylon stockings, kid gloves, and a hat with a veil. My parents never took vacations. My mother saw no reason to return to the old country from which her family had escaped—and she was afraid, if she left America, that she'd never be allowed back. To my father, relaxation was another name for idleness. The minute I could afford a plane ticket, I started making up for my childhood.

The difference between travel then and travel now is not just that it has become more commonplace and affordable but that I've reached the age when I feel every trip could be my last—and therefore each should be extraordinary. Obviously others hold the same view since so many marvelous destinations are overrun with people my age and so many companies are specializing in cruises, treks, and study tours aimed at the fifty-plus set.

I have a hunch that much of this midlife traffic is motivated, consciously or not, by the same heightened sense of mortality that propels me out the door. I want to get around while the getting is good—before I have to worry about wheelchair access, before it's too late altogether. I also know that travel yields rewards far beyond its monetary value, that travel memories can prop up the sagging spirit and recompense us retrospectively for losses we have yet to know. As the poet Yehudah Amihai put it:

> Travels are the soul
> Of this world.
> Travels remain forever.

But there is an irony here. Whereas young people take to the road to find themselves, most of us who are older travel to lose ourselves. In a strange place where no one knows us and our history, we are able, if only for a week, to reinvent ourselves, to be ageless, to act as young as we feel. How liberating it is to leave behind all one's telltale labels and social insignia. When we get wherever we're going, nobody knows or cares who we are, and we don't have to do anything to maintain our image. We can try new things, make fools of ourselves, fail grandly, and answer to no one. We have no decision-making responsibilities more weighty than whether to swim or read, no clock constraints more pressing than getting on the tour bus before it leaves, and no one with greater claims on our time than ourselves and each other.

What I've just described, in essence, is the freedom of youth—to be unencumbered, carefree, and unapologetically self-pleasuring. Travel takes us back to that nirvana and makes life simple again. The years fall away. We carry relatively few possessions. With a lightened load and a tabula rasa identity, we're free to reclaim the abandon of our younger days; free to go dancing at midnight or make love at noon; free to read trashy novels, spend the morning in a museum and the afternoon at the zoo; see five movies in four days and drink three margaritas before dinner.

Travel may be more expensive than everyday life, but that kind of freedom, that kind of freshness, is priceless.

*Letty Cottin Pogrebin is the president of the Authors Guild, a founding editor of* Ms. Magazine *and the author of* Getting Over Getting Older; Deborah, Golda and Me; *and many other books. She is also the editor of* Stories for Free Children *and the codeveloper with Marlo Thomas of* Free to Be You and Me *and* Free to Be a Family. *She and her husband live in New York City.*

## PART TWO

# SOME THINGS TO DO

ANN JONES

✶ ✶ ✶

# Kenya on Horseback

*Four legs can go where four
wheels only dream.*

DON'T ASK ME TO *EXPLAIN* THE PASSIONATE ATTACHMENT OF girls and women to horses. It's a fact of life, now documented by experts. Animal behaviorists at Duke University report that although boys star as heroes in kids' books about horses, it's girls who actually get on those ponies and ride. Psychologists label the craze a "transient phallic illusion" of preadolescent girls—you know, before they kick their tomboy habits and settle down to be "feminine." I guess the experts haven't noticed that for thousands of grown-up women, horses are no passing crush.

My love affair with horses has a practical side: riding is a first-rate way to travel. It can take you just about anywhere, far beyond the reach of roads, and put you on intimate terms with landscape and weather, as you can never be in a vehicle. It gives you the freedom of hiking or biking, but the horse does all the work—and provides, in addition, a superior perch from which to take in the sights. Besides, a horse is a personality, a companion, a more or less cooperative pal. A horse is friendlier than a bike and smells better than the average hiker after a day on the trail.

Over the years I've explored a lot of out-of-the-way places on horseback, from the Yukon to Patagonia, from Australia's Snowy

Mountains to China's Altai Range. But I've always dreamed of Africa and the great plains of the Masai people—the Masai Mara in Kenya, sweeping southward to become Tanzania's Serengeti National Park.

Early one October morning, I met nine riding companions— including several couples and a widow from Wales—on the terrace of the Norfolk Hotel, the place to be seen in Nairobi and the mustering point for safaris. In their serious boots and cowboy hats, they stood apart from the crowd of pale, safari-jacketed tourists who waited to be collected by guides in tidy Japanese minivans. In the center of things, making the introductions, was Tristan, a boyish, square-shouldered former officer in the Blues and Royals—the Queen's own Horse Guards—and the man we were to follow for more than 200 miles across the plains of Kenya.

All day we drove west in two battered Land Rovers, bouncing and swerving around the potholes and throwing up streamers of dust as we crossed the Great Rift Valley into Masai country, where herds of bony cattle swam toward us in the dun-colored air. At dusk we climbed to our camp in the Loita Hills.

"You call this camping?" asked Linda, a London banker who was traveling with her husband. Incredulous, we examined the spacious tents, the cots and mattresses, the crisp linens and soft blankets, the sheepskin rugs, the bath towels, the English Leather soap, the ice bucket on the bar set up outside the mess tent. "I believe I can endure this," she said, popping open a cold Tusker beer. Out back, in canvas cubicles, were the latrines and, hanging from trees, the hot showers under which we would shed the dust of the day's drive. Chef Kalele was cooking a three-course dinner on an open fire. There would be candlelight and wine. "It's not camping," said one of the men, who was the only old Africa hand among us. "It's a real safari."

Picketed at the edge of camp were the horses: big, rangy Thoroughbreds crossed with a disease-resistant Somali line, fit and well muscled from hard work on the polo field. A little bay mare caught my eye and drew me in to scratch her neck. "Take her, if you like," Tristan said. "We call her Toroka—that's Swahili for runaway—because she ran away from a lion on her first safari." He pointed out the long scars on her flank, and suddenly I was filled with second thoughts. Why had it never occurred to me that lions eat horses?

The next morning we set off on a test run over grassy hills and through forests of pencil cedar and yellowwood dripping with diaphanous moss and busy with the flight of tiny yellow sunbirds. All at once the trees around us erupted with colobus monkeys flying from limb to limb, their white tails billowing like sails in the bright air.

We were headed for the edge of an escarpment for a sweeping view of one of the planet's last great wildlife habitats: the savannas of Kenya's Masai Mara. But as we cantered fast up a grassy slope, one woman's horse stumbled. I heard a surprised cry just behind me and glanced over my shoulder to see a flimsy bit of khaki streaking through the air with such velocity that I thought it must be a jacket, come loose from the saddle. But it was Anne. We pulled up and rode back to where she lay, crumpled and uncon-

I rode her up the broad valley, following the dry wash where the water came down in the rain…. We waded through acres of wild sunflowers as high as my knee, heading again for the wash with its telltale line of willows. And suddenly there were so many butterflies that we could make no progress, could not see for orange-gold fritillaries dancing before our eyes, landing on our eyelashes. Duchess was as astonished as I. I tried to find a bit of her I could stroke, but she was hoary with upfolded wings, and they covered my fingers. There was no sky; it was gold with butter. I do not know how long we stood, caressed by their gentle touch, shimmering statues intrigued by our attraction to those palpitating legs. Butterflies taste with their front feet; we were thoroughly savored. Duchess harrumphed indignantly as they tried to crawl up her nose, and we moved off.

◆

—Lucy Rees, *The Maze: A Desert Journey*

scious. Jill, who had trained as a nurse, took charge until Anne
came round and gamely agreed to be lifted back on her horse.
That evening she had to be borne to dinner in a chair, unable to
walk. "It's nothing," she said, for she is that kind of person. "I'll be
fine." A nurse herself, trained at a different London hospital than Jill,
Anne struggled politely for two days against Jill's diagnosis of her
ankle—"broken"—then boarded a medevac plane for Nairobi.

Anne's fall—happening so fast and so hard—made us all uneasy,
and on the second day, when we set out in earnest on an eighteen-
mile ride over the grasslands to a new camp, most of us tightened
girths and adjusted stirrups, and then did it all again.

We climbed steadily uphill on the third day, moving among herds
of long-faced wildebeest and natty zebra over tawny grasslands
that seemed to glow under a lowering gray sky. Each day as we rode
we came upon Masai settlements—such low-lying, unassuming
assemblages of sticks and mud and cattle dung that they were nearly
invisible. As we passed by in our dusty breeches and t-shirts, glorious women emerged from the enclosure of thorns encircling the
settlement. Tall and silent, they were resplendent in layers of brightly
printed batiks, broad collars and chokers of beads, and tiaras dripping with cowrie shells and bits of tin. Their ears, lacy with holes,
held ornaments of leather and dangling beads. *"Soba!"* We called
out the Masai greeting, and they broke into laughter. *"Soba,"* they
called back, waving to us across the centuries that separated our lives
from theirs.

Almost all the women carried babies, and toddlers clung to their
knees. The birthrate in Kenya is among the highest in the world.
The Masai population alone has tripled in the last thirty years. By
tradition, the Masai are nomadic herders, following the new grass
just as the migrating wildebeests do, and living on milk and blood
drawn from their precious cattle. But spreading farmlands are pushing the Masai, with their grazing cows and their close-cropping
goats, westward onto the high plains and into the hills. The Masai
have never hunted the wild grazers—"God's cattle" they call the
gazelles—but increasingly Masai cattle compete with God's for the
same grass.

We climbed to a dizzying 9,000 feet, skimmed along the high ridge at a lope and then began the long descent—some 2,500 feet to the great ocher plains that spread below us, dappled by scudding clouds. We did much of the descent on foot, scrambling down the crumbling red face of the escarpment one step ahead of our horses. Along the way we met Masai women, trudging homeward in solitary concentration to the treeless savanna, each woman bent double under a load of firewood suspended on her back from a strap looped over her shaved head. At night they sang together, invoking rain, and their voices drifted into our camp on the wind.

In the morning, when we set off across the plain, we rode under a scorching sun. The earth of these great savannas is hardpan, compressed from layer upon layer of volcanic ash. It supports a great variety of grasses, which should have been still green in October, except that the long rains of March and April hadn't come. Only short grass grew here, and it was dry, scattered in small clumps, with nothing but dust between. The wind raised the dust and sent it swirling. The intense light seemed to melt everything—earth, air, and the great drifting herds of wildebeest and gazelles—into a single, luminous color that was no color at all.

"This must be the 'endurance' part," Jill said. "I can feel the heat rising up through the soles of my boots."

We rode on, each of us deep in a private dream, as step by step our horses delivered up the land. Here and there the grass gave way to scrubby brush, ferocious with thorns; and as we zigzagged, ducking around the wait-a-bit bushes, we lost sight of one another in the brush. Instantly my mare was all nervous muscle, whinnying to the other horses and deftly leaping sideways, just out of reach of lurking lions that may not have been altogether imaginary. At times Tristan spotted them—and I peered down his pointing finger, squinting to make them out where they lay in the croton thickets looking out, invisible but for the twitch of a big, round yellow ear.

Day after day, the wild creatures were all about us, and only the big, velvety elands and waterbucks seemed to dissolve silently into the brush at our approach. The rest were bolder. Squads of baboons patrolled the grass in search of baby gazelles, their unusual carnivorous appetites a sign that vegetation was scarce. Impalas, sleek as water, lingered close at hand, watching us curiously, and then disappeared with a single dazzling leap. Warthogs knelt to root at the ground with their short tusks, hoisted their tails like flags and trotted off. Some creatures seemed oblivious to us, like the jackals and hyenas and vultures busy at their scavenging. Others were immovable, like the huge black Cape buffaloes being tidied by oxpecker birds, and the blue-flanked topis, on the watch for enemies, each one standing atop a tall termite mound like a solitary statue on a pedestal. Giraffes worked like topiary gardeners, trimming the lower edges of the desert date trees straight as hedges sixteen feet above the ground, then loped off across the plains, always in slow motion—like my mind, which had tuned to the cadence of the land.

When we reached the Mara River, we found great clumps of lolling hippos supporting babies on their backs and eyeing the crocodiles that drifted down, silent as logs. Near the river, where the bush was thick, a squad of elephants brought down the fever trees, munching thorns and all. This was why I'd chosen to cover this country the hard way: to be part of this slow drift of animals over the land.

All across Africa, where once there were islands of people in a sea of animals, there are now islands of animals in a sea of people—and the sea is rising, with the African population expected to double within twenty-four years. Discussing these things over dinner one evening, Tristan voiced the worst fears of conservationists. "When people want the land, they'll take it. And that will be an end to it."

Yet it's still possible—in the middle of the vast savanna on the back of a horse, or perhaps even in a Land Rover—to imagine a different future. It's possible to imagine that the Masai, who have always lived in peace with God's cattle, will find a way to carry on. Just as it's possible—when the only sound in your ear is the soft susurration of the wind through a stand of whistling thorn or the clear, bright cry of a fish eagle—to imagine that you and your horse can roam forever among the creatures of the great savannas.

*Ann Jones is best known for what she calls her "heavy duty feminist books"
such as* Women Who Kill *and* Next Time, She'll Be Dead. *She is also
the author of* Looking for Lovedu: Days and Nights in Africa, *a book-
length version of this story, and* Guide to America's Outdoors: Middle
Atlantic.

LYNN FERRIN

* * *

# Sex, Yams, and the Kula Ring

*In the South Pacific, on some enchanted*
*evening, you may meet a stranger*
*across a crowded room.*

MY FRESHMAN YEAR IT WENT DOWN TO TWENTY BELOW ZERO IN Syracuse. The sap froze in the trees and the branches groaned overhead. In the chill of my Anthro 1A classroom, we studied a people who lived about as far away as you could get, in that confetti of islands and atolls sprinkled across the southwest Pacific. Considering the simplicity of their surroundings—straw huts in clearings on coral islands—these people had developed an astonishingly complex culture. Elaborate rituals, mores, and magic invested every routine of their daily lives: agriculture, trading, canoeing, gift-giving, sex, marriage, death, inheritance.

The Trobriand Islands, off the coast of Papua New Guinea, were an ethnographer's supermarket. It was there that the earliest real fieldwork in anthropology was done, by Bronislaw Malinowski, from 1915 to 1918. He was the first to live among his subjects for a long period of time, learn their language—rather than just ask questions through an interpreter—and use his observations as research. In books that became anthropology classics, Malinowski detailed the Trobrianders' epic ceremonial inter-island canoe voyages, called the Kula ring; the magic spells that make their yam gardens grow; and their wildly promiscuous sexual practices.

It made for lively reading that dreary midwinter in upstate New York, and those tropical islands remained somewhere in the far corners of my mind. Years later, planning a trip to Papua New Guinea, I ran across a cultural tour that included several days in the Trobriands, and recalled the provocative works of Malinowski. I signed up, but I never expected to find the old Melanesian culture so wonderfully intact.

> ———)———
>
> That tickle in the base of your skull, the urge to see a place, can be triggered by a million different things. A passing word, a painting, a movie, a sudden surprising thought.
>
> ♦
>
> —Sophia Dembling,
> "The Tickle to Travel"

The Fokker 27 flew in over Kiriwina Island under dumpy clouds. In the low-lying jungle below were several villages, each with its center ring of yam houses and outlying gardens. When our band of seven tourists and one anthropologist-guide stepped onto the airstrip, there, beyond the fence, stood the people I'd come so far to see. They wore grass skirts and palm-thatch codpieces, their puffs of black hair filled with feathers and wooden combs. A lifetime of chewing betel nut had turned the smiles of the elderly into red slashes. A van with rust-holes in the floor took us to the seedy Kiriwina Lodge, among the mangroves on the leeward shore.

For several days we bounced around the island on faint coral tracks—the remains of roads built by Americans, who had an air base here in World War II. We combed for seashells on the windward beaches, went for rides in outriggers, bargained for exquisite artifacts carved from local hardwoods. Every afternoon we'd drive to a scimitar of talcum sand beside an aquamarine lagoon. The snorkeling was so fine I'd stay in the water until I was puckered, roaming through the coral gardens and out to where the reef dropped away to dark blue oblivion.

We watched the Trobrianders and they watched us. They are a handsome people, more like Polynesians than the Papuans on the mainland, and went to extraordinary lengths to decorate themselves each day. They painted their faces and wore garlands of hibiscus and plumeria. Young men wore *laplaps*—cloth sarongs—and tucked aromatic fresh grasses and mints into their armbands. The girls were bare-breasted, with saucy red banana-fiber skirts.

The village yam houses, open log structures with peaked roofs, bulged from the recent harvest and were trimmed with bright paint and seashells.

Malinowski's works did not prepare me for the stunning beauty of the island, with its moist breezes, lush jungles, and coconut palms bending to the waves. Iridescent butterflies as big as salad plates browsed in the morning glories. Friarbirds fluted in the trees. The chanting of fishermen filled the papaya sunsets.

At night the cooking fires glowed in the villages, and the smoke rose through the palms toward the crescent moon. The only other lights on Kiriwina were the bare bulbs in the lodge bar, where we drank with visiting expats. Later we lay on our cots in the straw-walled rooms, listening to the geckos clacking in the rafters and the mangoes pounding on the tin roofs.

One day we scrambled through a thicket of vines and betel palms to one of the many limestone caverns on Kiriwina. At the back of the cave we found a cold, sweet-water pool, undressed and slid into the water. I lay floating on my back, gazing out through the fringe of jungle around the mouth of the cave, where a black-and-white friarbird worried above its nest, and knew I wanted to be nowhere else.

On our way back to the lodge, we stopped in a village called Kudukwaikela. As we poked around, we realized

> *D*oes emotional honesty follow from being physically uncovered? We're half naked half the time, so maybe full disclosure is a logical consequence of unveiling the body's imperfections, of feeling exposed.
>
> ◆
>
> —Letty Cottin Pogrebin, "A Heart to Heart Workout," *The New York Times*

that the place was thick with anticipation. People were smearing their bodies with flower petals and painting stripes and polka dots on their faces. The old men were helping the teenagers arrange fans of cockatoo feathers and cassowary plumes in their hair and adjust their grass skirts. A toddler scampered around with a huge green and black butterfly struggling at the end of a string. We heard the blast of a conch shell. The youths scurried into a circle before the main yam house and began to dance around a band of drums and chanters. The only spectators, we watched from the huts until dark. We never did learn the precise reason for the celebration; whatever it was, it was theirs alone.

In the evenings we gathered in the lounge for lectures by our guide, Dr. Dana Keil, an anthropologist who had done his own fieldwork in Papua New Guinea. He told us about the *sagali*, a complex women's economic transaction system, and about the hereditary chiefs and their yam-growing magic and the Kula ring. "In the old days, the outriggers had sails woven of pandanus leaves, but those are all gone now, replaced by cloth." His words were still hanging there when an outrigger came around the point, its new pandanus sails flying like glory. It was testimony that, since independence from Australia a decade ago, money for buying products from outside has become scarce in remote areas of Papua New Guinea; people are returning to traditional ways.

Now, about the sex. Trobriand children begin sexual play almost as soon as they can walk, and become downright active as early as eight, sometimes even six years old. The adults tease and cheer them into the bushes. In adolescence they have the freedom to run through many lovers before choosing a permanent mate for a relatively faithful marriage—except during the yam harvest season, when the festivities can develop into orgies where, so to speak, everybody does everybody. In fact, a husband might rebuke a wife who's not keeping up with Mrs. Jones. Trobriand conversation is peppered with lewd expressions, and the islanders delight in singing songs of vulgarity that will curl your toes. With so much practice, Trobrianders have a reputation for legendary technique and gymnastics. (But not basic deduction. We were amazed to learn that they make no physiological connection between sex and conception. Babies are thought to be spirits that enter through a woman's head, often when she's swimming. If you don't want to get pregnant, stay out of the ocean.)

Mixing tourists into all this is a hoot. Every now and then islander boys would stand in the road as our bus approached, point down into their *laplaps*, grin and gyrate their hips. Locals have been known to prowl the Kiriwina Lodge after bedtime, rapping on doors. The right guest roster of young Australian plantation managers from the mainland can make the building jump on its stilts. One tour guide told me that just as he was warming up to a harvest orgy, he noticed that all his American charges were cowering in the bus, whining that the Trobriand men had been goosing them.

I was out bird-watching alone when I was jumped by a gang of pubescents out for grabbies. Infuriated, I started punching. At the same time I was struck by the absurdity of it. I was, after all, old enough to be, good lord, not their mother, but their grandmother. I kicked and shrieked until I'd managed to drag us all within earshot of the lodge. A guest looked over the fence. The boys scattered and I collapsed, disheveled but otherwise undamaged, into the bar.

That year I was experimenting with monogamy, but I was not above encouraging someone else to participate and then report back to me. Staying at the lodge was an Australian whose libido matched her ample proportions. She was sultry and very sexy. "Why don't you see if they live up to their reputations," I prodded her one night over gin and tonic.

"Naow, word'd get out. Anyway, why don't you?"

"I have a nice man at home. Come on. Otherwise I'll never know."

She contemplated a millipede tap dancing across the floor matting, then said, "Well, um, look at the bartender." She eyed the smooth copper youth polishing the glasses. We moved to the bar.

By the time I went off to bed she had worked the conversation around to his sex life. He was complaining that, at nineteen, he was considered an effete old man by the island girls. He feared that his magic was failing. I sensed that he knew his luck might be turning.

Next morning at breakfast she was sitting alone looking out to sea. "Well?"

"I kept him talking about it for hours," she said, "asking him more and more intimate questions. Finally I let him know he could come to my room. He showed up later with a bottle. Things got moving along."

"And?"

"Pah!" she said. "Not worth all the effort. All he knew was the missionary position."

In the Kula ring, which Malinowski described in *Argonauts of the Western Pacific*, outrigger canoes are used to carry a "treasure" on a ritual circuit from island to island, village to village, in the Trobriand and nearby archipelagoes. Two kinds of treasure are involved: necklaces and shell armbands. The necklaces travel clockwise, the armbands counterclockwise, and many are en route at once. A Kula object will stay in a village with one man for a period of time before it is carried to its next destination. A complete circuit for any given object—with all the accompanying ceremony—takes several years and covers hundreds of miles.

Kula treasure has no monetary value in itself; it cannot be sold. Its only function is to be possessed and traded. Merely having it for a short time gives its holder pride, social status, and the envy of his friends. And the Kula ring serves an important economic function—it establishes trading and social relations among vast numbers of people living on islands scattered across a wide area of the southern seas.

To our surprise we found that the Kula ring is still in progress. We made inquiries and learned that a Kula necklace had just arrived in Sinaketa, toward the southern end of the island. Sinaketa turned out to be a large village, with its huts arranged around a grassy common. And there, drawn up under the palms at the edge of the beach, was the Kula canoe, with its prow and rudder carved and painted with red and black designs. Its entire construction was logs and palm-lashing. We found the chief and after some banter, he agreed to show us the precious Kula. He emerged from his hut and held it up for inspection, gingerly, like a Catholic priest lifting the Host.

My Western eye saw only strings of cowries, clams, red shell money, and colored beads.

To him, it was the very embodiment of magic, the repository of all good.

Being somewhere like the Trobriands gives you pause about the ways different lines of the human family have worked things out: how to assure that there will always be more babies, enough to eat, comfortable shelter, the right thing to wear, a happy life together. The Trobrianders have their magic and their yam-harvest orgies and their Kula ring. We have—what?—McDonalds, the Easter Bunny, Madonna, realtors… Whatever would a Trobriand anthropologist make of us?

I hope it will always be so, because the difference between us is what gives the word *mankind* its definition.

*Lynn Ferrin was nine years old and knew she was in the wrong place: Texas. One day her father came home and announced the family was moving to Kuwait and her traveling and writing career began. Since then, she has roamed the planet by foot, horseback, kayak, canoe, ship, plane, train, and camel. Currently a freelance travel writer, Lynn was an editor and writer for thirty-seven years for* VIA, *membership magazine of the American Automobile Association in California, Nevada, and Utah. Her specialty is writing about adventure travel and public lands, and she most recently co-edited* Wild Writing Women: Stories of World Travel. *She has lived in a cluttered hillside cottage in San Francisco for almost forty years.*

LEILA PHILIP

*  *  *

# River of Life

*A journey into the wilderness
brings a new mother
closer to her son.*

A MEANDERING RIVER MAY BE A METAPHOR FOR LIFE'S JOURNEY, but running rapids in the Grand Canyon seems a particularly apt metaphor for being a mother. Paddling the river, you can never know ahead where the current will take you; the art of staying afloat is finding that line of current that will take you through the white water. If you let yourself get buffeted by distractions, you will flip. I had learned this on the fourth day of the trip when I ventured out in one of the inflatable kayaks. Paddling solo through miles of calm, I had been lulled by the incredible peace of the river, the red canyon walls holding the sky like great hands, palms up on either side. The river was so quiet that I lay back in my kayak and removed my helmet, letting the small boat gently spin in the current. I could hear the rustle of small animals in the bushes on the shorelines. This is the sound of time, I had thought, moving us forward imperceptibly. Then I began to hear the river guides strapping down gear in preparation for white water and readied my own boat for our shoot through the rapid.

"Paddle right," the guide whom I was to follow, had shouted as we picked up speed, "The water's big today." Ahead of me I could see a series of white waves. I cut right with all my strength, but as soon as I entered the tongue of the rapid I could feel that it was too much for me. The next thing I knew, twin walls of water were carrying me up higher and higher until my paddle was striking air. Then I was hit broadside by a wall of water and felt my small boat buckle. I was tumbling out and down into the terrifying cold of the river.

Later, rescued some distance downstream, and once again in my kayak weaving back and forth across the river, I felt great. I dipped in and out of eddies, and skirted rocks and river boils, hidden sleepers that could have flipped me again as effortlessly as a potato chip. I was freezing cold but I had survived. I felt as if I had been baptized by the river and reborn as my old reckless, adventurous, premotherhood self.

I will need that adventurous self today. I glance up at the canyon rim where all too soon the sun will appear as a bright bar, lighting the top strata then moving down through geologic eras to arrive at the base where I now stand. In the predawn darkness, blue shadows hug the nearly vertical red walls. Once upon a time, the land rose up and the river cut down deeper and deeper until it formed this deepest point in the canyon. In a few hours we will begin our hike out of the canyon via the infamous Bright Angel Trail. Each year hikers die along the trail from heat exhaustion and dehydration, and I will be setting out on the trail already tired from the rigor of the past week. The heat today is expected to be unusually high for September. Water is my main concern. As a nursing mother, I generally needed to consume an extra ten glasses of water a day even when I was not exerting myself. To avoid dehydration while hiking side canyons, I found that I needed to sip water every fifteen minutes, but the weight of my already loaded pack prevents me from carrying more than two quarts of water. Will it last until the first water stop at Indian Point?

By 1 p.m. I have reached Indian Point. I am dizzy with heat and fatigue, but I have made it without too much thirst. On either side of the trail, the magnificent walls of the canyon rise up so steeply, the red cliffs seem to shimmer in the heat. Far below the river snakes through the rock. I quickly eat the first of my three sandwiches and all my cookies, but do not feel the burst of energy I had expected. My legs are rubber. To make matters worse, it is time again to pump. The question is where? I look past the covered mule corral to the shaded rest area filled with hikers. After the wilderness of the river, this trail, a popular day hike down from the South Rim, feels like Grand Central Station. While I look around, a mule train arrives. Fifteen mules carrying tourists decked out in full cowboy regalia. I watch a ponderous couple awkwardly dismount and immediately pull out their video camera to zoom in on the oversize thermometer located on a pole just above a stand of cactus. The large dial reads 105 degrees. I walk over to the mule corral, hoping to find some shade nearby with a semblance of privacy. The ammonia stench of urine in the corral is terrible, but I am in luck. A narrow stream runs behind the corral and there is a perfectly located cottonwood tree, an ideal spot for pumping. Most important, it is empty, save for a woman whom I recognize as Kyla, the yoga teacher from my rafting group. "Hi," I say, walking up, and ask Kyla if she minds sharing the spot so that I can "do my milk thing" which is what I have resorted to calling my daily routine of expressing milk so that I can maintain my supply in the wilderness.

"No, go right ahead," she responds. "I'll stand guard for hikers, you can sit behind me if you like."

I am grateful for her help and take a seat on the roots of the large cottonwood tree, safely above the scurry of red ants, and begin.

After twenty minutes I am exhausted. I know I should express more, but I am simply too tired. I stop pumping and slump against the tree, paralyzed by the heat. Then I hear Kyla's voice. "Can I help?"

I turn to look at her, startled, surprised and touched, by her offer.

"Not really," I say, "Go on ahead. In fact, you should go on. I'm holding you up, and I think the coast is clear of hikers here. This is pretty much a one-man, I mean -woman job."

I watch as Kyla gets up, reshouldering her large backpack. She is in her thirties like me, but so fit and glowingly healthy that she looks twenty. She told me early on in the trip that she has no interest in having children.

"See you at the rim," I say, mustering cheer. She laughs, and waves, then turns to head up the trail, but then turns back and looks at me intently. She speaks so quietly that at first I don't hear her. "I think you're very brave."

Brave? Her words leave me stunned. I watch her slim figure making its way up the trail. In the past weeks of preparing for this trip, then setting out upon it, I have felt ridiculous, harried, exhausted, and apologetic. I have felt determined and at times, pouring my cups of milk into the river, jarred by a bolt of deep satisfaction, but I have never thought that what I was doing required bravery. Kyla's words, coming at this moment—me slumped in the heat so filthy and exhausted I could scream—shock me into a recognition that courage and glamour are not the same. All the difficulties I had taken upon myself suddenly seem worthwhile and of value. I resolve to push myself to pump for another ten minutes.

It is then that I hear a rustle in the bushes across the creek. The brown nose of a mule appears, followed by its head, front legs and, suddenly an entire mule train is crossing the stream not five feet from where I sit. My first reaction is annoyance. Every minute that I sit in the shade, the temperature back on the trail rises. I have lost so much time already, I don't have a half an hour to wait for them to amble by. I am tempted to keep on pumping, but remind myself that I am close to civilization now, and need to be more discreet than on the river where the lax rules of wilderness camping prevented modesty. I wait.

Mule after mule walks by, each one lowering it head to take a quick sip from the creek. I watch, nodding and sometimes smiling to the bobbing heads of bemused tourists, none of which return my glance. Finally, the mule driver who brings up the rear, rides up. "Howdy," he says, tipping his hat and nodding in my direction.

"Hi," I respond. I wonder why he is grinning so wide, the waxed tips of his curled moustache twitching. His mule, a pretty sorrel mare, looks at me dolefully before stepping on. Finally, they are gone. It is when I look down that I realize with horror that the front of my button down shirt is undone. In my exhaustion I had let it fall open. No wonder the tourists had looked away, while the mule driver grinned. Once again, it is a moment so embarrassing, it can only be motherhood. And this time I don't care. I am beyond considering anything except how to finish my business there as quickly as possible in order to get back on the trail. I will have to hurry to make it to the rim by five o'clock, when our pickup van departs.

Twenty-six hours later I am back in New York, holding my son Rhys while he nurses intently. Six months and eight days old now, he had not weaned while I was gone, and my husband, far from resentful at my absence, was bursting with proud news of his week alone with his infant son. I cannot stop staring at my son, I am so glad to be with him and my husband and at home. But I have only to shut my eyes for a moment, and I am once again in the wilderness. I can see the red rock, lit with sun as if on fire from within. I can see the stars, so many it seems as if the night sky is draped in lace. I can smell the gentle tang of tamarisk, and I can hear the river, rushing through the canyon like time. Once again I am aware of a paradox. I traveled away from my son, journeying into the wilderness, but I have moved, not away from him but toward him.

*Leila Philip grew up in Manhattan and upstate New York. She did a two-year pottery apprenticeship in Japan, then went on to get a master's degree in creative writing from Columbia University. She is the author of* The Road Through Miyama, *which received the 1990 PEN Martha Albrand Citation for nonfiction, and* A Family Place: A Hudson Family Farm, Three Centuries, Five Wars, One Family.

FRANCES MAYES

# Venice

*A romantic city gives a different
life a new outlook.*

THE PRIMO APPROACH TO VENICE IS NOT MARCO POLO AIRPORT
or the train; having driven around in the Veneto, and stopped in
Chioggia, I've absorbed a new sense of this watery location. I'd
always thought of Venice as a risen place which not long ago was
sinking and might sink again. Wandering in the Veneto, I absorbed
the real *geographical* sense, and I'm more awed then ever. The land
under Venice is often little more than the sandbars I used to wade
to at Saint Simons Island. The feat of establishing an empire on this
marshy archipelago shows that the settlers were strong on imagination. They wove willow dikes to keep away the sea. What madness!
Foundations were built on wooden poles, driven all the way
through the water and silty land to the packed clay substrata. The
hundreds of tiny islands were later linked by bridges, giving the
impression of canals carved out of a single island. Some waterways
were filled in, further changing the reality of the actual topography.

Instinct tells me that by learning to "read" the watery map, I
may be able to feel my way toward the source of this place's hold
on my imagination. I know already that it's not only Venice's
extravagant beauty that pulls me. My clues toward a solution may
begin with the realization that Venice's origins are against all ratio-

nal thinking: build your church—or your insurance company—on a rock.

Ed and I park in a remote garage, leaving most of our luggage in the trunk, and board a boat, which crosses a flat stretch of water and soon enters the Grand Canal. Holy Toledo! Holy of holies! Memory has abstracted the city into watercolor scenes. The reality of the dips of the boat, the working gondolas laden with fruit and cases of *acqua minerale*, the construction barges piled with boards and sacks of concrete, the mind-stopping, stupendous, fairy-tale, solid beauty of the *palazzi* lining the canal and reflecting in the water— I stand at the rail biting hard on the knuckle of my right forefinger, an old habit that returns when I am knocked silent. The beauty does not just pass before your eyes. It ravishes. I begin to feel the elation that a traveler experiences when in the presence of a place supremely itself.

Arriving in Venice seems like the most natural act in the world. Is it this way for everyone? The place is so thoroughly known through film, photographs, calendars, books. Is there another layer to this easy familiarity?

I'm feeling a rush of memories, and I want them to end by the time my foot steps out on the *fondamenta*. Venice was "our" city, my former husband's and mine. Although we went only twice, we'd loved the small flower-filled hotel, where we pulled the mattress off the bed when it squeaked. Our gondolier had a piercingly sweet voice and glided through canals, ducking under bridges. Well, yes, he did sing "O Sole Mio," but he also had a good fling with "Nessun Dorma." At the early-morning market, a vendor built a ziggurat of ripe white peaches. Every fish in the Adriatic seemed to be lined up glassy-eyed on ice, ready for the women with their baskets, and restaurant owners trailed by minions who balanced crates on their shoulders. Because I am cursed with a bird phobia, I hovered under the arcades of the Piazza San Marco while my husband walked among the thousands of pigeons then came back to describe the *piazza* from the perspective I never will see. We found the paper store with blank books bound in vellum and marbled paper. We tried the pasta with squid in its own ink. I loved the cycle of

Saint Ursula paintings by Carpaccio. Ursula, lying there in a tall bed, dreaming, while the angel bringing the palm of her martyrdom steps through her threshold. Four years later we returned with our daughter and had the pleasure of being in her happy company on those canals. She wore a straw gondolier hat, ran to pet cats who wouldn't be petted, left her drawstring pocketbook on a *vaporetto,* and cried for the loss of a dozen pieces of broken glass she'd collected on the trip. Odd what fragments of memory stay. I don't remember how she liked the lagoon, the bridges, the *piazza.* She loved the hotel tub's brass swan handles and spout. Strange how memory can reach *around* years and reconnect to the place and time where old loves are still intact. The memory rush subsides.

Many high waters have washed through Venice since then. Now I am back. With Ed. A different life. We'll make our own way here. I look over at Ed and have to laugh. He has the deep-space stare. "Venice," I say and he nods.

He's already tan, and leaning on the rail in his yellow linen shirt, with the pure glory of Venice racing behind him. I think he looks like someone I'd like to run off with, if I already hadn't. The prospect of days with *him* roving around Venice: *bella, bella.* As we enter the widest part of the Grand Canal, it seems to tilt. Soon we're bumping into the dock. "Heaven. Unbelievable."

"Yes, if there's no Venice in the real heaven, I don't want to go there."

*Frances Mayes has written for* The New York Times, House Beautiful, *and* Food and Wine. *She is also a widely published poet, food and travel writer, and novelist. She divides her time between Cortona, Italy and San Francisco, where she teaches creative writing at San Francisco State University. Her books include the novel* Swan, Under the Tuscan Sun, *and* Bella Tuscany, *from which this story was excerpted.*

DEBORAH JOHANSEN

\* \* \*

# Winter Walk

*Old friends share a New England mile.*

THE LAKE SITS LOW AMONG THE DECEMBER HILLS LIKE A MIRROR
in your palm, the skin of black ice polished smooth by the raw night
wind. Emptied of the last geese flushed from its shores, Tamarack
Lake remains silent, as expectant as the nearby stubbled cornfields
and the slate-gray sky banked up to the north, as ready as Greta and
I for the year's first snow.

One-half mile long and half as wide, the lake is bordered on the
north by a single stately row of tamaracks, hence its name. The trees,
at least a century old, add a graceful dignity to this rude landscape
stripped of its autumn brilliance and yet not cleanly muffled by
drifts of snow. The ochre branches—leafless now—glow against
the darkening sky in the late-afternoon light, their paler gold
reflected in the black ice below. This is what you first notice—this,
and the far pastures gone to seed, the hillside poverty grass gently
waving, a softness the color of chestnuts and wintering ponies.
Beyond lie the Catskills, an undulating horizon of pale blue and
softened indigo, melding softly into the haze.

Heading out across the field toward Lake Tam, we call it, I am
with one of its longtime residents, Greta Norberg, who is my friend
and my guide. More than anyone I know, she has perfected the art

of walking. German by birth, she has lived most of her seventy-six years on the lake among the hills of Dutchess County and knows them like a native. I've come from California for a traditional New England Christmas with my family, but stop for a preview of the season with her before driving on to western Massachusetts. She and I still cherish childhood winters beneath blankets of snow— hers in the Alps, mine in the Berkshires. Greta's mood turns bleak when the fields on her farm are not, by this time, similarly blessed with snow.

She is as lean, and often as unbending, as her walking stick which she stabs periodically into the side of the pathway. Our boots crunch into the crystallized mud. As we near the lake, the air carries the clean scent of snow—moist and chill. A slight breeze rustles the cattails massed along the shore. We push aside great whorls of plum-colored blackberry briar which has overgrown the path since last spring. A little farther on, the fiery orange and red berries of bitter-sweet catch the waning sun. Greta neatly clips a spray. "My winter bouquet for the kitchen sill," she says. "It will do me well until spring forsythia." Beyond is a stand of young sumacs, their bare branches tipped with velvet spikes of deep-crimson berries.

The low slant of light sinks behind a thin streak of cloud, and the breeze dies with it. Suddenly a heavy, even sound swishes overhead like labored breathing—the last geese of the season flying south, their honk-honking punctuating the silence. As we round the lake's eastern shore, the trail meanders into the remains of the Norberg's apple orchard, planted by Greta's father when her family first arrived from Germany. The thick, gnarled trunks seem barely to withstand their own weight, let alone support the confusion of heavy branch-es above. I remember these trees from five springs ago when I last visited, their small clouds of pink blossoms exuding a sweetness that overwhelmed the air. They stand now with a certain humble dignity, like the weathered figure of Mr. Norberg reaching up for apples in July.

Our path has all but disappeared in the high grasses that whisper to our knees. Greta points her walking stick at the cut in the far stone wall, course-correcting us back toward the lake. We pick our way among the granite boulders hefted aside by years of winter frost and occasional mischief of small boys. Patches of lichen cover the stones in rust, pale green, and white. A chipmunk peeks out from a crevice, pops up and, skittering the length of the stone wall, disappears into the woods.

Along the lake's southern shore, we, too, enter the woods, a second growth of maple, birch, ash, and beech among an older forest of hemlock. The dank air is infused with the pungency of rich, dark, loamy mulch—a thick carpet of rotting leaves and pine needles beneath our boots. On either side, soft, vivid green mounds of moss are intertwined with dark, leafy vines of partridge berry and ground pine.

The wind momentarily freshens, stirring the few remaining leaves on the beeches—stiff, translucent, little flags. Slim shafts of birch rise like white spires against the deep, green pines. Overhead the hemlocks rhythmically sigh and creak. A few wrens flutter among themselves, then streak off among the branches and are gone. I shiver against the growing cold.

Emerging into the meadow, we have completed our circle, a ritual of walking we share the few times I visit. The last of the sun is veiled—weak as milk—as we trudge up the hill to the farmhouse. In the diminished light the muted colors of the landscape soften and merge—the ochre deepens to umber, the tawny to chestnut, the pale blue-gray to slate. Among the last shifts of sea-

> *T*his lake is a knowing eye that keeps tabs on me. I try to behave. Last summer I swam in its stream of white blossoms, contemplating "the floating life." Now I lie on its undulant surface. For a moment the lake is a boat sliding hard to the bottom of a deep trough, then it is a lover's body reshaping me. Whenever I try to splice discipline into my heart, the lake throws diamonds at me, but I persist, staring into its dangerous light as if into the sun.
>
> ◆
>
> —Gretel Ehrlich,
> *Islands, The Universe, Home*

son, the lake remains still, in dark reflection. The surrounding emptiness and silence are complete. In the end, it is only we who hold out—two women in their own way—impatient for the deep and longed-for snow.

*Deborah Johansen is coauthor of five books including* The Spirit of the Monterey Coast, *a 400-year cultural history from Carmel to Big Sur. Although she is the only member of her family gone west of the Hudson River, she still has one foot firmly planted in New England.*

ALISON DaROSA

# Extended Family

*A homestay opens new doors.*

LIKE BOYS AND GIRLS AT A FIFTH-GRADE DANCE CLASS, WE SEGRE-gated to opposite sides of a youth recreation center. Us and them.

Nervous. Shy. Awkward. Thinking positive, but scared to death.

We were here in Delhi to meet the Indian families who were going to adopt us for the coming week. We'd move into the homes of these strangers, experience their lifestyles, share their meals, play with their children. We'd learn from them what it means to be Indian today.

And we'd learn about Indian hospitality, a concept that goes beyond words.

"In Sanskrit, the guest is next to the Lord," said Pulin Trivedi, who helped start the first chapter of The Friendship Force in India in 1990.

We would learn what it means to be treated like gods.

I was in India with the San Diego chapter of The Friendship Force, an organization that arranges homestays among members in fifty-six countries. After three days in Agra, where we learned about the history and culture of India and a little about what to expect living with an Indian family, we were in Delhi ready to begin our homestays.

All I knew about the family I'd been assigned to was their names, that she was Hindu and he was a Sikh, and that they had two children. I searched the room for men wearing turbans.

San Diegan Ruth Miller and I, assigned to the same home, watched others pair up with their families. It was a scarier version of that fifth-grade dance class: nobody was asking us to dance, and this time we'd be wallflowers for a week, thousands of miles from home.

At last, a royal-blue turban entered with a woman in a stunning emerald-green sari shot through with gold. The man in the turban wore a tailored, white dress shirt and rep tie. Both were breathless as their dark, smoky eyes scanned the room.

"Lyall?" I asked.

"Yes, yes," they answered.

We were all so relieved, we started laughing, nodding, shaking hands. Nervous laughter, sweaty hands.

Pritpal and Aparajita Lyall apologized for being late. They had come in two cars. Pritpal lugged our luggage to the white Armada sports-utility vehicle owned by Otis Elevator, where he is Delhi general manager. A company driver drove it off. The four of us and my camera gear packed into the tiny red Suzuki that Otis provides for the Lyalls' personal use.

The Lyalls drove us to their two-bedroom apartment, also provided by Otis, in south New Delhi. A big, bony cow, one of several that wander the neighborhood, occupied their usual parking space. Hindus believe that those who kill or eat a cow will rot in hell for as many years as there are hairs on the cow that was slain. We found another parking spot.

At the Lyalls' front door, we followed their lead and removed our shoes, placing them in a rack of cubbyholes.

Then we became aunts.

The Lyalls' children, Simran and Rohan, then five and eleven respectively, were waiting to greet us. We were introduced as "Auntie Alison" and "Auntie Ruth." Both of the children were shy and perfectly behaved. That would change soon enough.

Aparajita, thirty-four, who works part time as a travel agent, introduced the family's housekeeper, Shelia Saha, who said she was eighteen but looked closer to fourteen. She offered us frosty glasses of orange drink, then busied herself in the apartment's closet-sized kitchen.

The children were eager to show us to our room, which was really *their* room. They had moved to the basement, so Auntie Ruth and I would have beds.

Because of our visit, the family had installed a used air conditioner in that bedroom. I'd read that morning in the *Asian Wall Street Journal* that despite temperatures that frequently exceed 110 degrees in summer, only one percent of Indian households have air conditioners. That used air conditioner never worked for more than a few minutes during our stay, despite repeated visits by assorted repairmen—but Ruth and I discovered that comfort has far more to do with hospitality and generosity than room temperature.

To make conversation easier that first evening, Ruth and I dug through our bags for small gifts we'd carried from home. We gave the children marker pens and coloring books and the adults a picture book on San Diego. But it was Ruth, who was then president of the San Diego chapter of The Friendship Force and a veteran of many homestays, who broke the ice:

"Do Sikhs take off their turbans at night?" she asked.

They do. And Pritpal, then forty-one, was happy to demonstrate. We learned later that it takes about thirty minutes to wrap a lengthy stretch of soft cloth into a turban. Pritpal was happy to demonstrate that, too.

Dinner that first night was *channa dal masala*: lentils with vegetables and brown rice. Aparajita ate with her fingers; when she used soft flat bread to sop up the sauce, I felt right at home. After dinner, all of us convened in Pritpal and Aparajita's small bedroom, where there was a working air conditioner. We sat on their bed or on the floor and talked. It became a nightly ritual.

Behind closed doors that evening, Ruth and I whispered like fifth-grade girls. We were happy with our dance partners.

The next morning, over Western-style omelettes with ketchup, we discussed an article in the *Sunday Times of India* by Gail Sheehy. It was on the changing roles of women, and it was enough to drive Pritpal to the nearby squash court.

That morning, I learned that in Hindi, Aparajita means invincible. As we became closer over those days, I came to understand that Aparajita was perfectly named.

A member of the Brahman class, this Hindu woman defied her family and its long-held tradition of arranged marriages to wed for love. Marrying a Sikh took extraordinary courage.

"It was hard—but not *very* hard—because I moved to the city and lived away from my family and had a lot of support from friends," she said. "My friends come from all backgrounds."

But that morning, talk was less personal: "Thanks to television, even women in villages are putting their foot down, saying, 'I contribute,'" Aparajita said. "It has been less than ten years since satellite dishes and cable television began providing exposure of other cultures to Indian women. Before that, it was only India TV. Worldwide television is making a big difference—and even in the poorest slums, you will see TV."

Aparajita said that a bill then being considered by Indian lawmakers would reserve 33 percent of the seats in parliament for women.

"It is tremendous progress," she said. "Especially when you consider that it is only a two-year-old law that makes it illegal to abort female fetuses just because they are female."

Aparajita said female infanticide is still practiced "in very small pockets."

"The government is clamping down," she said. "But the issue is taken up only when the male population gets very high in some states."

We talked about poverty in India—and she acknowledged that she and her family have far more than most.

"The infrastructure is poor in many villages, but nobody is hungry anymore," she said. "There is no income tax on agriculture, so there is no food shortage."

While most Americans think of the impoverished majority when they think of India, it is important to remember that the nation's burgeoning middle class is equal in number to the entire population of the United States.

As the week progressed, we spent more time laughing at our-selves, eating with our fingers, shopping together at outdoor markets, being astounded by everyday life. We spotted relics of ancient cities scattered almost everywhere; enjoyed the mind-numbing nirvana of oil treatment/scalp massages available at corner beauty salons for about $3; discovered that a dozen eggs cost 48 cents while a single roll of toilet tissue runs $1; ventured into the circus that is Delhi-driving.

Nearly three million vehicles—and assorted animals and people—clog the roads in this city of eleven million. Cars, camels, buses, water buffaloes, trucks, cows, motorized trishaws, dogs, taxis, elephants, bicycles, horses, and hundreds of thousands of scooters merge in a perpetual blaring traffic jam. Nobody pays attention to signs posted to encourage some semblance of sanity: "Lane driving is sane driving." This circus would be more fun, if it weren't so dangerous: on average, five people die in Delhi traffic accidents every day.

But traffic didn't deter us. One evening we visited an outdoor shopping bazaar where Ruth and I each bought a *salwar kameez,* a pajama-style Indian outfit, and long

> *W*hen we drove to the markets of the old city, we were hit by a rock-video kind of intensity: hawkers, jostling crowds, blaring Hindi film music, pigs, cows, goats, chickens, parrots, diseased dogs, bicycle rickshaws, one-armed lepers, legless beggars, ragged children. On the streets surrounding Jama Masjid, the largest mosque in India, the smells of incense, jasmine, and sewage mingle with the delicious aroma of Indian bread puffing up in the oil of a frying pan. Photographs and films cannot completely capture the sensory overload. Until then, I had always been slightly disappointed to find the foreign countries I visited in some way shadows of what I had imagined. In India that first day I was incredulous.
>
> ◆
>
> —Elisabeth Bumiller, *May You Be the Mother of a Hundred Sons*

Indian dresses. By the end of the week, we felt more comfortable in our Indian clothing than in our Western skirts and slacks.

As a family, we visited a Hindu temple and a Sikh *gurdwara*.

"She is Hindu," Pritpal joked, pointing to Aparajita. "I am one of the nice guys."

But there was nothing funny about the stories they told of the 1984 Hindu riots in Delhi, following the assassination of Indira Gandhi at the hands of her Sikh bodyguards. Whole Sikh neighborhoods were torched, and as many as 5,000 Sikh men and boys were butchered. Aparajita dressed her husband in a disguise to hide his conspicuous long hair and beard; Hindu friends risked their lives hiding him in their home.

Pritpal and Aparajita each took separate days off work to show us the tourist sites of Delhi: Embassy Row, the Red Fort, Connaught Place, the Birla Temple, India Gate, Humāyūn's Tomb, ruins of the various cities of old Delhi.

But when I thumb through the notebooks I filled during those excursions, it's not the descriptions of ancient temples or historic tombs that tug at my heart. It's the flying elephants and silly airplanes, drawn with orange crayon in a five-year-old's hand, that I treasure. It's pages filled with tied tic-tac-toe games and huge block letters: S-I-M-R-A-N.

Those drawings remind me of a pigtailed little head so filled with imagination and things to say she couldn't spit the words out fast enough. I close my eyes and hear Simran's breathless, musical staccato: "Do not talk while I'm saying to you…" she would command, sputtering wonderful stories of elephants that fly and use their trunks to pump swimming holes full of water for children to play in.

The drawing also reminds me of her brother Rohan. Serious and kind. Thoughtful and studious. And always a gentleman. I remember sitting cross-legged with him on his bed, playing checkers. He was a tough opponent, but then, I had a harder time differentiating among the buttons, baubles, and pieces of candy that replaced a slew of missing checkers.

I remember the morning I joined Rohan at his Delhi Public School, where he was among fifth-graders receiving a Scholar

Badge at a ceremony honoring top students. I sat beside his parents and shared their pride.

That night, we celebrated by going to dinner at one of Rohan's favorite restaurants: El Rodeo, a Tex-Mex joint where the waiters wore cowboy hats and red bandannas and the menus were shaped like six-shooters. The restaurant, one of the few places in Delhi licensed to serve beef, is tucked up a narrow stairwell on Connaught Place, a huge traffic circle ringed by architecturally uniform, colonnaded buildings. It suddenly seemed stranger to be eating enchiladas than to be seeing cows on the sidewalk.

Toward the end of our weeklong stay, Friendship Force members and their families convened for dinner at a downtown hotel. Everyone turned out in their finest Indian fashions.

"This has been the best experience of my life," said a woman from California, who was wearing a royal-blue sari and a string of sapphires borrowed from her hostess. "We went to a safe deposit box to get these to wear tonight," she whispered, fingering the necklace.

Another woman from New Jersey wondered why I was taking notes.

"You're never going to be able to put these feelings into words," she said. "You can't intellectualize emotion."

I looked at the Lyalls and knew that she was right. India had touched my soul; they had filled my heart.

On our last night together, Pritpal and Aparajita took us to their special place—Lodi Garden, the park where they had courted. We strolled under the new moon. Aparajita and I shared secrets, the way longtime girlfriends do. It was impossible to believe we had been strangers a week earlier.

Later that night, at Indira Gandhi International Airport, when it was time to part, all of us embraced and struggled to hold back tears—some of us failed.

*Alison DaRosa is travel editor of the* San Diego Union-Tribune. *She is a three-time winner of the Society of American Travel Writers' Lowell Thomas Gold Award for travel writing. "Extended Family" won the 1998 Pacific Asia Travel Association Gold Award for Travel Journalism. She contributed to several other Travelers' Tales books, including* A Woman's World.

BARBARA RAS

# The Center of Nowhere

*A mother and daughter mush*
*Alaska's Brooks Range.*

A HUNDRED AND FIFTY SLED DOGS LIVE IN THE BETTLES DOG
yard—three times the number of people in this arctic village
arranged around an airstrip in the interior of Alaska. Nearly every
dog here is barking some canine version of "Take me! Take me!"
Puffs of dog breath rise into the dry April air. I look up from
harnessing, through the foreground of scruffy spruce, birch, and
cottonwood and beyond to the horizon, where the white peaks of
the Brooks Range jut dramatically against the deep-blue sky. The
dogs are all wild to run, wild to go with us on our four-day, 100-
mile journey into one of the last pieces of true wilderness left here
or anywhere.

John, our lead guide and musher, owns many of these dogs, and
he's picking among them, matching us and our dogs with a list he's
made up according to some mysterious calculus of dog-client-
weight-temperament. One by one, he points out the dogs that we
hitch up in a prescribed order. The lead dogs are first, which goes
against my impulse to start closest to the sled. The idea is that the
lead dogs will steady the others. But who steadies the lead dogs, I
wonder, which turns out to be a good question.

"Here's Buster," John says, presenting a gorgeous, blue-eyed husky with cream and black fur. He holds Buster up by the collar and hops him across the dog yard on his hind legs, since four sled-dog paws on the ground make more traction than you can control easily. "He'll be one of your lead dogs. He's a little more steady than Duke, your other lead, so always hitch up Buster first." We get Buster into a harness, head and legs through the appropriate openings and the rest laid out across his back, and hooked into the lines coming off the sled. He's remarkably obliging through it all, though slightly aloof in his bearing.

John brings over Duke, another 50-pound dog nearly identical to Buster in coloring and musculature, but definitely a loose cannon. "Don't let Duke get away from you," John says, with a bit of under-statement, hitching Duke to the lines. Hitched or not, Duke is leapfrogging over Buster, and getting him all lathered up, so that they're both pulling furiously against the sled, and bounding in wild, semilunatic orbits, spending energy I think they'd be better off saving for the trip. A word from John quiets both dogs. Until he turns his back. Then even with my best Arnold Schwarzenegger voice, I can't get them to stop their furious leaping, tangling each other in the lines, and yanking on the sled.

I want to get on with the rest of my team, so I leave them to it. Besides our two guides, there are four of us on the trip, and everyone else is further along than me in hitching up their dogs. Cyndi is helping her husband Eric with their team (she's ditched the idea of driving her own

*When* we climbed into the sled and I admitted feeling guilty about letting dogs haul me across the snow all day, [my friend] Rande insisted that the dogs loved to mush. "Listen," she said. "They're singing!"

They were, in fact, making a joyful noise, a yipping, yodeling canine chorus that didn't let up until Doug Hannah, their kindly owner, cried, "Hee-yaw!" and we were off.

♦

—Jessica Maxwell,
*Femme d' Adventure*

sled in favor of riding in the basket of his), so the two of them are nearly done. John's team seems to coalesce magically into place amid his help in getting the rest of us squared away. And our other guide Marie has been helping Anna hitch up her team. Anna is my twelve-year-old daughter—my partner on this adventure.

I manage the next two pairs, the team dogs in the middle, followed by the wheel dogs closest to the sled. In the end, a Duke, a Luke, two Busters, a Jackson, and a Tinkerbell, 300 pounds on 24 paws. The wooden sled, overfitted with cranberry-red canvas, is about eight feet long, shaped like an elongated shopping cart on skinny skis. At my end of the sled, there are handlebars. Actually the handlebars are just one semicircle of wood, but singular or plural, it's what you hang on to for dear life. Behind the sled are the runners, where I'll ride. I look down at my feet in the huge, insulated bunny boots I've been issued by the outfitters. They look too large for the thin slats of wood I'll be standing on five or six hours a day.

John circles his hand over his head—our signal to head out. The dogs see it, and they crank up, straining against the sled to be off. Their yapping makes a good accompaniment to my heart, which is beating up a little storm of its own. John's sled takes off. Then the sled ahead of me, with Anna driving. She vanishes around the first bend in the trail, in the scrawny collection of trees that passes for woods here. Then it's my turn to follow. I don't know if I'm more worried about losing sight of her or losing my grip. Marie is alongside me, helping to yank free the snow hook, a two-pronged iron claw that grips the snow and keeps the dogs from running off with the sled. I want to think, "Bend your knees, relax," but I'm reeling at the swish of the sled, the whiplashing speed of our take-off, the hush of the dogs, now that they are running, now that we are running.

They call this mushing, from the French command *marchez*, but it's more like waterskiing over snow, powered by quiet motors, furry dynamos, each with a distinctive gait that will become hypnotically familiar as we wend our way down the trail. This wending takes time, however, since at the first curve out of the dog yard, going at warp speed, I wipe out. I manage to tip the sled as John has instructed, so that on its side it'll drag to a stop instead of overtaking the dogs and slamming into them from behind. I get up out of the snow, relieved that I can fall and get up again in one piece, something that, as a forty-six-year-old, I haven't been practicing regularly. Not yet, at any rate.

Ahead on the trail, Anna leans on her sled. Between the otter fur trimming her hat and her sunglasses, I can't see much of her face, but I can tell from her stance that she's nonplussed by the delay. We are in the midst of snowfields stretching off to mountains that are jaw-dropping in their splendor. It is hard not to gawk. But here's Anna pulling a packet out of the front pouch of her anorak. Nonchalantly, she starts slamming down pastel M&Ms. We could be at the corner store back home in Berkeley, we could be anywhere.

John helps me untangle the dogs, and I get back on the sled, knowing that when the sleds ahead pull out, my team will once again be wild to follow. I can't remember to remind myself to breathe. I'm too busy preparing for takeoff, one foot on a runner, the other hard on the brake, one hand on the handlebars, while with the other I reach to pull the snow hook up out of its death grip in the snow. As soon as the hook is up, I throw it into the sled and hold on. The maneuvers aren't that complicated; it's managing to do them in the blur of the moment, the landscape rushing past, a funny dislocated feeling in my mouth that might be my heart.

Once on the straightaway, the dogs running silently, the sled swooshing more or less predictably on the trail, finally my heart stops trying to escape my body. We are heading up the valley of the Wild River, up into a central piece of the Brooks Range, an expanse of mountains that crosses Alaska east to west for 600 miles. The sky has the azure promise of spring. The air is still, and though the thermometer was at zero when we woke this morning, now at midday, it's probably up to twenty. Even with the rush of air on my face, I'm toasty, the good work of thermal underwear with a boost from adrenaline. It is hard to reconcile the mysterious words we studied on maps, the imagined deserts of ice, with this shimmering beauty of sun on snow, us in it, Anna up ahead, already letting go of the handlebars to snap pictures, and my six dogs diligently running.

✳

This dogsledding adventure was my idea. Some friends of mine had done a more ambitious version of the trip, and they made it sound irresistible. I wanted to have a wilderness experience with Anna before her adolescence took us on a wild ride of its own. Being with dogs was part of the allure. Because of Anna and the dogs she brought into our family, I finally discovered in middle age what puppy love was all about. I thought putting us with dogs in the wilderness would superglue Anna and me into a joyful closeness. I thought we would both speak in rapturous Muir-like sentences extolling untrammeled nature, wild beauty. I thought dogsledding would be an easy access to wilderness that we couldn't drive or wouldn't snowshoe. Hah. Hah. And hah.

At the end of our first day, when we reach the tent that will sleep all six of us, it looks puny in the wide pool of white at the foot of Mount Gilroy, rising almost 4,000 feet above. We pull in, unhitch our teams, and start setting up camp. John tends to the dogs. Marie unpacks the sled she's loaded with firewood and gear. Eric goes out to shovel snow into a plastic bin to melt for water and coffee.

I walk off into the snow well beyond the camp and stretch out, feeling the force of the cold earth with the length of my body. It's like a large ice pack on my aching muscles. I write for a while, grateful that my pen hasn't frozen as the gear list warned it would. I am also grateful for the blood that rushes to comfort my cold-packed body parts after I'm up and moving around again. Above me, the single saw-toothed shape of Gilroy is catching the sunset, turning peachy.

On my way back to the tent I pass John. He's going from dog to dog, paw to paw, checking out all the moving parts. The dogs flop onto their backs, give up their bellies for rubs, and leap gleefully for attention. At the tent I notice something surprising on a crate next to the vats of dry dog food John has been boiling into mush. A Bible. The gilt edges of the pages seem oddly fancy, oddly right.

At dinner we all gather in the tent. We sit on cots eating the chicken teriyaki that Marie has dished up. Except for Anna and me, everyone is in their thirties, and except for Anna, everyone is a little diffident at being cast together as a group of strangers stuck with each other for the next few days. Anna rattles on about her dogs at home, her stuffed animals, her friends. Marie, a Stanford graduate who grew up in Northern California, keeps drawing her further out. In the face of Anna's talkativeness, I say little. As the others manage to get a word in edgewise, I'm surprised that none of the talk is about Alaska. Everyone talks about home. Eric about his route driving a gasoline truck between western Virginia and Richmond. Cyndi about her mother, who doesn't know she's on this trip and will be furious when she finds out. John tells of his five-year-old girl winning the one-dog competition with Junior, his lead dog, pulling a basket sled. Outside the temperature is falling, and dusk goes on for what seems like forever.

The next morning dawns chiming with yellow, the sky cheerfully blue. After the night we've spent, it's a good thing the day is glorious. During the night the tent divided itself into factions: the snorers, the complainers about the snorers, and those in the middle being kept awake. Amid all this was the creakiness of the cots, bad enough when someone turned over. But when anyone tried to get up, they sounded like icebergs calving. The cot groans couldn't compete, however, with the zipper of the tent flap, which made broken chain-saw sounds every time the door was opened and closed by departing tent mates. If you divide the length of the night (already shortened by the extraordinarily long dusk) by a dozen goings and the same number of comings, you get an idea of how long any stretch of sleep lasted. Add in the twenty-four blasts of sub-zero air each time the tent flap was pulled back and—well, you get the picture.

But the morning is brilliant. Marie is whipping around the tent, packing with a vengeance. John is out feeding the dogs. Eric and Cyndi have already repacked their gear into all their little zipper bags and stuff sacks. I'm trying to organize for both me and Anna, who now that she's old enough to actually be of some help is beyond the age where she wants to. She has no scruples about slouching on her cot while I huff and puff over the gear. And given how sleep-deprived we are, I'm in no mood to struggle with her.

Later, after we've suited up in our Michelin tire-girl outfits, hitched up the dogs, picked up the picket line (an awfully light-weight name for a chain that weighs 40 pounds), and loaded up our sleds, I attempt to elevate the level of discourse. I walk up to Anna, who's got her hip stuck out in that whaddya-want stance. I should know better, but I can't help myself from asking, "So what do you think a mom and a daughter can learn from being out in the wild?"

In her best hell-bent-for-thirteen tone she says, "That we can't cope with getting along."

Finally underway. It's a relief to be alone. Alone with the dogs like good shepherds leading me into a river valley that carves its way through the mountains. Craggy peaks crown the horizon, circling 320 degrees. We whoosh into their midst, into monumental silence that dwarfs the sounds of the sled, the padding of dog paws on the snow. The beauty is austere. The purity is aching. For mile after mile, the snow is brilliantly, unwaveringly white, even on our trail, which has been previously traveled all season by many groups like ours. For those, like me, accustomed to the way snow grays and muddies in more populated regions, the natural authority of this whiteness is humbling.

We are in boreal forest, the last tree growth before tundra. It doesn't look very forestlike, however. It's more like a sparsely scat-tered field of trees, scraggly black and white spruce, many growing no higher than ten to twenty feet and no wider than a foot at the base. If you were of a mind to do some tree-hugging, you could probably get your arms around three or four of these at once, if it weren't for the fact that there are distances of several yards between one tree and another.

Now, ahead, the trees begin to cluster, bunching up in denser growth. These stands of taller, sturdier trees signal water, or in our case, ice. The sled, even with my foot on the brake, slides around wantonly. When the smooth ice suddenly gives way to an over-flow—a rough patch where running water has bubbled up to refreeze in great heaves and ridges—it's like sledding over lava. The dogs slip and slide a little, but as a team, it doesn't slow them down.

Even with all my weight on the brake, the teeth of the rakelike metal strip don't get much purchase. My sled slips around behind my team like a caboose jumping the track. After a few wide arcs, I fall. I get up. But there's more ice, more overflows, and the trail over it curves through trees. A few more uncontrollable careenings and I fall again. Each time John anchors his sled and walks back to help me regroup. Each time Anna looks back impatiently, or takes pictures, or eats candy. Thankfully the dogs look ahead.

The ice mercifully behind me, I'm back in cruise mode. Me and the dogs. Luke, at nine, is the oldest on my team. He has that side-to-side run, not unlike a toddler with a load in his pants. Jackson, about twenty months old, pulls with one shoulder forward. "In order to give 120 percent effort," John says. Buster has a stiffness in his gait, the result of a dogfight a while back that had him on an IV for four days. My favorite is Tinkerbell, a sweet young thing that runs brightly, as if to live up to her name.

The presence of the dogs keeps wildlife at a distance. But there have been animals here, all along the trail. I try to inventory the frequent tracks in the snow—evidence of moose, fox, marten, and possibly fiercer mammals. Bear? Wolves? Occasionally a small bird flies alone across the trail—its sudden dart of life a reminder of how little movement I've seen in the cold, snowy languor around us. When two ravens join us, crisscrossing the trail, their company feels huge. It's no wonder the Athabaskan people native to this land attached such mythic significance to them. They believed that Raven was the prime power in the ancient world, that it was the raven that brought the sun to sky. Here above me, with sunlight gleaming off black feathers, the ravens swoop and soar.

We stop for lunch, and Anna flings herself into the soft snow on the side of the trail. I join her. We eat peanut butter on Sailor Boy crackers, trail mix, and the candy bars we helped ourselves to this morning. We rub the dogs. Thank them for their generous spirits. Mostly we just sit, flopped back on the snow, gazing out at the mountains ringing the horizon, the sky impossibly clear, impossibly cerulean. Four sleds' worth of dogs rest along four sled-lengths of trail and not one of them is barking.

A native legend tells of how dogs came over to the side of the humans when a big rift opened up in the earth, separating people from the animals who fled to the other side. Only the dog stood by at the edge of the abyss, begging to be rescued. A man called to the dog and urged it to leap across. The dog leapt, and landing short, hung on by its paws. The man pulled the dog up out of the brink, forever sealing the bond between the two creatures, and thus beginning a working collaboration that for centuries provided transportation to arctic peoples around the world.

> *The* eyes of wild animals are unfathomable pools. Most of what we see in them is ourselves, reflected.
>
> ◆
>
> —SueEllen Campbell,
> *Bringing the Mountain Home*

In fact, the first use of sled dogs occurred around 4,000 years ago in central Siberia, in the area north of Lake Baikal. But now native people rely on snowmobiles for hauling and transport, leaving dogsledding to sport and adventure travel. The well-publicized Iditarod Race, covering 1,000 miles from Anchorage to Nome, has put dogsledding in the limelight. It's also prompted a few t-shirts, including the one that appeared after Susan Butcher won the race four times in the late 1980s: "Alaska—where men are men and where women win the Iditarod."

We mush on into the afternoon, traveling at about six miles an hour when we're on flat terrain. The valley opens gently into expansive vistas, and we spread out. Far ahead, John and his team are tiny in the distance, the arc they're tracing like the swirl of a waltz across a vast white floor. In the nearer distance, Anna follows, floating gracefully, swooning into the curves. I wonder why John chose to put Anna behind him and ahead of me. I think about her moving into adulthood, not looking back, me trailing her from behind.

As the land gets hillier, John slows his team to close up the distance between sleds. Going uphill, the dogs look back, a silent plea that means, "Get off and run behind the sled, or at least help by pushing off with one foot." Going over the top of a roller-coaster hill, my sled is airborne, slamming down the hillside and threatening to overtake the dogs. I ride the brake as hard as I can, hunching down over my sled. The tense white of my knuckles spreads all over my body. Beyond me, Anna rides tall and sleek on the slope below. There's something a little insouciant in the way she puts one foot on the brake, as if slowing down were an afterthought.

Tonight we make camp in a mining cabin in a little nook of the valley. Next to it is a cache, a miniature cabin on stilts that looks like a playhouse, but actually serves as a larder. Storing food away from the house reduces the likelihood of wildlife dropping in for a bite to eat and no doubt removes the temptation for midnight snacks. We delight in the coziness of mattresses on the floor and the luxury of an outhouse. An outhouse with a view onto a mountain that leaps into the air right out the (doorless) doorway.

The Brooks Range feels old, and it is. Geologists date its formation to 150 million years ago (making it more than twice as old as the Rockies). The peaks are rugged for their size, craggy, monumental, even in the afternoon light, now softening them with tints of honey and amber. The shades on the mountains move into lavender and grays with the gradual deepening of dusk. Each day lengthens by eight minutes, a pace that'll add about an hour of daylight per week. The long light means our chances of seeing the aurora borealis are postponed till darker skies, past midnight.

In the wee hours, Eric and Cyndi wake me, whispering, "Lights." I rouse Anna and we throw on parkas. Outside the relative warmth of the cabin, the air, maybe twenty below, slaps us awake. Above us a shimmering green banner spans the sky. There is no wind. The hush is dense. With the sky so still, the dance of the lights appears all the more vivid, as the colors run through a range of greens, changing intensity and mood, by turns wistful and wild. When a power surge pulses across the arc, the green goes from mint to Day-Glo.

Thankfully, no one talks. We watch, enthralled by this otherworldliness.

Arctic peoples believed the northern lights were the souls of animals dancing in the sky or torches lit by the dead to help hunters find their prey during the long dark of winter. Scientists attribute the auroral displays to solar winds interacting with the magnetic force of the earth. After traveling through space at speeds of one to three million kilometers an hour, the winds brush past us, releasing electrons into the atmosphere that we see as color and light. Standing here in the middle of the night, I can barely believe Alaska, let alone solar winds. I give in to the spell of the lights, the way their eerie beauty belongs to this stillness, this cold.

Before we go back to sleep, the dogs pick up howling, some sudden urge passing from dog to dog, then by twos and threes, until all twenty-five of them are head back in full neck-stretching wails. When they get to the end of the song, or the roll call, they all know it and come suddenly, in unison, to a full stop. The total silence of the night resumes its uncanny hold.

Later, someone talking in her sleep announces, "Oh, my God, that's cool."

Halfway into our third day, I'm falling less. Except on ice. I watch John, then Anna, cross the worst ice and overflows successfully, then watch them turn around to watch me. By now I have my own mantra about falling. It comes from an incident in *The Snow Leopard*, Peter Matthiessen's account of a long Himalayan trek. Faced with crossing a particularly rickety bridge, his Sherpas decide to take off their packs before venturing on. The first man to reach the other bank waits for his bedroll to be thrown across after him. But the throw misses, and the bedroll drops into the icy stream below. Matthiessen expects nasty tempers, fights, what most of us might imagine at the thought of sleeping in a wet bedroll in the freezing cold on a remote Himalayan trail. Instead, they all laugh, even the Sherpa with a wet bedroll. I tell myself that falling is just another wet bedroll. I tell myself to surrender the idea of control.

But surrendering isn't getting me past this excruciating stretch of ice we're crossing. My sled keeps sliding out from under me, and no matter what I do, I cannot seem to get more than 40 feet without falling again. John and Anna have disappeared around the bend, and the thick growth of trees around the curves of the creek hide them from view. Marie comes up from behind to get me back on track. I'm sore and tired. Hauling myself out of hip-deep snow in massive clothes, again and again, is taxing even my bedroll policy. Marie says, "What can I do to help?"

"I have no idea," I say, nearly in tears at her kindness and my ineptitude.

"I could take the sled across for you. Or I could ride with you and then walk back to get my snowmobile," she suggests.

"Will we both fit on the sled?" I ask.

Ever cheerful, she says, "Sure." She gets on the runners behind me, reaching around my waist to grab onto the handlebars. We figure out how to position our hulking feet in our oversized Bunny Boots, and off we go.

Marie leans hard into the curves, the sled up on one runner, almost vertical. I mimic her. It's a private lesson, and it's working. I'm euphoric at finally getting what I've been doing wrong. But when we round a deep curve, my euphoria lurches to panic. A dead tree fallen across the ice has gone right through the handlebars of Anna's sled. The sled hangs there, empty. The snag sticks through the handlebars about a foot and a half, piercing the space that Anna had been riding in. John is coming down toward the sled with an ax. Finally I see Anna on a snowbank, doubled over, holding her stomach. I run toward her, trying not to imagine what I'll find.

"Are you okay?" I ask over her bent head.

She looks up. Her face is white, except for two round flushes of pink on her cheeks. She's not crying. "I think so," she says weakly.

"Did it break the skin?" I ask, hugging her. "Let me see," I say. Without resisting, Anna lifts her layers of clothing to show the veiny white scratches on her belly, her skin mercifully intact.

"What happened?" I ask.

John, ax in hand, tells me, "I came around the bend and there was this mean old snag hanging into the trail. I was heading straight for it, and I jumped off my sled to avoid it. Then I looked back to warn Anna—she was heading straight for it. I yelled. She kept on going, but she didn't jump off her sled. She kept scooching back on the runners as the snag came at her. Then I saw it catch her handlebars and Anna went flying off backward. I couldn't tell if it rammed her or what. I ran back here, and luckily she wasn't hurt bad. Had the wind knocked out of her, though."

We laugh. It's that nervous release of tension. An adult reaction. I wonder if Anna will be offended. She looks up. She laughs too. John chops the limb off to free her sled. We cheer. "What do you think we should do, Anna?" I ask.

"What do you mean?" she says.

"Well, do you want to ride with one of us? Maybe with Marie on the snowmobile?"

"No, I'm fine," she says. "I'll just ride on my own sled."

At the end of the day, we are back at the tent. This 300-pound Weatherport feels almost like home. We finish unhitching the teams, laying the dogs out along their picket lines. John and I stand together, shoulder to shoulder. There's a lot to do, but there's time for this, too, gazing out at the way the light falls over the mountains into our little hollow.

"That was quite a day," I say. We talk about Anna's mishap with the dead tree, retelling it the way stories get retold on trips like this.

"You've taken this trip a bunch of times this season," I say. "Does it ever get boring?"

"It's still a thrill. That's why I do it. That and watching the dogs run and taking care of them. They're my biggest joy," he says.

"It's a big responsibility owning so many animals," I say.

"Yeah, and each one of them is a little different. Some need more TLC. And they need a lot of food. I trucked 5,000 pounds of dog food up from Fairbanks. That's just for the winter. A winter diet for 47 dogs costs $1,000 a month."

This is the last trip of the season. John talks about going home to Galena, his village on the Yukon, home to his wife and girls.

My girl, meanwhile, is bustling in and out of the tent. She's helping Marie with dinner, specifically with dessert, still the big deal of the meal for Anna. She comes out of the tent and sets a cheesecake on the snow to chill. "Pretty big refrigerator," she says gleefully.

The big refrigerator makes it easy for us to carry food. We've had filet of sole, pork chops, and oddly summery side dishes like corn on the cob and strawberries. And it enables John to carry the frozen Spam-like loaves that he's now hacking into serving-sized chunks with an ax. Gray jays flutter around the dog food. They swoop down to get scraps of the chicken fat and beef liver that make up the meat. "That's why they call them camp robbers," Marie says, gesturing at the birds.

A little later a flock of snow buntings arrives in our clearing. These white and black birds, the most northern land breeders of arctic species, are making their way back north to their breeding grounds. I haven't seen any snow buntings since the Bettles' dog yard, so their presence here harks back to the beginning of the trip, and the progress of spring.

Our last day is different. The dazzling blue has given way to more motley coloring, gray skies streaked with white clouds. The wind whips the snow into little eddies. I am finally getting the hang of it. It's my birthday. I am forty-seven. And today I haven't fallen once.

After each crossing of killer ice, each steep drop, John looks back. It must be a relief to him to see that I'm still standing. Anna looks back each time too, signaling her approval with a thumbs-up.

At the crest of a hill we've been climbing steadily, Anna disappears. I follow, taking the downhill in stride. Even the thwacking of the sled sounds happy.

We level out. I think about this trip, the unexpected splendor of the isolation, the unanticipated appeal of the stillness and cold. I think about Marie, who told us about living for months on a lake not far from here, and how a week ago I would have described it as being in the middle of nowhere. Now I'd say it's at the center.

I think about things I've read about people's fascination with the arctic, which until now seemed unfathomable. The eighty-year-old man Barry Lopez describes in *Arctic Dreams*, who looks back on his travels by dogsled. Lopez says, "He spoke to me with the tones of someone remembering having once fallen in love."

Yes. It is like that. Rapturous. Like the light on the land. The mineral quality of the air and the snow. And the hold of the peace that permeates this landscape.

Anna interrupts my reverie, gesturing wildly from her sled, some distance ahead. I can't figure out what she means. She keeps on pointing up into space, and when I look up I don't see anything. Finally, she drops her snow hook, and waits for me to catch up. It's the first time that we have met like this on the trail. "Look!" she squeals. "A rainbow around the sun!"

I look up. Pale colors surround a pale sun.

We stand alone on a stretch of trail, the dogs quiet, Anna and I not talking, just looking up at the sky together, and beaming.

We mush on, the dogs eager, smelling the dog yard. We're on the river now, the middle fork of the Koyukuk, minutes from Bettles. It's a wide, flat ribbon of ice. John does handstands on the handlebars of his sled. Anna is riding backwards, the inevitable look-ma-no-hands. I'm riding with no hands, too, applauding wildly. We are all a little giddy as we head for home.

*Barbara Ras is the author of* Bite Every Sorrow, *which won the 1997 Walt Whitman Award from the Academy of American Poets. She edited* Costa Rica: A Traveler's Literary Companion, *a collection of contemporary Costa Rican fiction in translation. She lives in Athens, Georgia, where she is an editor for the University of Georgia Press.*

*  *  *

# Ndume

*A young zoologist tracks
mountain gorillas.*

DAMP GORILLAS YAWNED AND SHIFTED HEAVILY IN THEIR NESTS AS morning mist rose reluctantly from the tumbled vegetation on the slopes of Rwanda's Virunga volcanoes. Nestled under warm blankets in my tin hut below, I also yawned, hearing the day's crop of excited tourists starting to gather outside its protective walls. Rwanda in the early 1980s was not a household word in the Western world— pregenocide, pre-refugee crisis, pre-Zaire rebellion. But word was starting to spread to the traveling public that it was possible to trek in this part of Central Africa and see mountain gorillas at close quarters. My role as a young zoologist was to encourage the gorillas to tolerate small groups of visitors daily, all paying high fees that would help conserve both apes and habitat. The gorillas were great, but the visitors? I yawned again in anticipation of the same old questions—questions about gorillas, sure, but also about me. I suppose a rosy-faced, curly-haired English girl leaping about the volcanic slopes in pursuit of hairy apes should have expected variations on the what's-a-nice-girl-like-you-doing-in-a-place-like-this question, but it was still tiring. Fastening a welcoming smile in place, I emerged reluctantly into the sunlight.

You could never be sure where the gorillas would be, or even whether you would find them. They made it easy for us by tramp-ling a swathe through the undergrowth; and we would search for their night nests, then follow the signs left that morning. Sometimes they led upwards, leaving the bunch of tourists gasping for breath in the thin air at several thousand feet of altitude. Other days they would make for the bamboo zone lower down, where the ground cover was sparse, but we could follow their progress by the scattered remains of excavated bamboo shoots. Often the trail led across the unmarked international border into Zaire, and our Rwandan track-ers would become nervous. Trigger-happy patrols from the Zaire Army might mistake us for poachers in the thick vegetation.

I had to admit there were often interesting visitors in these daily groups—a wiry, ninety-year-old Australian grandmother deter-mined to see gorillas in the wild before she died, and putting some of the flabbier tourists to shame with her fitness. Michael Crichton, traveling to overcome writer's block—charming, erudite, and absorbing the experience like a sponge. And in today's bunch, an executive of a European airline that had refused to adhere to inter-national wildlife conservation treaties. A captive audience on his day out, I could regale him with evidence that his company was transporting ivory to the Far East. Oh yes—that would make strug-gling for hours along muddy tracks, over tangled nettles, thistles, and ferns, much more entertaining.

Ndume and his family had moved downhill, towards a swampy area along the edge of the park. Tracking them through the forest, we could hear the squeals of Rwandan children playing in the pota-to fields below, and the calls of their mothers echoing up the slopes, as they bent over the rich soil to tend their crops, runny-nosed babies fastened tightly to their backs. Extremes of temperature and heavy rains make this a harsh environment for people. Streaming colds and hacking coughs are common, as are childhood diseases like measles and mumps. Crops, however, thrive in the rich volcanic soil, and the ability to garner two crops a year of potatoes and beans supports one of the highest human population densities in Africa. Both these factors are bad news for the gorillas. Besieged in an island of forest, along the summits of the Virunga volcano chain, they are now confined to a high-altitude area, with their access to the warmer, lower slopes progressively reduced by land brought into cultivation. Bringing tourist dollars into the local and national economies provides an incentive for their conservation and helps them survive. I had to remind myself of this as I shepherded my merry band closer to Ndume and his simian family.

Ndume was a particular favorite of mine; a young male coming physically into his prime, but mentally just emerging from adolescence. The old leader of his family group had died not long before, and Ndume was only just getting used to power. He could make the daily decisions about where the group went, and when; he could sort out squabbles amongst the females and between unruly youngsters with a mere warning grunt. But he also had to defend his family against danger. Fortunately there was not much obvious danger to challenge him—leopards no longer roamed the slopes, and poaching was minimal. He would still roll lazily onto his back, and tolerantly allow the youngsters in the group to climb up his huge bulk. But it was not quite clear what category I, and my small group of tourists, came into. Friend or foe—interesting and potentially amusing, or worrying and possibly dangerous?

We could hear the gorillas singing as we approached. It is not widely known that gorillas sing, but it is the only word I can find to describe the phenomenon. Just occasionally, on a sunny day, with plentiful food and in a relaxed mood, the group would make these pleasant little noises to each other, tuneful sighs, a refreshing change from the staccato retorts emerging from their other ends—they are vegetarians after all, with kilos of plant matter journeying along several feet of gut each day. The singing stopped as they became aware of our arrival—inept humans scrambling over a mountain of tangled undergrowth with all the delicacy and stealth of a rugby football scrum. The park guide and I made throat-clearing noises, which we fondly imagined mimicked (I nearly said aped) their own contact calls. Only us, it was meant to impart: we come in peace.

We emerged on our hands and knees at the bottom of a small clearing, sloping gently upwards to where the group was resting in the heat of the midday sun. "Just stay here quietly," I whispered to the tourists. "Remember the advice of your guide—remain calm and quiet. Do not make rapid movements, try not to appear threatening, and don't run if he charges—it is usually only bluff." Ndume rolled onto his side and, picking his nose lazily, observed us with adolescent curiosity. Peace and tranquillity.

The transformation to panic was instantaneous. One tumbling infant lost its footing and rolled a few feet down the slope towards us, causing its mother to leap to her feet and bark in alarm. This was too much for Ndume. As if realizing he was supposed to be on duty, he leapt up with a start and charged. But it was a slope, and he was on us before he knew it, almost skidding to a halt right above my lowered head. Senses tuned tightly by the adrenaline rush in both species, the air throbbed, and time—proverbially—stood still. I trusted this animal, but a brief moment of doubt flitted across my mind as he towered above me, and I could feel his warm breath, smell his fear. I know I was smiling, even when he lowered his head to mine, bringing his huge canines and powerful jaw to within millimeters of my hair, touching a swollen finger to

---

——— ☽ ———

*J*ane Goodall…related an exchange between the signing gorilla Koko and trainer Penny Patterson. A researcher was visiting them, and Penny wanted Koko to exhibit her intelligence. Penny held up a piece of white cloth.

"Koko, what color is this?"

Koko signed, "Red."

Because the gorilla made an error, the woman asked again, "Koko, what color is this."

Koko again replied, "Red."

Exasperated, the trainer said, "Koko, if you want to eat supper, you'd better answer the question. What color is this?"

Koko leaned forward and picked a tiny piece of red lint off the white cloth, looked her caretaker in the eye, showed her the lint, and laughed, "Red. Red, red, red!"

◆

—Linda Hogan, "The Kill Hole," *Dwellings: A Spiritual History of the Living World*

my forehead, and sniffing the alien scent. The charge in the air was palpable—mingled curiosity and fear from woman and beast. Suddenly, like a teenager at an adult party, it was all too much. His point made, his courage vanishing, he wheeled around and strutted off, leading his family safely back into their Eden.

Turning, my face suffused with the joy of a religious convert, I grinned at my tourist group. I could hardly speak. They could hardly see. One by one, six gorilla watchers lifted reddening faces out of the ground into which they had melted, and out of the nettles they had found there. Quaking in their boots, and taking submission to a fine art, they had missed the whole thing. Marching back to base, with swelling welts from the nettles on their faces, and minds released from fear, revised versions of the encounter started forming which would no doubt be recounted over many a dinner table in the days, months, and years to come.

Those years have proven difficult for Ndume and his kin. Since my magic moment, gorillas have been at the center of dramatic human conflict—their forest habitat washed by waves of war and refugees, invaded by weapons, disease, mines, and other dangers. But they are still there. Even now, I let my mind wander, and readily recover the imprint of Ndume's face resting there. Does Ndume do the same for me? As he rolls over in his midday rest and looks up to the sky, is my image conjured up in his reflections? I know he is fine, I know all his children, his daily traumas and strife. He cannot know of me and mine—that I have also had children—three blond-haired sons, that I have moved to another country, but still work for his safety through the African Wildlife Foundation. I would like him to know, I would like to feel that knowing me has changed his thoughts as he has changed mine. A moment in time—blue and brown eyes reaching across the species barrier, with no hope of return.

*Rosalind Aveling has worked in wildlife conservation since graduating as a zoologist in England in the 1970s. Primates are her first love; their conservation has taken her from the rain forests of Sumatra to the volcanic slopes of Rwanda and Zaire. Based now with her three sons in the urban jungle of Nairobi, Kenya, Rosalind works as head of program development for the African Wildlife Foundation.*

$\ast \overset{\ast}{\ast} \ast$

# Girl Kayak Guides of Juneau

*Good advice for the girl
guide in all of us.*

IF I WERE IN JUNEAU RIGHT NOW, I'D BE THINKING ABOUT TAKING a nap. Naps are a very Juneau thing to do. Jane, a self-styled "girl guide," told me that while we were feasting on smoked salmon and reindeer sausage at Eagle Beach not far from downtown Juneau, Alaska's tiny capital. We had paddled our sea kayak—a long, narrow boat, swift and silent as a shark—to a beautiful outlook where humpback whales rode the chilly waters and eagles huddled in black trees. Way off on the horizon, mysterious peaks pierced the clouds that hover perpetually over the steel-blue Gulf of Alaska.

A lanky girl with bright brown eyes, Jane stood on the shoreline and scanned the channel for squalls. Then she scanned the black-sand beach, which gave way to lush meadows of fireweed and rye grass. She listened to the squawking of ravens, flying up to stands of Sitka spruce. She sniffed the air, which smelled of kelp and wildflowers. Finally, she yawned.

"Boy, I wish I could take a nap right now," she said. "We're real nap-oriented here. My boyfriend has what he calls a safety nap. He'll spot something dangerous. And he's like, 'Whoa!—time to take a nap!'"

What a revelation. Where I live near Seattle, the lights at

Microsoft burn all night. I never nap without feeling that I've taken a sad and possibly fatal turn toward sloth. Now here was Jane, an adventurer, promoting naps as a safety tip. And here was I, a failed kayaker, hanging on her every word. The truth was that before I met Jane, I was thinking about giving up sea kayaking, because I simply wasn't strong enough to stay out of trouble on saltwater.

Just a month before, I had gotten myself in a nasty mess on Puget Sound—the wildcat waterway on which Seattle perches, some 900 miles of icy water south of Juneau. I crossed a shipping lane with a group of kayakers on a glorious summer day. Suddenly, a current caught my boat and tossed it to the right. Everybody else went left. I kept trying to turn the kayak, but it was like trying to turn the head of a rebellious horse. Next thing I knew, I was headed out to sea. I couldn't see a single member of my group, not even their white paddles going up and down—a sight that, from a distance, looks like a flock of tiny, elusive white birds.

Then the wind rose. I had to fight both the current and the chop. I panicked. I knew that kayakers, even experts, died on the Sound every year. My biggest fear was that I would flip the kayak and either get trapped underneath or fall into the icy water and be unable to struggle back into the boat. "There is no lonelier, more desperate maneuver when you are far from shore and help," my kayak manual said. "Whatever can go wrong will go wrong, made worse by cold, fumbling hands."

I knew I should conserve my strength, in case the kayak capsized. But I kept thrashing around, because I couldn't think of anything else to do. Luckily, a woman from our group finally spotted my uplifted paddle—which she said looked no bigger than a handkerchief in the wind. She doubled back and towed me, humiliated, to shore.

How I longed to be courageous like Jane, who soothes angry bears with compliments: "I see you, bear. I respect you, bear. Brave, brave bear." Jane, who can tell a storm is coming by the smell of the wind. Like the Tlingits who settled this lovely, rain-drenched land, Jane makes tea from a prickly plant called devil's club. She can out-paddle a squall and survive by her wits.

"My first year in Juneau, I lived in a cabin, without heat or running water," she confided, as we climbed into our double kayak to paddle back to our starting point. "The cabin was on an avalanche chute. Every night I had to think, Now, where am I going to sleep tonight? I had seven escape routes."

She laughed. "But, hey, it was cheap and available. And avalanches bring trees down with them. If an avalanche comes down the hill without hitting the house, you can get your firewood for free."

Juneau draws many women like Jane—adventurers from the Lower 48 who climb the near-vertical streets in drab raincoats and yellow, knee-high neoprene boots rolled partway down. It is a tilted town of brightly painted gingerbread houses pressed up against a muddy mountainside, with water everywhere. You can't drive from Juneau to any other town, because the longest road fades into wilderness after 40 miles. You step outside your front door into a maze of wild rivers and crumbling glaciers and slippery peaks.

On my wildest days, I like to pretend I have what it takes to be a girl guide. Strength, courage, know-how, and patience. How thrilling to rate a chapter in Jane's memoirs, which she plans to call *Girl Guides of Juneau*. Where Jane works, girl guides tend to be tall, cool, powerful blondes of few words. But Jane was like a younger version of me—small-boned, dark-haired, and talkative. She made me feel that, given the time and inclination, I too could be a guide. I could give up my desk job and survive a winter in southeast Alaska without running water or electricity.

All the way back to Juneau, I did the paddling. Jane sat behind me, steering the boat and critiquing my technique. "If you keep jerking back like that, you're going to flip the kayak," she warned, as we skirted the edges of a forlorn island, its tumbled-down buildings covered with moss. Even though it was a balmy day in mid-July, she had insisted that we don life vests, plus waterproof jackets, pants, and boots.

"You wouldn't want to fall into that water," she said. "It's 45 degrees. We become animals at that temperature. We thrash around. We go insane."

I loved Jane's stories about careless sailors sent to the deep, hapless tourists who choked on poisonous mushrooms, reckless ten-derfoots who thought they could conquer Alaska without study-ing it first. She taught me that what I lacked wasn't strength but know-how, not courage but cunning. She showed me how to pad-dle with the power of my entire body, not just my arms. She made me pay attention to the currents and read the wind—a kayaker's greatest enemy.

"You have to look," she kept saying. "You have to be aware."

Suddenly, I got it. The kayak skimmed the water like a sailboat blown by the wind. Chum salmon leapt all around us. An eagle soared overhead. My heart soared too. I remembered why I had started kayaking in the first place. Because I love sea kayaks—boats as gaily painted as kites, so sleek and light that they feel like part of your skin. Because I longed to explore the wily, hard-hearted gor-geous Sound—every island, sea cave, twisted channel and river mouth. Because I was tired of standing on the shore while other people set off on adventures.

Back here in Seattle, 900 miles down the Inside Passage, rain falls all winter. When a Yukon Express blows down from Alaska, rain pounds so hard on the roof of my house that it wakes me up at night. So I read trashy novels. I lift weights to prepare myself for kayaking. I remember the mantra of the girl guides of Juneau.

"Always be prepared," Jane told me. "That's what the wilderness has taught me. I never leave my house without my raincoat—even when the sun is out."

Always be prepared. That's good advice for venturing anywhere. Have seven escape routes. A compass, map, and whistle. When in doubt, take a safety nap.

*Candace Dempsey's adventure writing appears in* Solo: On Her Own Adventure, Gifts of the Wild, *and* Women in the Wild.

DIANE RIGDA

# Scorpion Hunting

*The author gets more than she bargained
for when she accepts a ride with
scorpion scientists in Tunisia.*

DO NOT FALL.

Wear long pants and the heaviest shoes you have.

Stay close behind and keep the lid on tight.

Tight. Keep the lid on tight. Yes, I should remember my responsibility. I am in the Saharan black of night in central Tunisia, toddling behind a group of French scientists and a Tunisian Health Minister, carrying a Tupperware container full of writhing scorpions. We have been hunting for scorpions and need several hundred before the day after tomorrow.

Scorpion collecting may seem like dangerous work, but in fact, this newfound activity proved relaxing compared to walking alone around the average Tunisian town. I had just punched an overly amorous boy in the stomach for cornering me while wandering the central casbah of the last town. Braced for further approaches, I almost ignored the local gentleman breakfasting in Matmata, at the simple Hotel Berbere, where I was staying.

Nonetheless, Zacariah and I struck up a friendly conversation over our tea and bread. "I was in Matmata to see the historic troglodyte dwellings, and today I am en route to the desert," I told him.

"Fascinating, those white cave dwellings. I am here from Tunis, helping some researchers from France," he responded. "We're going to Medenine today. Would you like a ride?" he offered. I considered and accepted. I got more than a ride. And the ride did not come free.

I knew this would be no ordinary venture as I observed Zacariah carefully load the back of his extended-cab pickup truck with boxes of some of the most deadly scorpions in the world. Each of five cooler-sized boxes contained dozens of labeled glass receptacles with air holes containing individual scorpions. A bit of ice surrounded the tubes, rendering the beasts sluggish and preventing deadly overheating.

"Each night," Zacariah amiably explained, "I must haul all these scorpions into my hotel room for safekeeping. If anyone were to break into the truck and open those boxes for any reason," he shook his head, "it'd likely be fatal." Also when the sun comes up, it can get too hot for the creatures to survive. They must be kept alive.

We drove up the hill to pick up the rest of Zacariah's group who were staying at more expensive lodging. The three scientists, affiliated with a French university, agreed to have me along. Zacariah, from the Health Ministry, was the only Tunisian member of the team, and on a similar budget as me, which explains our taste in cheap hotels.

Settling into the truck, three of us were to rotate places in the backseat. Zacariah drove with windows rolled down, and had a "Beethoven's Greatest Hits" cassette vibrating in a small boom box nestled next to him. Beside me, Therese was a petite French woman with tousled, mousy-colored hair, and the typical pursed lips required for speaking fabulous French. I started off by sitting on the hump in the middle. On my other side was Marie, who was tall and athletic with longish gray hair loosely pulled back, sporting fashionably loud plaid shorts. Her dignified and erudite husband Herve sat in the passenger seat.

"*Alors,*" I began in French, "tell me about your project."

"We are studying scorpions, trying to develop an effective antivenom treatment to protect local villagers against scorpion stings. *C'est très important*," Marie emphasized.

"To do this we have enlisted the help of the Tunisian Health Ministry," she glanced at Zacariah, "to find a suitable cross-section of specimens to study. We need at least a few hundred live beasts to take back to France."

"On average, 100 villagers die each year from scorpions in central and southern Tunisia," Zacariah added.

"You are welcome to help, you seem interested," Marie offered.

Help? I knew nothing about scorpions. Wouldn't it be dangerous? "What can I do?" I asked.

"Well, we could use your help collecting them. We'll show you tonight," Marie said matter-of-factly.

We soon stopped to eat a full meal of rice, chicken, and salad, supplementing it with plenty of cold water and bread. Whether an early dinner or a late lunch, this would be our only meal of the day since we had work to do. Zacariah discreetly stacked the lethal boxes beside his chair against the wall inside the restaurant. On that very slim chance that someone might break into the vehicle, even during our meal stop, every precaution had to be taken.

After paying the bill, we reloaded the truck with our mysterious boxes. Our next task was to find a hotel. Medenine lacked choice in accommodation so we all compromised on our budgets and checked into the same hotel. The boxes remained in the truck with Marie looking after them. I was to share a room with Therese. By the time we finished our hunt and returned to this town that night, it would be nice to have a room arranged.

Anticipating a few hours to get to the scorpion site, we still had time to provision with batteries, water, gas, and warm clothes. We weren't even going to start our quest until the sun went down. We headed out for Biazghaia, a tiny village about one-hour's drive off a main road into nowhere. Our truck puttered up and down switchbacked mountains, often on dirt road. Each time we drove through a village, my companions couldn't help but cringe when they saw a barefoot child.

"So what happens to someone who gets stung?" I asked.

At the very least, there's pain at the sting site accompanied by itchiness and swelling, I was told. This pain is purported to last 30–60 minutes, at its most intense, and the best treatment is to do nothing, keeping the victim calm. If possible, apply ice to reduce swelling. A scorpion has the ability to control precisely how much neurotoxin-type venom it injects and can sting without imparting any at all. Oh, to be so lucky.

I felt prepped with a good healthy dose of respect for our night's quarry. After ample bouncing, we arrived just before twilight. Every head in the village peered out of all available windows and doorways. These were the locals who would help us find the area with the worst infestation.

Zacariah explained our purpose to a few men who stepped forward. They sent for two teenaged boys who squeezed into the back of the truck to show us the way to the scorpions. The boys came equipped with sandals and cheap local cigarettes. Though both boys looked deceptively worldly puffing on smokes, one innocently admitted that his dream was someday to see the sea. Amazing since it wasn't more than a one-hour drive from his village.

We randomly rumbled over rocky sand, as directed in French by the boys. Twenty minutes later, we stopped near a solitary house, lit from within by a single lamp. Why would anyone from a village venture so far away? My question answered itself when we got closer—water.

An extended family had set up house near a well, protecting and selling the water. In these desert regions, water is the most precious commodity. In the previous village I had noted a well-padlocked reservoir in the ground securing water against thieves. Here this lone family assumed responsibility for this well—a well that required them to tolerate not just desert isolation but also a heavily scorpion-infested environment.

Under a star-filled, moonless sky we readied ourselves. I dressed warmly.

Scorpions come out at night to eat. They don't ingest solid food, but suck body fluids from their prey. Scorpions prefer live prey and forage for any number of crawling, feathered, or flying game.

Just about anything that moves, whether slightly bigger than themselves or smaller, qualifies. This includes a menu of mice, small lizards and birds, snakes, locusts, beetles, and other insects. As desert dwellers, the Tunisian species can go more than six months without water or food. Our captives won't need much upkeep.

So what does a scorpion have to fear? Aside from humans eating them for traditional Chinese medicine and scientists like us capturing them to study, lizards and birds enjoy an occasional scorpion. To truly savor such a feisty delicacy, a predator must have developed thick skin to protect from stings or partial immunity to the venom. Many species of scorpion eat each other, too.

Scorpions are easy to find with UV-flashlight (black light) because their bodies fluoresce green. They don't sense the light, so they are easy to grab if the tong-wielder is quick. Shy, scorpions hide under rocks or straggly brush. They don't attack unless startled or provoked, I'm told. If roused, a scorpion scuttles sideways frighteningly fast, either to attack or more likely, to run away.

We split into two teams, a leader carrying the black light, another carefully following behind with tongs, to pluck each scorpion by the deadly tail, and finally someone following in the rear with a plastic box to hold the catch until we got back to the truck.

The terrain was uneven and rocky. I nervously reminded myself repeatedly to step carefully. I let my eyes adjust to the starlight and looked away whenever the flashlight went on. My rugged shoes and blue jeans protected me while upright, but if I fell, I could be vulnerable to a startled scorpion.

My shoes crunched on the stony ground as I closely followed Herve who wielded the black light. When we spotted a scorpion, Therese with the tongs would gingerly reach for its tail. I waited nearby and, extending my arms, peeled the lid open just enough to allow the squirming captive to be dropped inside without letting any escape. To be really sure, I would shake the container from side to side just before opening the box in order to disorient those already inside. I could feel all those armored bodies chink against the plastic sides and each other.

Occasionally, Therese would miss and the scorpion would

scuttle away. Then, we either had to kill it by stepping on it or try again to catch it, because a riled scorpion can be erratic and dangerous. Each time that happened, I had to suppress an involuntary squeal of horror while shimmying out of the way. Sometimes if we spotted one and it disappeared down a hole, one of the boys would use a spoon to dig it out. I silently cowered, wondering if he wasn't worried about getting stung on the hand.

There really were scorpions all over the place, including above our heads. "What?!" I asked. Marie poetically pointed out the Scorpion constellation. Sleepily I followed in ever-increasing concentric circles, helping to clear the area of scorpions. We found every color from black to light gray and even yellow. There were frequent surges of desperate scrambling from within the box I was carrying that I tried to ignore.

We took a break around midnight to cut open a watermelon. We stood around the back of the pickup truck and slurped the sweet fruit flesh, spitting seeds. Marie and Herve examined the Tupperware contents and placed the biggest and most rare of our find into individual glass tubes and labeled them. The rest were carefully sorted by size and species, placed into larger tubes, and marked. Each tube was sealed with a perforated rubber top and fitted into a rack. Every time the box of tubes was opened, the person opening it carefully inspected to make sure nothing was loose, before reaching inside.

When it was sufficiently late and we'd found almost 100 critters, we packed up the truck and headed back to the village to drop off the boys. There the scientists finished labeling and separating out the choice scorpions, then paid each boy five Tunisian dinars ($5), a good price in spite of the danger.

For the long road back to our hotel in Medenine, I perked up while listening to Zacariah's garbled classical music cassette. By 3:30 A.M. Therese and I bade each other *bonne nuit*.

The next morning I revised my original plan in order to accompany them for one more night. Admittedly I was lured by their talk of really large scorpions near Tozeur, our next destination. I let myself get caught up in their enthusiasm.

With direction and a mission, we groggily ate a quick and lean breakfast of bread and tea and were off again, driving most of the day. From Gabes we sped on to Kebili through uninteresting, mostly flat, sandy plains with occasional trees and spiky bushes. Hot and hungry, we devoured a lunch of chicken couscous and salad in Kebili, again in full view of our collective catch.

We took a minor road that led to white Saharan sand dunes with a few palm trees and rocks scattered around for texture. The simplicity of the whiteness against the trees and their shadows was riveting. Here under the shade of a big rock, we broke open another watermelon, spitting seeds but careful to collect the rinds not to spoil such a place. Sticky, we helped each other rinse our hands and face with spare drinking water that had turned unappetizingly hot in the car. We hit the road, hidden completely from time to time, due to a mild sandstorm blowing sand elegantly across the road in ribbons.

The occasional souvenir stand, in the middle of nowhere, sold pastel sand roses chipped from the nearby dry salt lake, the usual postcards, stuffed camels, and, to the amusement of my companions, scorpions. While they identified species preserved in Lucite key rings, I picked one out for myself.

We arrived in Tozeur in late afternoon. The French installed themselves at the expensive Oasis Hotel. Zacariah and I scuttled off to the cheapest hotel in town, not far away. Later, he woke me up from a hasty nap, and we loaded the truck with equipment and scorpions, then went to the Oasis Hotel for the others. With no need for a guide this time and thankfully not far to go outside of Tozeur, we headed out into the twilight.

We only went as far as the local garbage dump where scorpions reputedly like to congregate under the heaps of rotting trash, feeding on insects that are attracted to the rubbish. We didn't have much success there so we moved on to the palm grove and hunted in the shrubs along the road. Though we found fewer scorpions and they were relatively far between, those we did find were indeed bigger, about twice as large as last night's take.

★

This night, we found some so large that we had to separate large from small so the big ones wouldn't eat all the little ones. "Look how mean they are," Herve noted. "What are they doing?" I asked. I saw a five-incher fatally jab its tail into its neighbor.

"That behavior is because our captives are in distress. But when scorpions mate, the male stings the female to sedate her enough to complete the process. In some species, the female then kills and eats the male." Looking inside the Tupperware container I had just been carrying, I saw wriggling scorpions amid varying body parts, a pincer, a clump of legs

Task complete, we returned to the expensive hotel, where we exchanged addresses and bade farewell.

"The paperwork to get these live scorpions into France must be *compliqué*," I remarked, expecting an exasperated *oui*.

"Oh no, no problem." Marie absently volunteered.

"Really, on an international flight?"

"We take them as carry-on and don't say anything."

"*À bon,*" I nodded and wished them luck. I had earned my ride and now set off to be just another lone tourist.

*Diane Rigda traveled solo for twenty-one months in the Middle East and Africa, and is currently freelance writing about her experiences, both good and bad. She lives in San Francisco, California.*

MARILYN LUTZKER

# Bathing Suit Anxiety

*Self-doubt gets the cold shoulder.*

BATHING SUITS ARE DEFINING ITEMS FOR THE AMERICAN FEMALE. I am told that this is true for the slender and well-shaped, as well as for those of us at the other end of the scale. "Do I dare appear in public in this?" is an all too familiar chorus of self-doubt. I have never been able to make peace with bathing suits. As a chubby child, an embarrassed, overweight teenager, and then a more accepting—but still overweight—adult, bathing suits were bad news.

But now I am a traveler, alone, on my way to Iceland—a land of fire and ice, of glaciers and bitter winds, of bizarre rock formations and waterfalls, and a land where swimming is the national passion. The traveler—determined to experience the essence of a country—suppresses the old anxieties. I pack my ancient blue bathing suit—the one with the skirt that is supposed to hide all defects.

It is early June. The temperature in Reykjavík is ten degrees above freezing. Sixty years of bathing suit anxiety, buttressed by the suspicion that a sensible woman does not go to an outdoor swimming pool in forty-two-degree weather, is battling with my more recently acquired spirit of adventure. I set off for a quintessential Icelandic experience.

Perhaps it's anxiety (and not an increasingly cold wind) that makes me pull up my hood and tighten my scarf as I walk to the outdoor pool. Certainly it is my middle-aged body (and an echo of my teenaged self) which says, I can't believe I'm doing this!

Although the average temperature in Iceland is fifty-two degrees in summer and thirty-one degrees in winter, every community—including Grímsey Island at the Arctic Circle—has a year-round outdoor swimming pool. The pools are fed by the underground geothermal springs that also provide the island's heat, hot water, and electricity.

Reykjavík, Iceland's capital and largest city (population 160,000), has nine pools. Each has its own combination of waterfalls, hot pots, Jacuzzis, saunas, solariums, water massages, and water slides. Each has its regulars and its own atmosphere. I select Vesturbaejarlaug because I am told by the hotel concierge it has the "most serious" atmosphere. "You will be comfortable there," she reassures me. She doesn't know about bathing suit anxiety.

I pay 150 krona to the cashier at the entrance, receive a locker key, and follow the signs to the ladies' locker room. I recall a brief, unambiguous note in my guidebook: *In Iceland you shower before going into the pool; you shower before putting on your bathing suit.* I fight the urge to turn back.

I feel foreign, fat, and out of place, but the other women in the room greet me with smiles and show me what to do. I am reassured to see that, although they all appear trim and fit,

> The beauty of my body is not measured by the size of the clothes it can fit into but by the stories that it tells. I have a belly and hips that say, "We grew a child in here," and breasts that say, "We nourished life." My hands, with bitten nails and a writer's callous say, "We create many things."
>
> ◆
>
> —Sarah, *I Am Beautiful*

most are far from young. I carry my bathing suit to the shower area where the attendant—with graphic gestures—makes clear that water alone is not enough. (This high standard of cleanliness eliminates the necessity for heavy use of chlorine.) So I soap my body and shampoo my hair.

Finally, I am ready. Garbed, washed, and warmed by the hot shower, I open the door to the outside only to see a long staircase between me and the pool. Why is it that the ground-floor locker room is for men?

As a sensible woman, my first approach to the pool is to deeply submerge my big toe. Eighty-five-degree water feels very nice in forty-degree air; the rest of me soon follows the big toe.

For ten minutes I swim leisurely laps. I relax and stop worrying about how much of me is covered by the skirt of the old blue bathing suit. My eyes move between mountains in the distance and wisps of steam rising from the warm water surrounding me. I refuse to notice the gusts of wind blowing the steam away.

But the mind and body move on. What will happen when the cold air (and the breeze) hit my deliciously warm body? Inch by reluctant inch I rise from the water. The air is still cold, the breeze is still fresh, but even with all my 5 feet 2 inches out of the water, I am amazingly warm and comfortable. On to the next adventure: hot pots!

Vesturbaejarlaug complex has three hot pots; 98.6 degrees is the coolest. I join the seven people in that first pot; three are in their twenties, the others are closer to my age. Aside from a brief smile and nod as I sit down, no one pays any attention to me, or to my blue bathing suit. Although most of the men and women are chattering and laughing, two men appear to be relaxed close to unconsciousness (despite a sign warning about the dangers of falling asleep). As I linger—and linger—and ten minutes becomes twenty, I understand.

There are fewer people in the second pot, and I join them only briefly. One man, with the wrinkled skin of a person who spends considerable time in hot water, is in the last one. I cautiously dip the old reliable big toe in the steaming water; I pull it out with incautious speed.

It's time to leave. Two hours of hot water warms the blood—and blunts the memory of that cold wind. I have no fear of the walk back to the locker room (although I still resent the men on the deck level). I take another hot shower and use the hair dryer hanging on the wall.

I walk back to the hotel with my hood open and my scarf in the day-pack. Somehow, today, I no longer care about my appearance in that old blue bathing suit. But, I'm not sure I'm ready for the bikini-covered beaches of the Caribbean.

*Marilyn Lutzker is a retired college librarian. After publishing numerous dull but useful books and articles about using libraries, she is now writing interesting stories about her travels. She has always lived in the world's most provincial city—New York—hence the need to see the world.*

# The Stowaway

*Children save the day in
the Mexican desert.*

COAT HANGERS, EXTENSION CORDS, FILM, GOLF BALLS, CLOTHES-pins, Dijon mustard, kitchen matches...my list of things to buy was carefully thought out and long. With the VW to tote my purchases, I didn't want to forget anything. We had been living in Colima for six months and were heading back to California to renew our tourist visas. Then we would enter again and apply to take up residence as *inmigrante rentistas,* a permit allowing us to live in Mexico without frequent trips to the border.

Going up the 2,300 miles to Berkeley, we planned to travel light: just ourselves, Sam the dog, and seven guitars. Mexican guitars are popular in the San Francisco Bay Area, and we expected to make enough on these, even after paying duty, to help cover the cost of our journey.

A couple of hours before we left, I dropped over to tell my friend Rosita that we would be gone for a month and to remind her to water our plants.

"How lucky you are going to the United States. Oh, I wish...*No importa.* Never mind."

"Can we bring you something from California?"

I thought about my list and how full the car would be but after all she was taking care of the plants. I could certainly bring some little thing.

"Well, yes, some drip-dry sheets, king size, six sets with flowers. Big towels to match."

As I was leaving she called after me. "Do you mind if I phone my sister Mariki?"

Mariki soon turned up at our house in a new white Renault car. We promised to oblige her as far as we were able, with lace-trimmed guest towels, plastic flowers, rolls of ribbon to make little fish figures, and magnetic strips to fasten these as decorations on her refrigerator. She wrote down on my scratch pad the colors, sizes, and prices.

Mariki was followed in five minutes by Yolanda and the list in my notebook grew to include cranberry sauce, blueberry pie mix, and a big sack of Milky Ways for her five kids.

Mari Lu and Stella had already put in their bids for Corningware. Dr. Nicasio needed a special battery for his ophthalmoscope. Sergio felt it would be easy for us to find a windbreaker exactly like the one he had seen on sale in San Diego three years ago.

As we were leaving the house the telephone rang. "Don't answer it," Bill said and locked the door.

Though parts of Mexico are heavily populated, there are also miles of primitive countryside where there is no one, or perhaps just a cabin or two back in the bushes, a cornfield, a patch of maguey, a burro.

We were on such a deserted stretch, between Tepic in the mountains and Mazatlán on the coast. I had been driving. It came time to change places, and I stopped the car and turned off the ignition. When Bill got into the driver's seat and turned the key nothing happened. We are both in a mechanical category where all we know is that our VW engine is in the rear of the car. However, we dutifully got out, looked the engine over, got in again and tried the starter. No action. We did this several times, then sat in the car wondering what else to do. Several cars whizzed by. None stopped.

It was afternoon and darkness would come in an hour or two. We remembered scary stories of bandits on this very highway who raid foreign cars and strip them of everything. In our case they wouldn't get much unless they wanted to start a mariachi band.

The view, while lonely, was a splendid one. A vast stretch of low rolling hills clad lightly in cactus, pepper trees, tamarinds, and scrub mesquite, with an occasional cornfield making a patch of green, and cattle making spots of black. In the distance, lofty gray-blue mountains.

There were no houses in sight. There was no one walking on the road. No more cars passed.

Suddenly a squeaky voice came from nowhere.

"My name is Rodolfo. What are you called?"

I couldn't see anyone. Do bandits usually introduce themselves? I stuck my head out the window and there was Rodolfo, squatting beside the car. He was wearing an oversized pair of chopped-off pants. He looked about nine years old.

"Where's your father, Rodolfo," I said. "Where's the town you live in? Our car doesn't want to start and we need a mechanic."

Rodolfo repeated his first statement. In order to speed things up I said, "My name is Celia."

Bill, on the driver's side of the car, was engaged in conversation, too. I heard the words. "Julio…Jesús…Luis."

In a few minutes there were nineteen—I counted them—small boys, none more than ten years old, and some barely able to walk. They swarmed over us, staring in windows, climbing onto the roof, crawling under the chassis. There were no adults with them. I got out of the car and took Rodolfo by the shoulder.

"Our car is discomposed," I told him urgently. "It doesn't want to start. We must find a mechanic quickly. Where do you live?"

"I can write my name, which is Rodolfo," he told me at once, "but I have no pencil. Have you a pencil?"

The crowd of kids closed in around me. Rodolfo gestured at them.

"My friends," he said.

I felt in my pocket.

"I did have a pencil," I told Rodolfo, "but I lost it in Tepíc." I could hear echoings in the crowd of children.

"She lost it in Tepic…Where?…In Tepic."

Rodolfo picked up a small stick from the side of the road. In a patch of sand he painstakingly scrawled an R.

"Now the mechanic…the town," I said. "There must be a town?"

Rodolfo added an O to the R in the sand. "We can all write our names," he told me, "except the small ones." He gestured disdainfully at Juantio in the bushes. "But we have no pencils. And we have no paper. Are you sure you have no pencil?"

"I have no pencil," I said firmly. "Not now. If we could possibly find a mechanic my husband might have a pencil."

"Under the palm tree," Rodolfo said. He finished writing his name in the sand. A dozen shrill voices said. "Under the palm tree."

"Where is the palm tree? Do you really think there is a mechanic under it?"

"Yes, we will take you there. But afterwards, the pencil."

A detachment of seven little boys escorted me, four in front and three behind. Bill and Sam stayed in the car to entertain the other twelve boys. Sam reacts with fury to any strange hand at the car window. Faced with a couple of dozen miniature hands he lay down and pretended to sleep.

Looking back I could see children peering in windows, toying with windshield wipers, kicking tires, jumping up and down on bumpers. Looking ahead, I noticed a lone coconut palm with a man sitting under it. Beside him lay what looked like a heap of car parts.

"There," said Rodolfo, pointing proudly, "a mechanic."

*Mexicans are fiercely nationalistic, loyal, and proud of their culture. In spite of their poverty, Mexicans are remarkably generous. For their countrymen they provide a free educational system (83 percent of the populace is literate, according to government statistics). Similarly, travelers may find complete strangers stopping to help them. Big families will sometimes take in foreign visitors and treat them like royalty—feeding them and entertaining them and taking them along on their outings.*

◆

—Rebecca Bruns,
*Hidden Mexico*

"Are you a mechanic?" I asked, when we reached the tree.

"No, I am not a mechanic. I just like engines. And parts of engines."

"Will you look at our engine? It doesn't want to work, and we are trying to get to Mazatlán before dark. Will you come and look at it please?"

"It's too far away."

"No it isn't, it's right over there."

The man yawned and got to his feet.

"Well, if it's that close."

Twenty minutes later he had finished tinkering.

"Try the car," he said. It started! It worked! "It ought to get you into Mazatlán; that's only 70 kilometers, and you can get real repairs there. If you stop, keep the engine running."

We paid him generously and prepared to get under way.

"My pencil!" cried Rodolfo. "Our pencils!" all the children yelled. Bill and I looked carefully through our pockets and around the car. No pencils.

"But here's some change to buy pencils." Bill handed over coins. The crowd of children melted quickly away. The mechanic had already returned to his palm tree. We left.

Very soon we realized that something was wrong. As a dog, Sam is smarter than we are about some things. He ran to and fro on the backseat whining and barking and looking upward, then at us, accusingly.

Sam can't stand to see us robbed of anything, even the garbage, and this was his warning behavior. Bill stopped the car, keeping the engine running, and we checked for what might be missing. The guitars were all there, the camera on its shelf, Bill's wallet was in his jacket. But we seemed to hear someone shouting.

Bill got out and immediately discovered a clue hanging over the edge of the car roof—a small bare foot. Following it up, he came on Rodolfo crouched in the baggage well on top of the camper, his eyes closed tight, his mouth wide open for a howl, which presently came.

"Come down, Rodolfo. I'll help you."

Another howl as the boy's hands tightened on the brackets at the edge of the well. No getting him down. We turned and headed slowly back the few miles to the palm tree, keeping in mind that Rodolfo was riding the roof.

The mechanic was fitting two pieces of metal together. He looked up and scowled, "What happened?" Then he saw our cargo.

"Rodolfo!"

"Papa!" Rodolfo climbed down and they were fondly reunited.

"My son, I didn't even know you were gone. Rodolfo, my life, you have come back to me!" cried Papa.

Rodolfo gave a sob. They clung to each other. Papa looked up at the camper.

"So high! So dangerous. What a journey!" Rodolfo gave a louder sob.

While searching the glove compartment for a piece of Kleenex to dry my tears at this affecting reunion, I came on a stub of pencil. I picked it up and stuck out my arm to Rodolfo.

"Here Rodolfo. Here's your pencil. I didn't lose it in Tepic after all."

He leaped forward, grabbed the pencil, and gave me a wide grin. Before the car could start moving, however, this changed to a frown. Then his mouth opened for another yell. "Paper! I have no paper!"

I pulled out an old scratch pad from the glove compartment and tossed it to him. "Here's your paper. *Adíos*, Rodolfo."

We had driven some miles before I realized that I had thrown Rodolfo the pad containing the list of purchases for our Colima friends: Nicasio's battery number, the size and colors of Mariki's fish ribbons, the name of Yolanda's blueberry pie mix. The pad also had important phone numbers to call, a notation of Bill's eyeglass prescription, the address of a friend in Nogales.

"Well, anyway," I told Bill, "I won't forget the sack of Milky Ways for Yolanda's covey of kids. For the rest, it's sort of a relief."

*Celia Wakefield was brought up in New England. She has traveled extensively, contributing travel articles to magazines such as* Punch *and* The Atlantic. *This story appeared in her third book,* Under the Tabachin Tree: A New Home in Mexico.

## PART THREE

# GOING YOUR OWN WAY

# The Lushes

*The Italian countryside, a good book,*
*and a cheap bottle of wine brings a*
*group of friends closer together.*

IT WAS LATE AFTERNOON IN CENTRAL UMBRIA, THE SKY WAS fading blue like an old pair of Levis. It was our first day there all together. We were lazy, some of us just waking up from short naps, sleepy and disoriented; one of us had just reluctantly given up the hammock, having spent the entire day there, sleeping, reading, swinging. By the time the two big bottles of wine had been opened, the vapors scenting the air around us, we were all awake, ready for the first evening of our trip. We sat around the table, the five of us, the two bottles of wine like sentries at each end. Bread, cheese, and fruit decorated the table, and a book of poetry beckoned from the center.

We sat outside behind the old stone house looking out on a lush valley of scrub oaks that turned various shades of green and brown as the sky darkened. Two poplars on the side of the house—the poplars that supported the hammock, "the sacred poplars" as we came to call them—rustled, background music behind us. In the valley somewhere, beyond where we could see, was the village of Castel Rigoni, and beyond that the city of Passignano and Il Lago Trasimeno. For the moment though we didn't care about the rest of the world, the rest of Italy, or even the rest of the valley below us.

It was just us, Elena, Laura, Judith, and I—my reading group from Berkeley—and a new addition from Wales, Sarah, out in back of the house sipping wine, tasting the ripe, sharp cheese of the area, reading poetry.

I picked up the book from the center of the table. "Who's turn to read?" I asked. A nightingale sang in the distance, and I flipped the page to "Water Snake." "I saw him/in a dry place/on a hot dry day, /a traveler/making his way/ from one pond/to another." I took a long pause, then finished reading the poem. We all took in a breath of cool Umbrian night air, let it back out slowly.

How did we come to be here, in this stone house in central Umbria, reading poetry, the sky and the countryside overwhelming around us? Sometimes in Berkeley it took us months to find an evening we all had free to read poetry or sip wine. When my reading group had first formed, years before, we were a casual group of friends from work who got together once a month to discuss Toni Morrison, Barbara Kingsolver, Italo Calvino. As we got to be better friends, as we all quit our jobs and moved on to different places, we still got together when we could. And sometimes we even pretended it was the reading that brought us together.

But by the time we went to Italy, the group was about much more than reading: It was about getting together to drink red wine. It was about getting together to tell secrets, gossip, forge closer ties, and more recently practice our Italian. And sometimes, we still read, a new poetry discovery, or a short story heard on NPR sent away for to read to the group during long evenings in front of one of our fireplaces sipping wine.

It was during those evenings that Elena talked often about Casa di Fiore, the 200-year-old stone farmhouse in Italy her parents had bought 25 years before and where she'd spent a large part of her childhood. Elena's mom was Italian, her father British. She'd lived one of those exotic international lives. "It's so beautiful," she'd tell us, "I don't even know if I can describe it." And then she tried: "There's a fireplace as big as my living room. And when I was a kid, we had horses and we'd ride to town, my mom and I, to get groceries. And there are hills we used to hike through every day, my brother and I, scouting out the territory." She paused, a glazed look in her eyes. "And then, there's gelato," she added, "have I mentioned the gelato? And, my God, the wine. Good cheap, jug wine, It's a staple."

We loved to hear her stories, all of us in my reading group travel bugs, all of us in my reading group hardy red wine drinkers. But when she finally said to us one night in Berkeley, "We should all go to Italy some time, stay at my parents' place. It'd be a blast," we thought she was kidding.

"Sure," Laura said, "That sounds great."

"Right," I added.

"I'm serious," she said, "We could do it."

And two years later, a miracle had happened: we had done it. It hadn't been easy. I had to save money in an empty jug of wine all year long and then still had to borrow some from Laura who insisted we do the trip in the traditional Socialist way: "Those who can afford it, help out those who couldn't afford to go. That's the only way to do it, I insist."

Elena had called a friend in England and asked her to join us. We all liked Sarah immediately, felt as if she'd been a part of the group forever. It took her a little longer to warm up to us, to adjust her preconceived notion of how we'd be. "You're all from California," she told us, her Welsh accent charming. "I thought you'd all be tall, blonde, tan. God, I was dreading it. I thought you'd be traipsing around the house in string bikinis or something!"

Everyone but Elena had arrived early that morning in Rome. Elena had been there a week already, visiting with her parents before they took a small trip so that we could have the house to ourselves. I'd gone to Spain for a week beforehand to visit friends, so flew in from Madrid to Rome. Laura and Judith flew in from San Francisco, and Sarah from London. We all met at the airport, and Elena drove us the 90 miles from Rome to Casa di Fiore.

The road up the hill from Lago Trasimeno was narrow and windy, and Elena handled it like a real Italian, that is, like a race-car driver. She'd learned to drive in Italy, so I like to think she felt it was her duty to scare us all and swear impressively at other drivers. *"Che stronza, idiota,"* she shouted. She had hand gestures to match and used them liberally.

When we got to the top of the mile-long driveway to Fiore, Elena pulled off and stopped to talk to Alfredo, Fiore's caretaker. Alfredo had a face chiseled with age, and a body that bent slightly forward. He came to the car window, curious, intrigued by all the women in the car. When he smiled, everything about him changed: the wrinkles disappeared; his body straightened. *"Madonna,"* he exclaimed. *"Tutte donne, tutte donne belle."* We had tried to learn some Italian before we went, so we all knew enough to understand *donne belle*. Beautiful women. We smiled and laughed as he continued to shake his head back and forth.

We said good-bye, left Alfredo, and began the descent to Casa di Fiore. The dirt road that led to the house was lined by oak trees and Scotch broom. I imagined wild boars hiding among these trees, roaming these hills. I thought of going truffle hunting one day. The road wound around for three-quarters of a mile, and then we turned the bend to see it. Casa di Fiore, the house we'd heard so much about. It was glorious, breathtaking, like a vision form a fairy tale or a dream. It sat large, peaceful, and stoic in the center of the valley, its red-tiled roof glistening in the sun. Red shutters opened the house to the countryside around it, and two chimneys rose proudly from the roof. A pergola of bougainvillea shaded one side of the house, and white sheets blew in the wind on the other. Pots of blooming flowers were scattered around the grounds, the image impressionistic, like a painting.

We gasped and Elena stopped the car while we caught our breath.

"Wow," Laura said finally, "You've talked about this place a lot, but I never knew it would be like this."

"It's incredible," I added. "It's so…"

"Magical," Elena finished the sentence for me.

We parked the car and before we began unloading, Elena ushered us inside to see the interior of the house. Inside the house was as spectacular as it was from the outside. It was multileveled, tiered like the hillsides around it. The walls measured a foot wide, large stones from the area used in their construction. Elena's parents had spent years fixing up this house, a labor of love, and every nook and cranny attested to it. A small alcove off the living room contained a vase of flowers and a few books scattered about. A fruit bowl on a large antique credenza in the living room overflowed with local offerings of grapes, oranges, and plums. Two large jugs of red wine sat waiting for us on the kitchen counter with a note from Elena's mom. "Benvenute a nostra casa."

"I guess you've told your parents something about us," I said to Elena.

We each had a room to ourselves. Mine was upstairs, a small rectangle with a twin-sized bed, firm and sturdy, with a brass headboard. There was a small desk under a window that looked down on the pergola and a side patio. Elena's mom had left a vase of flowers in each of our rooms, a small welcoming gift she'd gathered from the Umbrian countryside.

One person from my reading group hadn't been able to come, so she sent along Mary Oliver instead, or rather *New and Selected Poems* by Mary Oliver. The book was like a sixth member of the group, an amiable traveling companion, one who gives a lot yet asks for little in return. A quiet whisper every once in awhile, louder in the evenings, *Open me, read me, ponder my words.* We left the book in the middle of the table out back and treated it like a sacred talisman. I remember the first night there when I took the book in my hands and held it tightly to my chest, the hardness of the cover cold yet strangely comforting against my body. How I flipped the book open, the words of the poems hitting me, hitting all of us, more powerful than the first sip of a good Chianti, as refreshing as the taste of gelato on the tongue.

What was it? Was it us? Was it Italy? Was it Umbria? Or was it Casa di Fiore that imbued everything we did that week with magic, made every action significant, every gesture deep and meaningful, every word spoken some unbelievable truth? Perhaps it was the combination of all those things. A country bursting with bright flowers and friendly people. Villages that glistened golden in the afternoon sun. Beautiful men and women, inside and out, who smiled heartfelt appreciation at our attempts to speak their language. A house whose fireplace really was as large as a room and whose surrounding countryside of forested hillsides and sweeping meadows seemed populated by fairies or angels, or both, spirits whose feet didn't touch the ground when they moved. And of course, the good, cheap, jug wine probably didn't hurt.

Every day we experienced some adventure around the house, the surrounding countryside, the village, or one of the nearby cities. We visited the gelato stands that lined the lakefront in Passignano. By day three we'd found the best place and even befriended the young girl behind the counter. She'd see us coming and wave while we were still a block away. *"Le signorine da California. Buon giorno,"* she'd shout.

Every day Sarah attempted a new flavor and a new and creative way of saying it. Zabaglione became *"zip-bag-li-oni,"* and tiramisu *"titromusueli."* We laughed for what seemed like hours each time she said the names. "What do you call that flavor again?" one of us would ask her, feigning innocence, and then there it would be again. "Something odd. A very strange word. Something like *zip-bag-li-oni.*"

We bought pottery from local merchants who gave us free cups because we bought so much. We flirted outrageously with old men in cafés, sipped the best cappuccinos we'd ever had, ate things like potato rosemary pizza. We took a boat out to the island in the middle of the lake and had a picnic at the old monastery there.

And every night as the sun sank into the Umbrian hillside, we lit candles, drank unbelievable amounts of red wine, and read poems to each other. The reading of the poems was like a ritual, like a Quaker ceremony in which you speak only when the light inside you, the light that is really God speaking, wants to be heard. In the center of the table the book lay, and when one of us felt called by the light, the muse, God perhaps, we read a poem to the group. There were no rules really. We could, of course, read the poems on our own. But none of us ever did. We saved Mary Oliver for our times together. Our favorites were the poems about nature, the ones that spoke to us there in that countryside with those trees around us, the quiet nights darkening the hillsides, the fireflies flickering over the valley.

By our sixth day, we were so in love with Italy, with the Italian countryside, with Italians, and with each other that we wanted to stay there forever, live off the land, live with each other. "We could figure out a way to do it," we each said in turn. "I could quit my job." "My boyfriend could come here." "There's no reason we have to live in Berkeley." Of course, we knew that we couldn't. But the fantasies fed our desire and the desire our fantasies.

That day, our last day together before Elena's parents came back to join us for a short time before we left, we decided to take a long hike around the countryside. Elena had told us of hidden springs, wildflowers that grew only in certain areas. She'd try to find them for us, lead us on the journey.

Elena had warned us many times about vipers. They were deadly and unfortunately no strangers to the area, killing one or two people every year. Her family kept an antivenin in the refrigerator which had to be taken within fifteen minutes of being bitten. She cautioned us again before we set out on the hike. "Everyone has to carry a stick,"

> ——— ♪ ———
>
> *I*t was this incredible feeling of freedom of being together and away and bonding. One evening we came back and Shana and Tamara had made dinner while the rest of us had done the laundry. They were sitting on the porch in rocking chairs, cackling their welcome. And they really were *cackling*. We talked about how this is what it will be like when we're old ladies, cooking and doing the laundry and coming together again. Perhaps after our partners die (did we say this out loud or was it a fantasy?), all of us reunited and cackling some more.
>
> ◆
>
> —Mira Wasserman, on a weekend away with her college roommates

she told us. "Make lots of noise when you walk. Whack it around.
Let them know you're coming. Remember," she added, "they're
more afraid of you that you are of them."

"That's what everyone always says." Judith practiced whacking
her stick—thwamp, thwamp, thwamp—testing its strength. "But I
don't buy it."

"If they're green, they're okay," Elena said. "The green ones are
harmless. It's the brown ones you have to watch out for."

We packed lunch in our backpacks, bottles of water and wine
included. We started the trek in a good mood, all of us carrying our
sticks, singing songs from our repertoire that ranged from Dylan to
the Indigo Girls. Elena led the way, like Beatrice leading Dante
through the underworld. "We'll go along this path first," she told us.
"It's not too steep and not very overgrown. A gentle decline." We
passed through meadows of tall grass sprinkled with wildflowers. We
petted the noses and rumps of horses we encountered along the way.

"Okay," Elena said eventually. "Everyone's up for a long hike,
right?"

We nodded.

"I want to find that spring we used to go to when I was a kid. My
brother and I, we used to think it was the fountain of youth. That if
we drank its water, we'd never grow up, we'd stay kids forever."

"Let's find it," I said, intrigued by her words. We whacked the
earth harder with our sticks as she led the way.

After a short time, we came to a closed gate, fastened with two
looped ropes joining a post to the gate. "I've become an expert at
these gates," Laura told us. "Elena showed me how on our walk
yesterday. You have to be careful to reclose them so that the horses
don't wander off."

She stepped in front of all of us and unfastened the gate, opening it so that we could pass. "Thank you," I said as I passed through,
feeling as if I were leaving something familiar behind. When we
were all on the other side, Laura refastened the gate, proud of herself. "There, the horses are safe," she said.

"There's only one problem here," Sarah pointed out. "Laura,
you're on the wrong side of the gate." Laura looked around her and

realized she'd neglected to pass through the gate herself before she closed it.

After the gate, the terrain became rougher and wilder as we descended farther into the valley, the path narrowing until there was no longer any path for us to follow.

"Don't forget to look up," Elena warned us. "The brown ones hide in the trees sometimes."

For an hour or so, we waded through marshy ground, the musty smell of the earth intoxicating around us. It was like a jungle, and I was glad we had Elena as our guide, someone who knew her way around the area. At one point, we had to crawl on the ground to get through some of the brush.

"Do you think we'll find the path again?" Judith asked.

"Do you think the spring is this way?'

"I'm not sure exactly where it is," Elena said. "But I can always get us back to the path. Don't worry."

We kept pushing on, anxious to find the spring of eternal life, all of us thirsty and tired, in desperate need of a break. By the time we were just about to give it up, call it a mutiny, insist that Elena take us back to the path, we heard it, music: the sound of running water somewhere ahead.

"That's it," Elena exclaimed. "I knew we'd find it." We trekked on, following the sound of the water until finally through a clearing in the brush we saw a patch of dappled sunlight, the glimmer of water. It was like an oasis, green grass, large rocks, and a spring of water, life-giving and fresh.

We spread our things out on the grass, took off our shoes and socks, waded in the water, It was like discovering a new world, like being in a place where no one else had ever been before.

Judith stripped down to her underwear and went all the way in. "It feels great," she shouted to us from the center of the spring. "I think it does take some years off."

Soon we'd all stripped down and were wading in the water, splashing ourselves and each other, like nymphs from some ancient time. After a while, we got out and sat on the rocks, dangling our feet in the water. We bathed in the sun, happy, relaxed, rejuvenated.

"There's something I want to tell you," Laura said, as we lay there, the sound of the water accompanying her words. She sat up straight. "I haven't known how to tell you." We all sat up straight, it seemed important. "Michael, you know Michael?" We all knew her best friend Michael; we'd taken Spanish classes together years before. They'd gone to college together, and she was godmother to one of his sons. He'd married many years ago and divorced soon after when he discovered he was gay. She'd been through a lot with him.

"He's positive," she told us, as she scooped up a handful of water and poured it on her legs.

We were all silent for a long time. And then finally I said, "Laura, I'm so sorry. You know," I tried to reassure her, "that can still mean a lot of time."

She looked at me in anger first, then softened. "He's had it for awhile," she told me. And then I saw the tears in her eyes. "I'm so mad at him. He didn't feel like he could tell me. He's known for two years."

Elena got up and put her arms around Laura. "We're there for you. You know that. We're there for Michael, too," she added.

"I just wanted to tell you. I knew I'd tell you on this trip. So that we all could know. Maybe I should bring him back some water from this spring." We sat in silence for a long time offering quiet solace before Laura finally said, "Why don't we open the wine? I think it's time." She reached in her bag, pulled out a bottle, then rummaged around for a corkscrew.

We ate some food and drank freely from the bottle, toasting Michael, toasting good friends, toasting eternal life.

After about an hour Elena got up and said, "We should probably continue. It's all uphill from here. But I know a couple places we can stop and explore." We looked at her suspiciously. "I'll get us back to the path. Don't worry."

We put our clothes back on, gathered our things together, and followed Elena. She led us again through swampy earth, over streams and through thick forests. We continually pounded our sticks on the ground. Every viper in the valley must have known we were there. As we began our climb, the heat poured down on us. It was as if we had a mission though, each of us determined to make it to the top. My thighs hurt, and my shoulders were beginning to ache from carrying my pack. The smell of the oaks around us was overpowering. We climbed until we reached a clearing and could see all of the valley spread out before us, like a gift, like a sweetmeat offered from the palm of a child's hand. Way off in the distance we could see Casa di Fiore, like a dollhouse, miles away.

"We're so far away," I said. "It's unbelievable we've come this far."

"There's one more place I want to take you before we head back," Elena said. "Just a small detour." She paused. "To the house of the gangster."

As we worked our way around the hillside, Elena told us the story of Lorenzo, a small-time Italian gangster who'd amassed enough money to buy property near them and then paid to have power lines brought into the valley. "It was easy for my parents then to hook up to the lines. Before that we didn't have electricity.

"The house has been abandoned now for ten years, since the night a car of gangsters—no one knows exactly who; they were never caught—came and pummeled the house with rounds and rounds of gunfire. He was in there with a young actress from Rome, just the two of them. They were both killed that night. The villagers still talk about it. And some people say they see her at night, a tall, dark beauty in a white dress, a bullet hole through her heart."

We approached the house from the back and could see immediately its incongruity with the surroundings. It was a testament to the seventies, overly modern and overly overdone.

"No one really missed him when he died," Elena told us as we got closer.

The house had been ransacked by kids in the area, so there wasn't much left inside. Trash and torn up couches and beds. We could see the remains of the sunken living room, what was left of a large and ostentatious bathroom. And bullet holes, everywhere we looked, tons and tons of small precise holes in the walls and front door.

It was eerie being in the house of a gangster, in the house where two people had died. I secretly hoped the young actress did roam these hills at night, some small compensation for having died so young, so violently: to roam freely in a valley as beautiful as this one.

"Okay, next stop, Casa di Fiore," Elena said as we finished exploring the house.

"A glass of wine before we go?" someone suggested. We all nodded our heads. I poured the wine, and we rested a moment on the front porch of the ruined house. "A toast to the spirits in the valley," I said.

Again it was up, up, up, even steeper this time around. We barely talked to each other now, the effort to keep going our only concern. Finally, we reached the top, and all we could see before us was a field of wildflowers, like candy, like colored marbles, like a playground for the angels.

No one said anything. No one moved first. We did it collectively. To all of us, it looked just like one of the fields over which Julie Andrews skipped and sang in *The Sound of Music.* And all of us felt in our bonded friendship as powerful as she, as if we too could take on the Nazis and win. We joined hands together, all five of us, and skipped over the field, through the flowers, singing, out of tune, but beautifully, brilliantly, "The Hills Are Alive with the Sound of Music." We ran through the meadow laughing until we were crying. And then one of us said, and later on, no one would remember who it was: "My God, we sound like the Von Trapp Family Lushes."

And there it was, in an instant, the perfect name, the christening of my reading group: The Lushes.

The next day we planned to take it easy, clean up the house for Elena's parents, and then go to town for a fancy dinner at night. I awoke early in the morning, made a cappuccino, and headed outside to breathe the cool morning air. Judith was the next to get up and join me outside. She had a funny look on her face, as if she had a secret, some surprise, a mystery to reveal. Finally I asked her, "What, what is it? What's going on?"

"You don't remember," she said, laughing. "I don't think anyone remembers."

"Remember what?" I said, thinking hard. "Oh," I finally exclaimed, remembering it was her birthday, "you think we forgot.

No, we didn't," I lied. "We've got something planned. Don't worry."

When everyone was up, I managed to whisper it to them all, that it was Judith's birthday. Sarah came up with a plan that we all quickly agreed to. "We'll make her a cake. Secretly. Have it with our lunch."

"How will we keep her out of the kitchen?" I asked.

"We'll keep her busy cleaning." It wasn't fair really. It was her birthday, and we'd all used the house for a week. But it was the only way we could do it: "Judith, can you vacuum the upstairs?" "The whole upstairs." "Judith, will you do the bathrooms too?" "Has everything been dusted?" "The bookshelves too?"

Meanwhile the rest of us stayed in the kitchen fashioning a cake with no recipe and the strangest of ingredients, anything we had on hand. We had to make it quickly while she scurried around cleaning by herself. The smell of it cooking permeated the house, and we knew that she knew what we were doing, but we kept up the charade anyway. We didn't have time to let it cool before we covered it in icing, the icing melting in a heap all over the plate and onto the table.

While the others put the final touches on the cake, Elena asked me and Judith to go outside and check the cistern in the well. "I need to water the flowers before my parents come back, My mom would kill me if they weren't taken care of. Can you make sure there's enough water in the cistern?"

We had to lift a large cement slab over the well to check the cistern. We stood on opposite sides of the cement slab, took a couple deep breaths. "Bend your knees," Judith said. "We'll lift it on the count of three, then move it to this side." We squatted down and when she said, "Three," we began to lift.

I didn't see its head, and I wasn't expecting to see one there. I didn't have my stick or anything else with me. Judith saw it from the corner of her eye. She didn't have to explain much. I knew exactly what she was talking about when I heard her warning from the other side of the slab, loud and clear. "It's a brown one!"

We froze for one second, then dropped the cement slab back on top of the well. About a foot away from the left side of my body, the viper writhed in pain before it stopped, dead, half its body trapped inside the well and half of it out. We looked at each other in shock before I fell to the ground shaking. Judith came over and sat down with me next to the well. We sat there in silence for a long time, the laughter of the others in the house echoing strangely in the valley. Finally, I shouted to them. "We killed a viper. Come quick."

"We didn't mean to kill it," Judith told them when they arrived, saddened at taking a life, even the life of a viper.

After we ate cake, sang Happy Birthday, we went to Mary Oliver for comfort, for answers. "'When Death Comes,'" Judith read from the book. "'When death comes/like the hungry bear in autumn;/when death comes and takes all the bright coins from his purse/to buy me, and snaps the purse shut;/when death comes/like the measle-pox;/...I want to step through the door full of curiosity, wondering:/what is it going to be like, that cottage of darkness?/.../When it's over, I don't want to wonder/if I have made of my life something particular, and real./I don't want to find myself sighing and frightened,/or full of argument./I don't want to end up simply having visited the world.'"

I raised my glass, "A toast to the viper. A noble traveler."

"Like us."


Elena's parents came back that afternoon, and that night we took them out to dinner at the fanciest restaurant in Castel Rigoni. We tried to tell them everything that had happened, but were careful too, trying to make a good impression, hoping they'd invite us back one day. We each had only one glass of wine with dinner, and when the waiter asked if we wanted more, we politely shook our heads no. Elena's mother seemed disappointed, surprised, "You're in Italy," she said. "You should take advantage of the wine. *Bebe. Bebe.*"


We don't sing many *Sound of Music* songs anymore although we did a year after Italy, the next summer when Judith got married. We pooled resources and bought her a gigantic bottle of Chianti with a long, sexy neck. We taped a copy of "How Do You Solve a

Problem Like Maria" and changed the name to Judith. Then in the middle of her reception, we put on the tape and sang along to it. And there we were again, a group of women hiking through the hills of Umbria, sipping wine, reading poetry under the starlit Umbrian sky, conquering the world. She gave us all the quintessential Italian gesture, the thumb on the nose, the four fingers waving.

We're known as The Lushes to each others' families and friends and even strangers on the Internet. "How are The Lushes?" someone I've never met before who's in a book conference with me on the Internet asked recently.

"Fine," I responded, "up and down, you know. Life. We're planning another trip to Italy."

"That sounds like a good idea."

*Pier Roberts lives and works in Los Angeles, California. Her stories have appeared in* Travelers' Tales Spain, Travelers' Tales Turkey, Her Fork in the Road, Escape, *and* Atlantic Unbound.

# Outside the Frame

*Changing continents forges*
*new identities.*

I WAS THREE YEARS OLD WHEN I WAS FIRST PHOTOGRAPHED. IT WAS a garden party for children—or at least that's what I assume it was. Dressed in a frock spattered with gold polka dots, a round brocade hat trembling on my head, I am in the arms of a radiant father. None of the little girls is on the ground. Each is held aloft by a father or an *ayah*, but not a mother. There are no mothers in the photograph. The only other ladies besides the seventy beaming nannies are the governesses, who look English, standing at the edge of the crowd in strawhats and summer dresses.

In the next photograph, I am older—already solemn at the age of nine or ten, looking at the world with wider eyes. Dressed in white lace but without the round brocade hat, my head seems bigger, my body contorted in the manner of a young girl beginning to grow. I look ill at ease seated in the lap of a gentleman. He is an elderly man with an air of distinction, dressed in a black coat and a black bowtie, unsmiling, slightly stern, despite me on his lap. Poised on his right and left, and behind him in a row, are more gentlemen in black. Among them is my father. They are a group of men who seem to know each other, bound in the portrait by the colour black, a colour that connotes formality, solemnity, ceremony. Some of them though have small, white garlands around their hands, a touch that softens the gravity of their demeanour. The garlands tell me that it is an after-dinner portrait. The garlands also evoke the sense of a Deccan night scented imperceptibly with jasmines, the small, white flowers of summer that women in back rooms of the house would knit into strings and send out for the men to wear on their arms. After the last of the lush mangoes, the gentlemen would dip their fingers in crystal bowls circled by the white garlands. Slipping them casually around their wrists they would walk away carrying the fragrance of an enclosed garden.

Dinner parties such as these were a regular summer ritual in our house. As were good food and camaraderie.

But the good life, it would seem, was designed only for men. Page after page in the old album unfolds groups and groups of them, ceremonially dressed, naturally guarding a rite which they deemed was bestowed on them. No women are part of this rite except those from abroad, usually the West. Dressed in gay chiffons, wide plumed hats, and high heels they seem at ease with men. Do the men enjoy their presence and also accept the fact that the women in the portrait have forfeited their claim to privacy, a tradition treasured amongst women of Hyderabad?

My mother remains absent in the only family portrait that rests on the last page of the album. Her seven children are grouped solemnly around a father, proud in the colour black. The inscription below the picture reads *"Hosh ki Duniya,"* Hosh being my father's pen name. My mother, it appears, has no claim on this happy world which she has helped create.

Where was she when the portrait was taken? In one of the back rooms perhaps or standing behind a *chilman*, the ubiquitous bamboo curtain designed to conceal women from the outside but not the outside from them. My mother, like all mothers of children photographed in the garden party, remained behind the *chilman*— their part of the house which was never allowed to enter the picture frames that ceremonially documented the high points in a family history.

The inside though was like a little city in itself. Enclosed but not shut, this city of women, defined and strengthened by its own norms and rituals, was charged with essences that gave the house its sense of being. From here generated the aroma of food and flowers, the exuberance of henna that stained feminine hands, the rainbow dyes that coloured yards and yards of cotton that garbed the bodies of women; the tinkle of bangles, the glitter of jewels, the chatter, the tales, the gossip that served like a social glue binding woman to woman in a circle, where their supportiveness became their strength. Even their survival.

I was among five sisters who grew up in this world, which I took for granted. My mother, like all the other women, was part of a landscape that I never questioned nor tried to explore. It was the men on the outside who held our fascination. Larger than life, their attentions mattered. Father, the only familiar male figure, who dominated a world outside, also filled the inside forcefully and invisibly. He embodied the ideal, exhibited courage to look into the future, nourished the tenuous links between the outside and the inside and helped create balances that spelled harmony within the family. His will governed the essential patterns of our life. He set paths for us to travel on, paths that would lead us into a city bigger than our own. He gave us names that were to become our identity. Names normally given to boys he gave to his five girls as if he saw implicit in them the roles that would be their emerging destiny.

The black Plymouth that drove us to school had dark draperies. Seated in the back seat we felt suspended like spring dolls in a magic box. We emerged every morning from a house that in many ways was like a citadel. It had high white walls, courtyards that were never without flowers, and stone terraces above which the sky stretched. The outside always beckoned. Once I pulled at the dark draperies and tried to peer out. The *ayah*—who combined the roles of matron, guardian, and, to a lesser degree, servant—rebuked me. No one was to see us, she warned gravely, for we were little treasures to be claimed in time by those who had earned the right to it. Twenty years have passed. I have still not been claimed. The old *ayah*, I have learnt, died some years ago. Her little treasures, unguarded, have scattered, have been pushed into worlds where Plymouths with dark draperies do not exist.

Many other things have taken their place. Albums filled with pictures of women looking into the camera with unveiled eyes, for one. I am among them: sad-eyed at seventeen, leaving home; with hair cropped and a bag slung over my shoulder at the top of the Empire State Building in New York; hiding rubber boots under a sari while struggling to walk over the Michigan snows; seated among strangers from lands whose names were once part of a school atlas; laughing without concealing my mouth with a hand; dressed in a formal black sari with my hand resting timidly in the hand of a man with smiling blue eyes; proud in a gown that conferred on me a distinction; dancing at a New Year's Eve gala in New York's Grand Central Station; behind a polished table with senators in Washington; in front of the Eiffel Tower; throwing coins in a marble Italian fountain; sailing down the Rhine; riding a horse on a Colombian ranch; trembling in a Siberian autumn; drinking toasts with *mao tai* at a round table in Peking; deep in conversation with luminaries, monks, men, women, children; beaming again with a family of seven, grouped now around a mother, whose head is serenely draped and whose eyes, though watery now, continue to watch. She has finally stepped out of the *chilman* and entered the frame. My father is dead. The citadel that he raised with pride and love to house his happy world has been sold. His children have scattered. They come together once in several years in Bombay where in a flat with several windows lives their mother. Beyond the windows, the sea and the sky meet in a haze of grey and blue. There is no horizon.

"What is at the end of the sea?" asks my young niece, tying a jasmine garland she has knitted, around my mother's greying braid.

"There is land behind the haze and people and houses they have built. Each house is a dream realized," says my mother.

"Where is your house?" asks my niece.

"Where my children are," my mother tells her.

Home for her children, too, continues to be where she is, where everything touches roots. Sounds, of a distant courtyard that once housed a city in its precincts, return. Tiny and staccato, they break the surge of the waves outside. Spaces no longer enclose the sky or the earth. I go down to the beach in a dressing gown. Men sit by the limpid waters and defecate. Women dressed like men go jogging. My little niece builds castles in the sand, gets bored, wants to play another game. "I do not know many games," I tell her.

"What then did you do as a child?" she asks.

"I looked at the world with wide eyes," I tell her. Though I had not seen the beach when I was her age, had not gone for a walk even on the street where we lived, and never seen a city other than the one where I was born. And yet I had known of the sea and the hills, of the mythical rivers and the lands to which they brought water and life and sustenance. Games were played indoors. We would pitch our stakes at pachisi and cards, play "lonepart" with servants in the outer courtyard when father was away, listen to music played softly in our rooms, and read books by Jane Austen, Marie Corelli, and the Brontë sisters, turning the heroes of fiction into our own; also, when the nights were lit by a round paper moon we would climb up to the stone terraces and sing sad songs.

"I lived in a veiled city of women so I never went anywhere," I tell her.

"Where is your veil then?"

As described in the great Indian epic, *The Ramayana*, the Lakshman Rekha is the protective circle or line drawn by Lakshman, brother of the hero-god Rama, around Rama's wife Sita. Sita is instructed to remain in the circle but is tricked into crossing the protective boundary by a demon in disguise and is abducted. In contemporary interpretation, her decision to leave the "safe" space created by her male protectors and step over the line has come to represent the crossing of a threshold and opens myriad interpretations of how women can and should act.

◆

—Shana Sippy,
"The Lakshman Rekha"

she asks. "It blew away in a strong wind," I say, wondering if it really did.

"I think of you—demure, tentative, rather frightened, very warm but in semi-purdah, asking sophisticated people to tell you what they never will," comments a writer friend. I have returned to the circle, to a family and a country which is not on the outside but is part of me. While returning to them, I have returned to myself, to the calm centre of the land and its life, quietly inherited it, and resumed from where I had left off. I have returned—though with eyes that have learnt to see and perceive. The sense of being veiled, however, continues to cling. I have graduated from the magic box into the hurly-burly of a working world. I no longer peer at landscapes. They have begun to peer at me as I move amidst them. I have become a "mem-sahib," one who symbolizes the new species of women who have crossed the "Laxshman Rekha," the mythical line that was not to be crossed even by the gods.

The years move, the seasons change. I move with them seeking my peace, my alternatives. The road which I have travelled has emerged on its own. And the road that lies ahead is not clearer; the landmarks emerge only on arrival. People tell me I have "arrived." I do not know what it means. For I never planned a career, just grew into it. Hence I make my norms as I go along. They cannot be shared with others as they are strictly mine. I have not yet found a face that suits a "modern" woman and a graph that determines the patterns of her life. I continue to live out an experience for which I have yet to find a name.

*Anees Jung was born in Hyderabad, India. Her father, Nawab Hosh Yar Jung, was one of the principal advisors to the last reigning Nizam of Hyderabad. She was brought up as a child in strict purdah, but later went on to study at Osmania university and the University of Michigan, Ann Arbor, where she received a master's degree in sociology and American studies. Jung has been the editor of a youth magazine, and has written for newspapers. She is the author of several books, including* Unveiling India: A Woman's Journey, *in which this story appeared.*

PAM HOUSTON

# On the Rocks

*A river guide learns a lesson.*

IT WAS EARLY JUNE A FEW YEARS AGO, AND NEARLY THE PEAK OF the runoff when I almost drowned in Cataract Canyon on the Colorado River on a trip that put an end to both my need to run rivers when they are at their most difficult and my marriage. There were five people on the four-day trip, divided by gender between two oar-frame rafts. I was rowing one of them, and my husband Mike was rowing the other. It was not the first time a judgment error landed me in the river, moving downstream fast with big rapids ahead, my boat floating nearby, upside down and useless, though it was the first time I found myself in such extreme conditions. It was also the first time I narrowly escaped being responsible for another person's drowning. That person was J. J., the only other woman on the trip.

It was high water. A heavy snowfall and a late spring combined to give Cataract its biggest runoff in nearly a decade. The river had increased in volume from 6,000 cubic feet of water per second to more than 70,000 by the end of May.

I've been running rivers for more than ten years. I started because I was in love with a man who did it, and I thought in order to keep him, I had to do it, too. It is strange to think of that beginning now, because the river is so much a part of me that those words seem like they belong to another woman. When that man and I broke up— only three river seasons into our relationship—the first thing I did was buy my own set of gear. I was afraid of the river in those days, and in a way I still am—though the fear I had then was based on ignorance, and the one I have now feels more like respect. Now I can read the river as easily as a poem. Now the river talks to me, and I have learned through the years how to listen.

It takes three days of floating from one of the last road-accessible put-ins near the potash mine southwest of Moab, Utah, to get to the beginning of Cataract Canyon. For three days your boat drifts lazily through canyon country so orange-red and labyrinthine that you can forget yourself, forget you are on one of the major stretches of white water in America, forget that just past the confluence of the Green and Colorado rivers are twenty-five rapids that at high water will come at you so fast you won't know what hit you—twenty-five rapids that had already claimed four lives that spring.

That's how it was for us, on our girls' boat/boys' boat trip, floating past places with names like Dead Horse Point and Coffee Pot Ruin, baking in the hot sun. Occasionally we mustered enough energy to argue politics or films across the two or three feet of river that separated the boats. When it got too hot, we rolled into the water and hung on to the boat rope, letting the river pull us gently and quietly along. We cooked elaborate dinners with fresh herbs and a cooler full of organic vegetables. We drank microbrews and took turns picking songs to sing by the fire as we watched darkness crawl higher and higher up the canyon walls.

What I'm saying is that this section of the Colorado starts out as one kind of trip and then becomes another. We hit the confluence late on the third day and spent the night close enough to Rapid 1 to lie in our sleeping bags and listen to it roar.

When Cataract is running at more than 60,000 cubic feet per second, all twenty-five rapids are big, but only a few are technical. In other words, there are only a few times when you have to work against the river. But it's kid stuff, really, compared with the Big

Drops: Rapids 21, 22, and 23, one of the most famous sequences in North America, where the river plunges 60 feet in about two miles.

Rapids are classified according to their degree of difficulty, determined by how much maneuvering is required, how strong the hydraulics are, how hard the river works against you, and what the consequences are if you flip. Class I is easy, a riffle with no major obstructions. Class II signifies medium difficulty with some maneuvering required, III is moderately dangerous, IV is very dangerous, and V is extremely dangerous. Class VI is a life hazard, foolish to attempt. In Cataract, Rapids 22 and 23 are considered class IV, but some people would rank them as class V when the river gets big.

Like nearly everything else in the universe, the running of rivers is viewed differently by men and women, partly as a function of strength, partly as a function of psyche. No matter how fit I am going in, my male counterpart will usually have more upper-body strength than I do. And no matter how good he is at controlling his testosterone, I will usually have more patience than he. A man will almost always try to overpower a river. He'll jump into the fray without much planning and nose right up to the edge of a rapid, then change his position at the last second. He'll get himself into deep trouble only to muscle his way back out. By necessity or by nature, I do most of my work on a rapid above the V slick that marks its entrance. Hanging back and reading the water, I wait for the river to tell me where to be. The river offers men and women this way to be equal, with one small qualifier. In negotiating a particularly large and difficult rapid, a man can use my method, but I can't use his. That's the point I failed to remember the next day in the Big Drops.

I woke up early the next morning, which is one way of saying I didn't really sleep. Mike and the other men snored loudly while I checked and tightened every strap on my boat. I clamped down on my oarlocks until I knew I wouldn't lose one and practiced releasing the spare oar five times just in case I did. Mike was sleeping soundly for the simple reason that he had no fear of the river, partly because that was his nature and partly because so far in his brief career he hadn't been on the wrong side of an overturned boat. I had taught Mike to row the way I had been taught, and he had plenty of brains and more than enough strength to be a good boatman. What concerned me was that he didn't have nearly enough respect.

The sun was barely up, and it was already clear that the day was going to be a hot one. Not that I'd notice the heat once we got started, not that I'd notice anything except rocks, waves, and water until we were safely on the other side of Rapid 25.

It was on mornings like this, facing rapids like these, that I wondered why I ran big rivers at high water, why I ran big rivers at all. Was it for myself or my father, who wanted me to be Chris Evert? Was it for J. J., who wanted to be like me, or for Mike's big boat full of men? I have always said I loved to run rivers not for the rapids but for the landscape, the beauty, and the pace of life as it slows to an approximate river speed of six miles an hour. For the cooking and the camping and the nights around the fire with friends. Did I actually enjoy the challenge of the class IV and V rapids? Did something in me require this kind of challenge to remind me I was alive? If not, what the hell was I doing in Cataract Canyon right now?

When I first learned to row, a woman guide was a much rarer thing than it is today; and though there are more of us now, there's still a major difference in how the sexes are perceived. For a man, becoming a river runner is as easy as sitting in any bar in any mountain town and proclaiming himself one; for a man, to say it, is to be it. A

> *O*bserving the Hance Rapids, reverent boatman and renegade Wesley Smith said, "We'll have to offer extra prayers to the river gods to let us through."
>
> Although frightened of the big water, I disagreed.
>
> "No," I said. "You just have to put your boat in the right place." Wesley turned to me with a huge grin, delighted that I presumed our fates were in our own hands.
>
> ◆
>
> —Rebecca Lawton, "Imbrication"

woman who makes the same claim in the same bar raises more than a few eyebrows; for a woman, to say it is to give herself something to prove. I had run class IV rivers for three seasons in five states before I dared to give myself the title "river guide." Even now, twelve years and a couple of hundred rivers after I started, there's part of me that still feels like an impostor, like I'm waiting for some guy to tell me I've probably just been lucky so far. I hoped it wasn't his imaginary voice that drove me to the river at high water. Imaginary voices are tough to quiet. Either you find the courage to define yourself without them, or you let them push you until you die.

That morning, like most mornings, the questions were all a little bigger than I was.

I was filled with the kind of fear that manifests itself in me as stony silence. Maybe that's why I didn't argue when Mike said that he'd lead us into the rapid and that I should, for a change, follow him. It was the first time he'd offered, and part of me was happy to give up control. I had been leading other boatmen for so many years I had forgotten how much easier it is to follow, like when you are driving a mountain road on a foggy night and you can't figure out why the car in front is going so slow until it turns off the road and you don't have its taillights to follow. Mike believed he could lead us through the Big Drops safely, and for some reason I believed him.

Before we took off, J. J. and I pulled hard on each other's life jackets about a million times to make sure they wouldn't come off under any circumstances. That is probably the reason we are both alive.

Looking back, I realize we should have traded passengers. In my much lighter boat, the two big men could have thrown their weight against the front tube when we hit the big waves and kept the boat from turning over. Mike's bigger and more stable boat had so much weight in the frame and the oversize tubes that it was almost impossible to flip, even in the worst conditions.

Looking back, I understand that by letting Mike lead us into the rapids, I gave away the thing I was best at, reading the water, and agreed, however tacitly, to run the rapid boy-style, a method I don't have the upper-body strength to pull off. Looking back, I believe I should have known that Mike would be goofing around above the rapid, getting a drink of water, tying up his hat. Looking back, I understand that if I had only listened to the river, it would have told me, in no uncertain terms, not to run it. I'm too big, the river screamed. Your boat is too small.

When all is said and done, it's just this simple: sometimes you have to let the river be right.

I think there were five seconds between the time I got the inkling that Mike was entering the rapid too far to the right and the moment I saw his boat disappear vertically, right out of sight, as though it had fallen over the edge of a cliff, and I knew he had gone straight over a rock the size of a townhouse. Then there were maybe ten more seconds to try to get left before J. J. and I went over the edge of the rock ourselves. Then we hit the bottom, and two walls of white water, the whitest I'd ever seen in my life, were coming toward us like a set of fangs on an animal, and the nose of the boat was rising, already on the way toward its flip, and J. J. was thrown out of her seat and flying backward, actually flipping backward—over the top of my head. Then everything went wet and cold and dark.

I had looked at the rapid from the shoreline for a long time, and I knew, even as my arms and legs were tossed by the hydraulics as if they were somehow separated from my body and my lungs breathed in water, that the odds were against us. A wave that sharp doesn't give up its cargo easily, and it would very likely hold us under till we drowned. The wave tossed me into rocks and logs and even into J. J. once, but the water around me was so white I couldn't tell which way was up or down. And even when it finally spit us out and we bobbed to the top in the calmer water between 22 and 23— no sign of Mike or his boat—I knew what lay ahead of us might be worse yet: a life-jacketed swim through Satan's Gut.

Who knows why Mother Nature sometimes lets us make a mistake? Who knows why the river picks up some of us and shakes us and sets us down to try again when we haven't done anything to deserve it? The Gut picked us up and shook us, rattled us until our teeth knocked together. But it didn't break our bodies, and it let us go before we drowned. It carried us roughly but more or less safely through 24 and into the quiet-water backwash of an overfull Lake

Powell. There we went about the business of righting the boat, collecting stray gear, and rescuing one another.

As it turned out, the weight of Mike's boat and the men inside it had kept it from flipping when they went over the rock in 22, but the wave had filled Mike's boat with so much water he'd been unable to control it from that point on. Though it didn't seem this way to him or the others, he'd been at the mercy of Satan's Gut, too.

On the long float down the arm of Lake Powell toward Hite Marina and the takeout, it was as if we'd been on two different rivers, the men jubilant, elated, almost smug; J. J. and I quiet, grateful, dizzy with our luck and the amount of river water we'd swallowed, still not sure why or for whom we were there. I knew if I risked my life again, I didn't want it to be for those men or even for my father. The imaginary voices were so quiet I could barely hear them. I knew I'd listen next time the river talked to me.

I went back to Cataract Canyon that October, with a group that happened to be all women, when the summer runoff was over and the river was down to a comfortable 7,000 cubic feet. We did a lot of side hiking, gave one another river–mud facials, counted all the men we'd ever slept with, and bumped through the quieted Big Drops as elegantly and skillfully as Chris Evert might serve a tennis ball.

If it had been all women on the trip in June, would we have portaged the Big Drops? If mine had been the boat in the first position, would I have read the water any better than Mike did? If there had been men on the fall trip, would something have gone wrong that would have made me second-guess myself? Will I ever be able to say with absolute certainty that I am out here not because I need to prove anything to anyone but because it's where I belong? The questions run through my head like the river—constant, continuous, the answers lying somewhere downstream. I strain my ears, wait for the river to answer. The sun glints off red rock. I reach for my oars.

*Pam Houston lives in Colorado. She has been a contributing editor to* Elle *and* Ski *and writes regularly for Condé Nast* Sports for Women. *Her books include* Cowboys Are My Weakness *and* Women on Hunting.

BARBARA L. BAER

* * *

# A Russian Handshake

*Time and distance alter a friendship.*

THE AFTERNOON I MET LUDMILLA IN THE SITTING ROOM OF Madras Women's Christian College, she reached out to shake my hand and held me in her unyielding grip. She looked around, mischief in her light eyes. "Russia meet America," she said. The Indian teachers giggled behind the fringes of their saris. When she finally released me, Ludmilla beckoned with a stubby finger, "Come, come, America."

Before the day ended, I had broken two of the Christian College commandments. The first prohibited climbing onto the dormitory roof, which we did by means of a back window and fire escape, Ludmilla boosting me up ahead of her. The second forbade smoking anywhere on the campus. On the roof, she lit two Indian cigarettes. We exhaled expansively into the humid fuchsia sunset. From that premonsoon September until she returned to Moscow in June, Ludmilla Mikhaelovna and I broke any number of college rules.

As rain trees and flamboyants swayed in a light breeze and monkeys screamed over parrot cries, Ludmilla told me stories in which the leading man was a woman. An hour before sunset on a footpath between two villages in Orissa, a Bengal tiger materialized before her. The tiger's tail whipped back and forth. She made me see its black stripes as thick as swabs of tallow. Behind her, Ludmilla heard her guide's teeth chattering.

 Before that encounter, which ended seconds later when the silent tiger turned and disappeared into the jungle, Ludmilla—who taught anthropology in Moscow—told me how she escaped from the Andaman Islands in the Bay of Bengal by offering a head hunting priestess her Zippo lighter. She witnessed a buffalo sacrifice in the Valley of the Dead with a tribe called the Toda. No other outsider had walked into the interior of the Blue Mountains of Kerala with them. She swore she saw Toda ghosts, their waist-length hair in corkscrew curls, shepherd staffs in their hands. "They are like Hebrews," she said. "Lost tribe of Israel." With her words, the tribal peoples holding spears and staffs, the Bengal tiger, his black whiskers as thick as a horse's tail, all came to life.

For the rest of the school year, Ludmilla and I taught our classes, ate *kulfi*—a Muslim almond ice cream wrapped in edible silver foil—and swam in the rolling, warm Indian Ocean. "Here come the Russian and American ladies," the Indian teachers whispered. They must have wondered about friendship at a time when our countries aimed nuclear-armed missiles at each other.

> *We travel, some of us forever, to seek other states, other lives, other souls.*
>
> ◆
>
> —Anaïs Nin, *The Diary of Anaïs Nin, Vol. 7*

 I was twenty-four in the mid-sixties. In graduate school, reading about India and Gandhi, I'd yearned to begin the adventure of my life. I traveled 12,000 miles to Madras for my first job, teaching young Indian ladies Shakespeare, Dickens, Austen, and the Brontës. I'd never met a Russian, nor any woman like Ludmilla. She was a prodigious worker. After our long evenings, she returned to her room and wrote until dawn. "Much work, Barbara. Fulfilling plan."

 Ludmilla hedged about telling me her age, but she was in her mid-thirties. She said her hair had gone completely white when she was a child during the bombing of Moscow. She was stocky, with a broad, flat nose and the palest gray eyes that had a dark ring around the iris, like a Siberian husky. She dyed her shock of white hair a cinnamon color that faded to beige before she hennaed it again.

One night in April, Ludmilla announced she would return to Moscow in a month. I had noticed she was thinner since her last trip to Kerala, which I attributed to the heat. "I am not so good," she said. She placed my hand on her left breast. "Here, feel." She pressed down until my fingers felt the outline of a bullet-shaped hardness.

"I have tumor. I know one year," she said.

I accompanied Ludmilla and her trunks on the four-day train ride from Madras to New Delhi. We could have taken an express train or flown, but we wanted to prolong our time together, to slow down our last days. We sat quietly smoking and drinking tea from station concessions, looking out over villages on stilts, women bathing in the rivers, plantain and coconut groves, temple pools, red rock outcroppings like atolls in the paddy fields. I felt everything in a hundred hours—love for her and India and a growing resolve not to lose her.

At the last moment, I still couldn't bear to see her go. I jogged beside the runway in a scorching New Delhi wind, waving and crying as her Illyshin jet made white flames in the white sky. "I'll see you soon," I shouted. "I'll see you in Moscow. Soon."

I would see her again, but how? In the late sixties, during the Vietnam War, few Americans visited Russia unless officially invited, or went as political activists committed to staying there.

Within two years, I found a way to be in Moscow. I married a French diplomat I'd begun dating in Madras after Ludmilla left. Adrien was a young French intellectual who read Sartre while I explored the markets the way Ludmilla had taught me, following back alleys, ordering tea in small cafés, eating whatever I wanted as long as it was cooked. Adrien had a more delicate stomach and was careful what he touched with his long, pale hands. When he learned his next post could be Tashkent, 2,000 miles south of Moscow in the heart of Central Asia, he asked if I'd come along—

something between a proposal and an invitation to hitch a ride.

When we landed in Moscow, snow was falling, but I saw a deep Russian forest almost black against the white blanket over the countryside.

"Barbara, Barbara!" She crushed me breathless. I buried myself in her big coat and fur hat. She was all gloves and cold skin, a Russian mother I'd come home to. She must be all right. The lump must have been benign. I introduced her to my husband. Forewarned about Ludmilla's handshake, Adrien kept his gloved hands in his pockets and pretended he didn't know English. Ludmilla introduced us to Boris, not as her friend Boris, just "This is Boris."

Boris, the companion in black with hair pomaded like a melodrama villain, stayed with us every minute. When Adrien left for the French Embassy, Ludmilla and Boris toured me through Moscow. At night, she plied me with drink. The week became a vodka blur. Ludmilla brushed aside questions. "Barbara, I am fine, I am good." I realized somewhere between hangovers and staggering through the official exhibits that our intense, unauthorized friendship in the hot, starry nights of Madras could not survive a Moscow winter.

I felt relieved when we boarded our flight to Tashkent. Adrien was sure we had been followed and bugged during the week in Moscow. "With Boris, who needed following?" I asked. We laughed. We now shared an experience and a judgment about the USSR. But I wondered, did surveillance really explain why Ludmilla kept me at a distance? Was it because of my husband? I didn't know and couldn't answer. Adrien and I were on our way to a new adventure. Central Asia—Tashkent, Samarkand, Bukhara, the Silk Route between Europe and China.

Adrien was assigned to teach French at Tashkent University. At the first reception we attended, the dean of languages said, "Our students have never studied with a native speaker from America." From that day on, I had a job too.

While officials 2,000 kilometers to the north decided that winter would come to Uzbekistan on December 1st, an overnight deep freeze in late November caught Tashkent unprepared. When the workers at the boiler plant finally received start-up directions, the frozen pipes exploded. Our apartment, like most of the city, remained unheated and without water during the incredibly cold winter of 1967–68. Our language department closed for months because the students couldn't study in freezing rooms.

For New Year's Eve, the dean of the language faculty invited us to a party. More importantly, he offered us a bath in his apartment. We hadn't bathed in a month, no more than a dab of water where it was absolutely necessary. Unlike ours, the dean's apartment hooked up to natural gas from Bukhara. He hadn't been warming his hands over the same pot in which his dinner was cooking; he had been bathing in fragrant bath salts and cultivating his roses in a hothouse.

Half-submerged in the bubbly hot water of our host's large and beautiful bath, we drank champagne and listened to the talk outside.

By the time we emerged from our long soak, the guests had made a small orchestra of spoons and glasses. Everyone around the beautifully appointed table sang and toasted from crystal glasses, drank, and ate *pilmenis*, caviar from the Black Sea, spiced meatballs, imported herrings, hams, and cheeses. The curve of energy rose and rose, like a hot-air balloon, and then began to fall, suddenly plummeting before midnight as if the bad fairy Carrabosse had pricked it with her spindle. Couples began fighting. Drinkers shouted insults across the table. Our special friend, a Georgian poet who taught French, recited poetry and fell sideways onto the floor. His wife shouted reproaches he couldn't hear. Someone poured vodka down our poet's throat, and he was resurrected at midnight as the whistles and bells went off. Everyone toasted life, *zhisn*, and the New Year, *slovum godum*.

As the hours wore on toward dawn, through cigarette smoke and warm, sweet champagne that was giving me a whopping headache, I grew sad about Ludmilla. She was my reason for being here, and yet she was lost to me in her own country. India hadn't only been a vast, mysterious, neutral land between the two political blocs. India was where foreigners arrived with improbable dreams. In

India you could believe in communism, America, yogis, and ghosts. Two women could have a platonic friendship that was as close as love. India made us believe in all our possible selves.

In June 1968 when the school year ended, Adrien and I flew back to Moscow. There I caught up on the news—the Tet Offensive, the assassination of Martin Luther King, riots and burning in American cities. I joined crowds standing around walls posted with newspapers outside our hotel. Robert Kennedy had just been shot in Los Angeles. People were shocked, in tears.

The day I heard about Robert Kennedy, I walked to the Lenin Hills overlooking Moscow University with the intention of finding Ludmilla. Everything was green and in bloom. Girls were pretty in cotton dresses and boys lay sprawled in the grass. Below in lecture rooms, Ludmilla might be telling her students about the first time she saw the Toda people who stood tall with their shepherd staffs, the last of the Hebrews. I did not descend the hill.

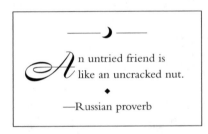

*An untried friend is like an uncracked nut.*

◆

—Russian proverb

After we left the USSR, my letters to Ludmilla went unanswered. Over the years, I have asked travelers going to Moscow to look her up, to give her my news and my love. Her books were in print but no one found her. Did she live to see Gorbachev's dismantling of the USSR? I suppose I will never know. Over time, Ludmilla Mikhaelovna has become an inner presence for me. Like her handshake, she does not let me go; her gruff voice still tells me stories in which the leading man is a woman.

*Barbara L. Baer taught English in India and Uzbekistan in the late 1960s. In 1998, 30 years after her first visit, she and her grown son traveled across Russia on the TransSiberian Railroad across eleven time zones—a journey as interior as it was extensive. She now publishes regional women's writing and art under the imprint of Floreant Press.*

*⁺*

# Italian Affair

*Healing takes many forms.*

LET'S SAY YOUR HUSBAND LEAVES YOU. HE LEAVES YOU LIKE HUS-
bands always leave in bad novels, abruptly, with a trail of lies that are
impossible, after all those sweet years, to believe. Let's say that for
weeks and then months you can barely eat or sleep or work. You lie
in bed while an Italian phrase keeps playing over and over in your
head: *Mi hai spaccato il cuore.* You have broken my heart. You have
cloven it in two. The Italian phrase at least takes you out of your
English-speaking mind for a moment, out of the ugly present and
into another realm of possibility. There is another world out there.
Where they take long lunches and drink good coffee and wine and
stay up too late after dinner. Where you will not run into your husband at the grocery store and will not have to hear his girlfriend
leave a message on the answering machine at the home where you
still live. Let's say you have a few friends you can stay with in Italy,
and you speak the language well enough. You can go there to forget. And then a fantasy flickers, and you think maybe an Italian man
might not be such a bad idea, either. So you book the flight and for
the next few weeks you stare at the trim folder and believe it's your
ticket to somewhere much farther away than Florence. To forget-
fulness, to contentment, to your old self in a new place.

Finally, the day comes when you leave messages on all your machines that you are completely unreachable, and you take off for Italy. You arrive in Florence and your dear friend Lucia meets you, walking with you along those narrow, cobbled roads to the Piazza della Republicca for a late-night glass of *spumanti secco,* and you recount, as best you can in Italian, the details of the breakup. She makes a gesture flicking her fingers under her chin that Italians use to say, economically, forget him, he wasn't worth it, life goes on, and you'll be better off. She tells you he was a nice intelligent man, but he never had the love of life you have anyway, the sense of *la bella vita.* She uses another swift gesture to tell the waiter to bring another round.

You wander Florence for a few days, taking in the ice cream-colored marble, the terra-cotta, the Brunelleschis, the Boticellis, and the Michelangelos. You walk past markets and boutiques, you bicycle up to Fiesole, and the view everywhere is lovely, but you always have the sense that something is following you close behind. Your Italian friends are in love this year, and it isn't convenient to stay long at their houses, so you make a plan to get far away from Florence, too.

And so you go to Ischia. Maybe you'll see Naples, Capri, Pompeii, and the Amalfi Coast, too, but your sights are set on Ischia. Something about a volcanic island with natural hot baths and long pebbly beaches sounds about right. Everything will be stucco white and washed with Mediterranean light. Everything else will be far, far away.

From Napoli you take the rickety metro to Pozzuoli, a fishing town destroyed by earthquakes and hastily rebuilt by people who know it is going to crumble again anyway. Everyone in Pozzuoli wants you to spend the night there, to tourist there, and they're sad when you ask only when the next boat leaves for Ischia.

The people you briefly encounter in the bars and shops in Pozzuoli don't know what to call you, a single American woman in your mid-thirties. You are certainly old enough to be a *signora,* and ought to be married. But there you are, *sola,* with no wedding band. *Signorina?* You don't fit. The eight-year-old girls call you *signora,* because you're older than their mothers. They ask you where you're from, and where your children are hiding. Where is your husband? He left me, you tell them, and they're startled by your response, uncomprehending. You look down at your shoes and say, "He died," because that they can understand. They nod solemnly and wave you off to the ship.

The air is fresh and cool on the top deck, the sun sinking behind the silhouetted island in the distance. Traveling by boat is romantic, pulling you away from shore, leaving a vast emptiness of water between your old life and an entirely new place. But as the engines warm up and the horn sounds and the ship belches black smoke, you realize you can't outdistance your sorrow, it hangs in the wet air and covers your face with salt water.

When the boat pulls up to Ischia's crater-round harbor, it is night. A bus circles the island on a windy road and drops you off seven miles away in Forio, the largest town. There, motorbikes race through the streets, tourist cafés have all-German menus, and souvenir stores sell stuff you would never dream of hauling home. You hate Forio: it is not the charming village you expected, you can't get a good meal anywhere, the red wine is sour, and the only saving grace is the *pensione* your hippie guidebook recommended, which is peaceful and cheap and clean with large tropical plants in an open-air stairway and a *signora* who is gracious enough after she grudgingly agrees to include breakfast in the price of the room.

In the morning, after *caffè latte* and a good roll, Forio isn't nearly so bad, and the *signora* recommends visiting St. Angelo, a smaller village with plenty of beaches three miles away. You climb aboard a bus filled with German pensioners in mismatching floral shorts and t-shirts and pass several of the thermal baths on Ischia, places that offer all manner of soaking and sweating and rubbing, amusement parks for the arthritic.

Finally the bus disgorges the last passengers onto a pedestrian-only zone, and noisy, tourist Ischia turns into the lovely Mediterranean haven you were dreaming about. In St. Angelo, you find a boat taxi that takes you even farther away, past the restaurants with sun umbrellas for rent, to a free pebble beach where you can spread out your cloth, lie down, and forget all the advice of American dermatologists for an sunny morning. From time to time you swim in the deliciously clear water, reveling in the freedom to swim and swim forever without hitting a wall or smelling chlorine.

Sometime after lunch you spot a building nearby with large palm umbrellas and a sun terrace on top and wonder, since it has no name, if it's a private club and whether you could go sit under one of those nice big umbrellas yourself. You hesitate, but decide, what the hell, you are a Blonde American Divorcée, and no one is going to complain if you tie your beach cloth around your waist and go sit on their patio and dry your hair in the sun. So you walk right in, making use of their shower on the way, and order a lemonade.

The waiter, who is tall and dark and, yes, handsome, is all too happy to give you whatever you like. You feel lovely sitting there on the terrace, drying off, and the square-bodied elderly German women doing the sidestroke in the water below feel beautiful, too, which is a nice thing about Ischia.

Then you realize what you really need is a salad and some good bread and a glass of white wine, which is so light on Ischia it might as well be water. After the coffee the waiter shows you to a comfy lounging chair on the terrace, where Germans are sunning them-selves in the all and all, and he tells you to have a nice nap. Afterward, he says, you can try the sauna and the *fango*, which after some confused description you realize is a mud mask with appar-ently special radioactive healing powers.

You go along with the plan: the nap, the sauna, which steams straight out of the volcanic hillside, scented with fennel; the *fango* spread all across your face and shoulders, left to dry and crack in the sun. When the *fango* is done, you have another sauna to rub off all the mud, and your skin is in fact unbelievably soft, and you race into the ocean for a refreshing swim before coming back to a hot pool in a hidden grotto. As the waiter climbs in with you, you begin to dimly realize he is not doing all of this for a better tip.

Finally he sits with you in the sauna and tells you that you have the most beautiful skin he has ever seen, the color of gold, so soft. And your body. What a beautiful body, so nice from so much swimming, so strong, so curvy. *Bella, bella.* He is, of course, saying all the things a Blonde American Divorcée is dying to hear, and in soft Italian. But he doesn't seem to have much of anything else to say. Here he is, the Italian lover you fantasized about. He's wild about you, he'll make passionate love to you, and he leaves you absolutely cold. Maybe, you think, you just have no desire for men at all anymore. So you leave, explaining you have to meet a friend in Forio, and you become just another fish that got away.

The next day you meet an American woman who has lived on Ischia for thirty years, and she and her friend, a 40ish photographer, take you in a '62 Ford to a hidden canyon on the island where mineral water comes pouring down through the rocks like a shower. Afterward, you lie on the beach and drink a couple of beers and have a cheerful conversation and the photographer starts telling you how much he's attracted to you. You swim out to get away, and he swims out after you and suggests that you two should spend the night together. He has some really great music you could listen to. Some Carpenters and some Fleetwood Mac. And he has studied yoga, and he knows that your energy will be good together. You have the perfect body, he says, you are the perfect woman for me. For a moment you consider going back to the waiter in the sauna the day before. You bide your time until you can politely say you have a phone call to make to the States and return to Forio alone.

Italian lovers, you realize, are as easy to pick up on Ischia as ceramic ashtrays painted with lemons. You go back to the *pensione* and read a novel and watch the ocean and realize it's just fine to be by yourself. You fall asleep making plans to move on the next day. A mosquito wakes you in the dead of night, and you write a twelve-page letter to your ex that you will never send, but putting it all down in a notebook in a *pensione* on Ischia seems to make it feel better. In the morning, you're ready to explore someplace new, alone.

At breakfast you say *buon giorno* to the *signora* and nod to the gentleman at the table next to you. You notice he is not German and you wonder about him. He looks remarkably like Bob Dylan did ten years ago, only less craggy, with shiny brown curls, a beak-like nose, and watery-blue eyes. He's wearing a long soft denim jacket and a tapestry vest and thick silver bracelets.

You're studying your hippie guidebook when he starts asking the *signora* some questions about the island. You join the conversation by asking her a question yourself without making eye contact with the man. When she leaves, you offer him a look at your guidebook. You speak to him in the third person formal, *lei*. You tell him what you know about the island and when he asks, you say you're probably leaving that morning but you're not sure, you still might want to climb the mountain first. He slips into the second person familiar, *tu*. You find out he is from Paris, half-Italian. He teaches art at a university, the philosophy of aesthetics. He first guessed you are German, but your accent is good and he can't tell, and you say you are from San Francisco, which you always say instead of America.

Your brain parts company with your mouth for a moment, and you tell him he has a face like Bob Dylan. He seems surprised at what a direct and personal thing that is to say, you American you, and you quickly add "ten years ago," though it's probably closer to five, and he doesn't really look displeased. Amused. Wasn't it strange, he says, that Bob Dylan just played for the Pope in Bologna? Has he become a Catholic or what? And what's with the hat?

It's always hard to know what religious phase Bob Dylan is in, you say. But the hat was *troppo* cowboy. The day the Stones play "Sympathy for the Devil" for the Pope, he says, I'll become a papist. You like his sensibility, and he says that if in fact you do climb the mountain, instead of leaving that morning, he'd like to come along. You shrug: Why not? Pompeii can wait.

In a few minutes you climb aboard a bus and notice that he, like you, has brought along a beach bag. He leans toward you away from the  Germans and asks you your name. "Laura," you say, with the pretty, rolling Italian pronunciation. He tells you his lovely French name, and you say, in your best formal schoolbook Italian, that it is a pleasure to meet him. He laughs.

The bus takes you to the highest road on the island, and from there you walk another couple miles until the road turns into a small brushy footpath and reaches the summit. From here, you really know you are on the island: water on all sides, Capri just obscured by the clouds. You sit on volcanic rocks overlooking everything, and he smokes and says there's no sight he loves more than grapevines with the ocean in the distance. You talk about all the islands you've been to, Stromboli and Sardinia, Crete and Santorini, and find you've both climbed to the top of Formentera, too, the tiny island off Ibiza. You go farther afield and talk about Iraq and Egypt, French politics, then Bill Clinton and Paula Jones. American politics are ridiculous, he says. Who cares whether the president propositioned her? At least Kennedy had better taste in women. We are far too puritanical, you agree.

At Mitterand's funeral, he says, his mistress was right there with his wife. Much more civilized. The problem with Americans, he says, is they think a little affair will destroy a marriage. How can you be so claustrophobic? It puts far too much pressure on the marriage.

On the way down the mountain, wandering through terraced farms with lemon trees, tomatoes and figs, he asks about your marriage. We're just traveling, he says, you can tell me anything. You tell him the story in brief, so in love, only married a year and a half when he left, a complicated psychological scenario. Did you have time for affairs? he asks. No, you say. But my husband did. Well, he says, that is all history. That is all behind you now, yes?

And are you married? you ask. "I'm not talking," he answers in English. That answers the question, you say. OK, he says, he has been married for ten years and has two children. I know better than to ask whether you had time for any affairs, you say, and he smiles, you're learning fast. You wonder to yourself whether you would have an affair with a married man with two children, and decide that in the United States, you would not. Then you figure that's why God made French men.

You find lunch, and then decide to go to a beach you've heard about, the Sorgeto, where hot water bubbles up from the rocks. After a swim, lying on the pebbles, you realize the rocks on the beach are not warmed from the sun but from inside the earth. The farther you dig down into the rocks, the warmer they are. You lie on your stomach to snooze and just when you're drifting off you feel a warm rock placed lightly on the small of your back and all the desire you thought was dead radiates from that rock through your entire body.

In the evening you find the only restaurant in Forio where Italians are eating, and you talk over pesto like old friends. You discreetly go back to the *pensione* at different times to your separate rooms. Later, when you tiptoe around the open stairway to his room, the eagle-eyed *signora* catches you walking where you have no business walking, and you realize you'd better leave in the morning.

So you have the bright idea of escaping these German tourists and going to Procida, a nearby tranquil fishing village, says the hippie guidebook, and the French aesthetics professor is game. After a crowded bus ride and a boat trip you land on Procida, which is charming in its 1950s Italian movie style, but the beaches are dirty and the *pensione* are deserted and the whole place is simply glum. After lunch you return to Ischia, and you suggest St. Angelo, and by evening you're back to the whitewashed village with the bright geraniums and fragrant jasmine and oleander. You're hot and tired but still in fairly good traveling spirits and when the hotel with the great view says it's full you ask if there might not be a private room to let somewhere nearby, and there is, with a terrace, and meals are included. You drop your things and rush to the beach to jump in. "*Lava tutto,*" he says. The feel of the water washes away the whole day.

Afterward, in the room, you mention that it's strange to share a room, it's somehow much more intimate than making love. He nods. "We've made a grand progression in a short time," he says, and then he picks up a big white towel and offers to dry your hair. A little later he thinks you are asleep, and he traces his fingers down the curve of your back and then he stops and you are desperately trying to come up with the right verb tenses. Imperfect subjunctive: "If you were to stop touching me," and then present conditional, "I would die."

Dinner is on another terrace, and the sun sinks red into the ocean. There are grilled eggplants and arugula salad and roasted potatoes with rosemary and tomato salad and *bruschetta* and that's just to start. Over a lovely piece of sole, he looks out over the view and starts laughing. We have found the perfect place, he says, delighted. "Gorgeous," you say in English, and he likes that word, tasting it like wine.

The next day you stretch out on lava rocks away from all the people as the sun washes over you. "*La vita e bellisima,*" he says, and you know that one of the things you have in common is a willingness to believe that life is truly beautiful at times and you should enjoy the pleasure of it completely. You talk about authors and films, Marcel Proust and David Lodge and Marguerite Duras and Martin Scorcese. The names and titles are a shorthand for what you can't express in your incomplete Italian, but it's enough. You are drugged with pleasure, lying on the rocks, going through cycle after cycle of swimming, drying off, eating, making love, swimming and drying off again. The next morning you ask what we should do today and he says, "The same thing we did yesterday. In reverse."

At some point it occurs to you that these four days are unique, that their particular beauty can never be repeated, and that probably you will never see him again. And you realize you may never have another lover like him, either. His lovemaking is like a long, languorous Italian meal, full of delightful appetizers and side dishes, a variety of simple, exquisite tastes, finished off by an unfiltered cigarette. "After thirty-six years you decide to take up smoking now?" he asks. You smile and tell him it is all his fault. When I get back, you say, I'm going to have to find a lover like you.

——— ) ———

*W*hen I return to my cat and my solitary life in Boston and resume the relentless hunt for companionship, I will think of contented Antonio on tiny Pantelleria, his simple life a never-ending stream of family, friends and foreigners. And I will wonder, in the end, which of us lives on the island.

◆

—Marguerite Rigoglioso, "Island Life"

"Inutile," he says, and laughs. Your only hope is to teach someone. Then he becomes more serious, avuncular. You'll find someone, he says. All you need is a man who is older than you and younger than me. A professor of literature who speaks Italian. There must be some of them in San Francisco. They're everywhere, you say, like German tourists.

Over dinner, when he's quiet, you ask him if he's thinking about school on Tuesday, and he says no, he's thinking about you. *Cara signorina*, he says, his only compliment. You dear woman. In such a short time, you know him better than most people do, he says. Then he laughs: you even know about his secret life. Maybe, he says, we will find each other again some time. I hope so, you say. You really shouldn't die before you see San Francisco.

The next morning is all business, a bus ride to the port and a ship to Naples where you practice putting distance between each other. In Naples, he helps you find the train station and your ticket and takes you to a very quick, noisy, wonderful Neapolitan lunch. He crosses the street to the train station and says send a postcard at Christmas. Then he abruptly says, "I'm abandoning you here," and kisses you on both cheeks, *ciao, ciao. Piacere*, you murmur, a pleasure, and he is gone.

He is gone, but on the train ride back to Florence, the sad feeling of loss that followed you to Italy doesn't return. You are lighter and happier and even, somehow, feel more beautiful. The physical miles of travel, you realize, can't make the pain in your life go away. But you have traveled inside, too, and it has expanded you, let you discover that *la bella vita* always exists alongside what is ugly, and you can at least find it for a time, if you look.

*Laura Fraser is a San Francisco-based freelance writer who is always in search of* la bella vita. *She is the author of* Losing It: False Hopes and Fat Profits in the Diet Industry *and* An Italian Affair.

# Three's a Crowd

*Sleepless in Seattle.*

IT REALLY IS OKAY, I TELL MYSELF, THAT I AM IN A HOTEL ROOM with my nineteen-year-old daughter, and a college boy I hardly know is napping on a rollaway bed beside the window, wearing only boxer shorts, whistling softly through his nose.

"Steve and I want to go down to the waterfront and have dinner together," my daughter says quietly. "Can you find something else to do?"

"Yes," I squeak. "Of course. Happy to." I can eat dinner alone, I tell myself. People do that. All the time. Some people go years without eating dinner with their daughters. Let her go.

I eat by myself in the hotel coffee shop, nonsmoking table for one. While I eat I read a book, which was Steve's idea, that boy's idea. The book is a collection of nature essays that I bought in the airport, so I am reading about ducks and feeling conspicuous. Wood ducks lay their eggs in tree cavities or nest boxes high in trees near the water. Twenty-four hours after the baby wood ducks hatch, they are able to swim around and feed themselves, so there is no reason for them to stay home any longer. The mother duck flies down to the leaf litter below the nest box. Then she sings a special song, the low, soft, duckish song that she sang to the babies while they hatched—*kuk kuk kuk*. When the ducklings hear that call, they climb out of the box one by one, teeter on the edge of the entrance hole, answer their mother, *pee pee pee*, and launch themselves into space. With little stubby wings, ridiculous imitations of wings, they can't fly a stroke, so they drop like stones, landing with a thump on their sternums. They pick themselves up, shrug their wing nubbins, and dotter off to the creek.

I close the book, marking my place with a salad fork. How can she sing that song, the mother duck? How can she force herself to sing the one song that will make her children leave the nest? Does she ever think, "I'll just wait a day, or two days?" Does she ever settle lower on her nest, feeling the little warm balls of babies pressing into the down on her breast, smelling the four close cedar walls of the nest box, listening to the soft songs of the river far below, letting herself believe, just for a minute, that her happiness will never end?

Late that night, long after dinner, long after I have called Frank to tell him that this is ridiculous, and he and I should have come together, just the two of us—hours and hours after that, it's the three of us again in the hotel room. An entire wall of the room is a broad curve of windows filled with the city below us—rows and rows of lights stacked to the edge of the Sound, and a fleet of freighters outlined in lights. Beyond them, darkness, and along the seam between black water and night sky, a narrow strip of sparkling light. My daughter is asleep on a bed beside me. Beyond her I can picture Steve sleeping in the damn rollaway bed.

This is absurd. Why did I let her arrange to meet him here at my conference? Why did I ever think this would work? Why couldn't they wait to get together until after final exams? I try to sleep, but I can't shut out the prickling lights of the city, and a song, maybe it's a song, will not leave my head. *If you love her, let her go.* Those aren't the right words. *If you love her, let her see.* Is this a song? Is this a sermon I am singing to myself? Have I heard this before? *If you love her, let her go, if you don't*…I'm too tired to do anything but let the words grind in my mind, reproving me. It's fine to know what you are supposed to do, I tell my song, but how do you make yourself do it? *Akrasia*, that's the Greek word: weakness of the will.

I'm a philosophy professor and I'm supposed to know these things.

I'm also a mother, and I know this: for parents, child-rearing doesn't have a happy ending, so we'd better look for happiness somewhere besides at the finish. I know this, my husband knows it, and the duck must feel it somehow.

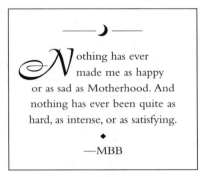

Nothing has ever made me as happy or as sad as Motherhood. And nothing has ever been quite as hard, as intense, or as satisfying.

♦

—MBB

When I wake up again, I sit straight up in bed, my heart racing. The sky above the city is pink, puffy, glowing. It swells and pulses, pressing into the pointed building-tops. What time is it? I swivel around to look for the alarm clock. Four o'clock, way too early for dawn. "It's a cloud cover, moved over the city." The voice comes from the rollaway. Baritone. I stare in that direction. What is he doing awake? "Beautiful, isn't it," he says. I can't think of any answer. To me, it looks like somebody's lungs. The globs of pink sway and push, incandescent reflections of the office lights in the high city towers and the spotlights on the trawlers in the Sound. Without answering, I drop back onto the mattress and force my eyes to close. The song moves in again.

When Erin was little, she wanted to learn all the songs I knew. "Sing it with me," she would say. "Teach me to sing that song." So we would sing a song together, line by line, quietly, tentatively, then all the way through without stopping, louder, in unison. Then all the way through again at the top of our lungs.

"I think I've got it," she would say. "Stop. Stop. Let me try it by myself."

So I'd be quiet and let her try it alone. If she got stuck on a transition, I would fill in a note now and then, but mostly I just listened. "Got it," she would say. "Thanks." Then for a couple of days, I would hear her singing alone, soft, clear, true, the sound coming down the stairs or around the corner of the house. Days later, maybe weeks, hearing her sing the song, I would hum a harmony part.

She would come closer and sing louder, and I would add my alto line, both of us confident, singing chords that raced and chased like two dogs running on the beach.

The first time she came home from college, she taught us new songs she had learned.

"Mind if I sing while we do the dishes?"

So she did. Turned the CD player up so loud that the bass buzzed in the woodwork, grabbed up a plate, hula-stepped across the kitchen, and plunked the plate into the dishwasher. Snatched the dish towel off the rack, danced over to Frank, hooked elbows, swung him around the kitchen, all the time singing to the music at the top of her lungs.

I roll over in the hotel bed, trying not to make any noise that might signal Steve that I am awake, and I bunch the sheet up against my ears. You are being dumb, I tell myself with real anger. Shame on you. What would the world be like if people were never allowed to leave their parents? It's good to sing by yourself or with your friends. I force my mind to a stop and I lie still, cold in a queen-sized bed that smells of travelers.

When I was thirteen, I had three friends. Together we were a quartet. We sang walking home from school. *Roses love sunshine / Violets love dew / Angels in heaven / I know I love you.* Four girls in sweaters too small, skirts too short, lipstick too bright, singing in four-part harmony, walking through the neighborhoods past small houses with big front porches and tall maple trees and sidewalks quarried from the sandstone quarry, walking slow, holding the chords practically forever.

My sisters and I made a trio. At night, when we had been tucked into our beds and kissed good-night, when the lights were turned out, we would lie on our backs and sing. After a while, our mother would come to the bottom of the stairs and call out, "Bedtime, girls." Then, ten minutes later, she would stamp halfway up the stairs and yell, "Don't make me come up there." We knew she would stay there and listen—demanding silence, alert for singing—so we sang in little puffs of air with hardly any tune, only soft simultaneous whispers, in our room upstairs on summer nights, with car lights sweeping across the curtains, and sometimes a car door slamming, and our mother sitting on the stairs.

When Erin and Jonathan were little, I would tuck them into bed, turn off the lights, half-close their bedroom doors, and then sit on the top step by the landing and sing until they went to sleep. I remember lullabies about train whistles, ragged owlets, an awful morose thing about lost children who died in the woods, and a cowboy lullaby my mother had liked. While I sang, I never knew if the kids were awake or asleep, so after a few minutes I would test them by singing more and more quietly and then fading away entirely, to sit silently, listening.

*Desert silver blue beneath the pale starlight…*

Long silence.

"Mom?"

"Yeah."

"Don't stop."

"Okay, but go to sleep."…*Silver winks of light along the far skyline…*

Good lord.

Now I sit in my meetings in the hotel in Seattle while Steve and my daughter ride the ferry across the Sound to Bremerton on a day so cold they will be huddling together in the lee of the lifeboats. I think I must have sung myself to sleep last night, silent singing, the old lullabies. We three had breakfast together this morning in the hotel coffee shop—I paid—and for all the conversation, I might as well have brought my book and read about ducks. I'm supposed to be listening to the panel of college deans, but that's futile. It's going to be all right, I say to myself, as if I were an accident victim, dazed, sitting on an upholstered chair at the Association of American Colleges. I address myself sternly: You will just have to learn a new part. Make it up as you go along, hum it softly, tentatively. Practice. Sing it alone until you're sure you have it right.

*Kathleen Dean Moore is the chair of the philosophy department at Oregon State University. Her essays and articles have appeared in* Travelers' Tales Alaska, North American Review, Northwest Review, Willow Springs, *and* The New York Times*, among others. This story is from her first collection,* Riverwalking: Reflections on Moving Water.

# Toiletopia

*A "business woman" plunges
into "Things Japanese."*

Behind a loud rap on the barn door stood my long-legged neighbor, a broad-brimmed, black cowboy hat shading his jowly face from a Montana spring sun. To my "Good morning, Joe!" he pressed a fat manila envelope into my arms and rolled forth deep and resonant. "Hi, doll! Here's everything you'll ever want to know about Japan, including how to go to the bathroom. Basically," he deadpanned, "don't squat with your spurs on." Joe's a retired Hawaiian Airlines pilot. His wife Adele is my travel agent.

Exactly a month prior to this morning, a paper had fluttered out of my fax machine in the corner of the hay mow, the area set up as my office in the seventy-eight-year-old dairy barn I call home. In an upright bold typeface, the letterhead read: Japan Toilet Association, with a Tokyo address. I glanced down to the "Very Sincerely" closing, beneath which three hand-brushed Japanese characters denoted the signature of one Secretary General Koo Ue. The letter was an invitation, composed by American standards in exceedingly polite language, to come to Japan and deliver the keynote address at an international symposium, all expenses paid! I gasped. The subject was toilets! Surely this was a joke.

Almost immediately measures of reality began to route my skepticism. Japan *did* have a National Toilet Day; I had mentioned it in an essay I had written. There *was* some sort of international toilet event. And the Japanese translation of my book, *How to Shit in the Woods: An Environmentally Sound Approach to a Lost Art*, had recently hit the bookstores in Tokyo.

Published originally in 1989, my book is an ecological message wrapped around a collection of toilet misadventures (gathered over fifteen years of guiding white-water rafting trips) and infused with compassionate advice for the urbanite venturing timorously beyond the security of a bathroom equipped with a door and a lock. The whole effort had stemmed from an outpouring of my heart at the sight of trashed beaches and trail sides.

The early seventies had witnessed a sudden rise in the popularity of white-water rafting, and professional river guides, becoming aware that group after group would be camping on the same beaches for years to come, took seriously the need to foster a garbage consciousness. During our pre-trip, put-in talks, the head guides (I one of them)

> *My* students advised me not to climb Mount Fuji. When I asked why, they responded in unison. "It smells. In the summer there are so many people and not enough toilets."
>
> That's all I had to hear.
>
> ◆
>
> —Amy Greimann Carlson, "Teaching Japan"

began to piggyback onto paddling commands and water safety education, potty instructions. A large paper bag, a shovel, and a roll of toilet paper, we informed everyone, would be conveniently stationed at the edge of camp. Men were to traipse downriver, and women upriver, with everyone depositing upon completion of their mission used toilet paper in the paper bag. The bag itself was to be incinerated in the campfire at the breaking of camp. Perfectly clear. Yet when it came to people adhering to our instructions, the system was a dismal failure.

Most weekenders from the city, unlike downright river rats,

lacked the kind of deep commitment to preserving the canyons that appeared required for a significant behavioral change in culturally shame-related toilet habits. Few had in mind to be "seen" bearing their personalized offering to the paper bag. In walking out from camp, I commonly encountered crumpled streamers of toilet paper tucked behind bushes or last week's soggy wads washed up by a recent rain. The condition of the poop itself gave off impressions of hastiness, ignorance, and embarrassment—but displayed, I must say, attempts at creativity. I found human excrement reclining openly on the ground, a peculiar kind of sculpture sprinkled with pine needles. I found it capped with a rotten log dragged clear across a hillside. I found it bedecked with tissue and squished under a rock, as though its donor was a maniacal deli worker, slapping together a midnight sandwich. Bringing about change was going to take time and patience as well as a persistent, direct discourse on the topic of poop—as though it were oatmeal on the breakfast table.

In my river journal, a book began to take shape. It spoke to the ill-at-ease outdoor neophyte on how to locate a squatting spot with privacy and vistas of grandeur with which to commune; to women, on how to avoid peeing in their shoes; and to all, even old-time ranchers and woodsmen, on how to excavate an environmentally sound hole. Since the day of its publication, the subject of backcountry human waste management—a most unlikely field for a career had I set out to select one—has stuck with me in the manner of pine pitch in a wool mitten: through new government regulations about the removal of feces from the wilderness; through a design revolution in portable outdoor toilets; and through a revised second edition.

The International Toilet Symposium in Toyama '96: "Toilets and the Environment" was no joke. I crowed at just how far a little book on poop might carry a person. *Wait a minute now*, this is serious business. *Business,* tee hee! I wondered whether the Japanese language contained as many euphemisms for toilet comportment as did English. My mind rushed ahead conjuring scenes. I imagined myself at a podium in front of a packed hall of black-suited Japanese environmentalists—all six feet of me. In dress shoes, more than six-feet-two. I'd be the brazen, boingy-haired American giantess come to the land of petite and historically soft-spoken women, elegantly coifed in shining black tresses.

"*Montamazon* goes to Japan!" Joe was calling it.

I was being asked to speak for 80 minutes, to set the tone for a worldwide exchange—28 countries, 800 people. On the topic of shit? I shuddered.

The next morning I began a fax correspondence with Secretary General Koo Ue that was to stretch over the next eight months, until the day I left for Japan.

In preparation for my trip, I arranged to have lunch with Yoko, my friend of half-Japanese descent, and her mother Yasuko, who had grown up in Hiroshima. I brought along a copy of the Japanese translation of my book. My wanting to be direct had primarily been the purpose in settling on the usage of the word shit, and I now was anxious for an opinion on how the term would be received in Japan. Yasuko was a thin, handsome woman, appearing taller than her five-feet-two. Her black hair was just lightly threaded with gray and her face bore but few wrinkles. Yoko speaks only a smattering of Japanese. She had warned me that her mother, as she ages, retreats more and more into her native tongue. Translating, therefore, amounted to Yoko's rephrasing our sentences into direct, simple English in the hope that her mother might understand.

In this manner, we exchanged pleasantries for the first half hour. Then I produced my book, and Yoko posed the question: "What do you think of the title, Mom?" Pointing to the Japanese characters beneath the English word shit, Yoko asked, "Mom, do you understand the word?" Yasuko's answer was to smooth her hands down over her abdomen and then earnestly point to the chair seat behind her. Yoko and I cheered at her comprehension. Then Yoko ran her fingertip beneath the characters designating my name. With slow dawning, Yasuko hooked the word shit to me and my trip, and a hand flew to cover her mouth and the end of her nose. Her eyes widened. She sucked in air, and giggled. It was a small, hesitant, guttural giggle—a sound unknown to me—at first low-pitched, then high. She peered again at the book cover, and then with full realization rocked backward with a slap to her thigh. The back of a hand next grazed her forehead. Then she buried her face in both hands, as if to hold a hurting head, and sagged over sideways until her cheek rested on the table top. Yoko and I stole a look at each other and howled. This did not bode well for my speech.

Yasuko had also brought along a book. She passed me a sweetly hand-bound volume for travelers entitled *We Japanese*. Compiled by a hotel owner, H. S. K. Yamaguchi, with the literary help of a Frederic de Garis, it had been published in English, in Japan, in 1934. The pages, though not rice paper, were thin and doubled. In turning a few pages, I noticed the acknowledgments placed heavy reference on a prior book: *Things Japanese*.

The day came when I was winging across the Pacific. With the shades drawn and the movie *Twister* on the screen, I reworked my speech, something I had been doing for weeks. I was still wrestling with how my subject might be recast for foreign ears. "The Japanese are toilet nuts, obsessed!" someone had told me. Well, fine, but they seemed also a quietly formal people, full of grace and elegance, or was it primness? And somewhat stoic. Yasuko's *We Japanese* had offered a discussion entitled "Japanese Emotion and Its Suppression." It began: "The Japanese are highly emotional but early acquire the habit of suppressing evidences of their deep-seated emotion, and encase themselves in an armor of inscrutability impossible of penetration by the Westerner." Things had changed in sixty-two years, the world had changed. Yet in homelands, cultural traits can linger through generations. Would my audience take to jokes about poop? What were the fine lines of these kinds of jokes? And what of the cultural mores of other countries attending?

Over the summer, any residual hilariousness concerning my trip had fallen away under a voluminous fax correspondence with the secretary general. The messages zinged back and forth, and the world's problems with human waste disposal again rose to greet me, though this time in ever-widening dimension and with ever more clarity. From a small monthly study group called Toiletopia, the

Japan Toilet Association was officially founded in May of 1985, and thereafter had been nothing short of a keenly focused organization. A promotional pamphlet entitled *The Restroom Revolution of Japan* describes the group as "entirely committed to the toilet, the only association of its kind in the world." Membership is comprised of a voluntary network of planners, designers, and researchers. With a far-reaching vision they seek to transform the unsafe and unsanitary image of public rest rooms, a largely expected condition worldwide, referred to in Japanese as the "Four K's"—*kitanai, kurai, kowai,* and *kusai* (dirty, dark, scary, and smelly).

The Toyama symposium was to be the toilet association's third international gathering. With a theme of "Toilets and the Environment," it would focus on the growing problems of human waste management in the wilderness (this is where I came in) as well as put forth compelling arguments for alternatives to the pervasive water-consuming flush system.

Not owning a laptop computer, I had brought along four copies of my speech for tinkering. Now with an occasional glance over seat tops to where cows and semis and 100-year-old trees hurtled across the screen—I hurtled likewise across the international date line—I pared and pruned on the first of the copies, striking phrases I thought might prove faux pas in other languages. It was tough enough presenting this topic in English. Now the task entailed a sensitivity to proprieties on a global scope. It's an oxymoron: decorous oratory on shit. The more I tweaked, the drier and flatter and duller the words became—in the running with stale tortillas. My usual directness, I couched until the pages bulged like overstuffed furniture. Left to my natural semantics, I might have covered the same hour-long terrain in a twenty-minute talk.

Flying in low over a wide, lazy-bending river, its flood plain seeded to rice paddies, I suddenly was on the ground in Japan. Purposely I had planned my arrival for two nights prior to the beginning of activities, thinking to allow myself a full day of rest and acclimation after a grueling trip. From Montana, it required four flights. The third, eleven hours in duration, deposited me at Narita,

Tokyo's International Airport. Then an hour-and-a-half bus ride across town to the domestic airport, and I caught the last Nippon flight to the island's east side. The final stretch was a drawn-out taxi ride through night traffic and rainy streets into Toyama proper. I was handed the key to my hotel room thirty-six hours after I had crawled out of bed in the barn.

Weary as I was, the taxi ride proved my first cultural thrill. The seat covers were white lace—yes, lace! yes, white! And the driver flexed his fingers over the steering wheel inside a pair of spotless white gloves. In the coming days, I was to ride in many taxis, each a bit differently appointed, but always the white lace and gloves. The back door panels in one were upholstered in lace sheeted over with clear plastic; from the underside of the dashboard in another hung a lacy skirt; and the headrests of many sported their own little crocheted slipcovers.

On each of my rides, I mused for a few moments on the immaculate state of these covers. I tried to envision the driver's morning. Did he (I never saw a woman driver) change them with each day's dawn? Were they supplied by the taxi company—a routine of picking up a carefully folded fresh set in the morning and then stripping and tossing it into a laundry cart in the evening? Or did the driver's wife dutifully launder them? Or a crew of women rotate them in the manner of hotel maids changing beds? The worried-about-the-future-of-the-earth part of me mulled over how many gallons of bleach nationwide were washing into waterways as a requisite of their perfect laundering? Of all my questions, I could answer only one: the source of desire for such presentation of a taxi. It embodied what I saw as the essence of things Japanese—cleanliness, beauty, and order.

The next morning, sunshine illuminating the tops of Toyama's tall buildings beamed through my window. The central city lies near the mouth of the Jinzu River, arms open to Toyama Bay and the Sea of Japan—Korea just over the western horizon. At Toyama's back, rural townships sweep up to imposing, forested mountains: the Japan Alps. The whole of Japan is only slightly larger than Montana and nearly as mountainous.

My hotel room was cramped by Western measure, though not the morgue drawer I had anticipated. Its bathroom was equally cozy. The centerpiece was a toilet-bidet combo equipped with three large control buttons and elaborately unclear instructions. Before departing Japan, I would encounter musical toilet paper dispensers and heated toilet seats, the latter seemingly better suited to a Rocky Mountain outhouse at thirty below. The fancier hotels, I was told, had computerized toilets. This may even have been one of them. After my first untutored experience with a bidet, I had permanently sworn off experimenting. It had been in the Bordello Room at the Panama Hotel in San Rafael, California, where my sweetie and I were ensconced. I was bent over the bowl, monkeying with the handles, when I received a sudden jet of piping hot water in the face—more accurately, face, hair, glasses, dinner dress. I had no desire for another such drenching or scorching.

——— ) ———

The Japanese advertise on everything, including handy tissue packets that are passed out on every busy street and in front of crowded train stations. These are especially useful since public bathrooms often have no toilet paper. This free tissue is a necessity—and it gives you something to read while squatting.

◆

—Kara Thacker,
"Time Well Spent in Tokyo"

The bathtub, however, was a different story and made up tenfold for any lack in spaciousness. It was short, but deep, and I sat upright in it with the steaming water lapping my chin. I wanted to wrench it out of the wall and check it through baggage for the flights home.

Refreshed by the long soak and a night's sleep, I dressed and took a stroll to an open-air market. The wide downtown sidewalks were laid in ceramic tile, which glistened in a light rain. A jumble of pedestrians and cyclists swung along at a brisk clip without rhyme, reason, or accident. Japanese cyclists are adept as circus performers, young and old pedalling ponderous loads. Today many rode one-handed in the need to guide umbrellas—in a cheerful, jiggling brilliance of color—through the crowd.

Near the market's entrance, I came upon a vegetable stall displaying carrots, the most remarkable carrots I'd ever seen—all symmetrically round and perfectly straight, each of precisely the same long length and rich orange hue. Setting aside for the moment my usual fondness for the haphazard, and also what manner of pesticide, herbicide, and growth hormone might have produced such clones, I purchased a bag of six for one yen (about a dollar American). Then being hungry, I tore open the bag and began crunching. The shopkeeper fairly fainted. Visibly shaken, he jumped behind a curtain, but emerged a moment later with a woman in tow. They whispered in stern consultation, then began to giggle. As I munched my way down the aisles, one after another Japanese vendor fell to shock, then titters, and I grinned back in a superb cultural exchange requiring no words. It said (I think): Americans eat raw carrots, Japanese eat cooked. I pondered the possibilities of their custom's origin. Had the bygone use of night soil (systematically collected human feces spread as fertilizer onto crops) once given rise to a tradition of cooking root vegetables? I was suddenly ready for the toilet convention.

That evening I browsed the symposium literature. Shortly before I left home, I'd received a late fax. Someone, it appeared, had thought better of my delivering the keynote address—instead, three of us would take to the podium, each for an hour, with renowned Japanese mountaineer Ms. Junko Tabei designated as keynote speaker and presenting first. Uno Winblad from Sweden, representing the World Health Organization, was scheduled second. The author of the shit book, quite appropriately, would bring up the rear.

Before climbing into bed, I laid out my staid black convention attire for the morning. I had determined earlier in the day to go with the original version of my speech: it was *me*, and I needed—half a world away from home—to hold close to what I knew. I rationalized: this was, after all, a *toilet* convention.

The intensity and depth of the international exchange that

spanned the next few days reflected a wide range of struggles—political and cultural and environmental—and the deadly serious concerns of sanitation, hygiene, and pollution. Aesthetics, in some of our minds, also ranked high—preserving that unexplored look to wild places.

Junko Tabei was a woman animated beyond her small stature. She bounced rather than walked, and her talk emanated from all parts of her frame. She spoke of her mountaineering experiences, especially the pristine beauty of Antarctica that inspired her not to leave the blot of her own fecal waste on the scenery. She had carried it out in a plastic bag tied to the outside of her backpack, where it froze and thwacked to and fro with the rhythm of her walk, until she could prop it on a sled.

Uno Winblad, in that he followed Junko and was wearing a choking ascot, presented a severe picture. His message from the World Health Organization was no more lighthearted. It stressed the global urgency of separating the components of sewage. The human body does not excrete sewage; it is a product of our technology—a mix of urine, solid human waste, and water. Each of us produces, over the course of a year, approximately 500 quarts of urine and 50 quarts of feces. We then combine that 550 quarts with 15,000 quarts of freshwater and flush it into a vast system of septic tanks, sewers, and treatment plants.

"Water," Uno went on, "is a scarcity in many countries." Sitting off stage, I thought of the stresses to water supplies I had known in the U.S., from urban bans on sprinkling to legislated household water quotas to arid western states' irrigation wars. Into my straying thoughts Uno's voice broke with this retinue of warnings: Our planet's advancing population is propelling us toward a world water crisis, and sewage flush systems that require billions of gallons of water are speeding us faster toward calamity. Increasingly, we can expect to see societies in which the rich flush, while the poor lack freshwater for drinking and bathing. The typical urban dweller of the next century (Uno was now blipping a little red dot around sketches on the huge screen behind him) is not going to live in a pleasant, comfortable flat or house, with paved streets and electricity, a sufficient, pure, and reliable supply of water, a flush toilet, garbage collection, and everything else that we tend to take for granted. Much of the world's population would inhabit squatter settlements that are predicted to mushroom in and around metropolitan areas.

This last set me, a person already on the low end of the income spectrum, to squirming in my chair. We can forget about watering flower gardens and lawns, I thought. And we won't—as in one drought I remembered—be joyously showering with a friend. This will be no ordinary living. A hard-edged picture passed through my mind, of the people in the convention hall living as a community on water dribbling from a long-distance pipe, houses with dirt floors, backyards heaped with discarded washing machines and dishwashers, all of us reduced to spit baths with bandannas.

Uno was merely the messenger of the day. Everything is telling us that our sanitation methodology must change. And it doesn't seem too much, I wanted to add, to adopt a goal of access to a decent toilet—one free of the Japanese Four Ks—for everyone.

My turn to speak was coming soon. With Uno's being a tall man, the lectern had been set atop a large plywood box, relieving me from the necessity of kicking off my shoes and assuming a semi-squatting posture (too ridiculously symbolic of my topic) to reach the microphone. The three young women interpreters with whom I'd met over breakfast, each to take on twenty minutes of my talk, were tucked in a booth at the side of the stage. I walked to the podium, pausing part way to bow from the waist and smile. (A bit of my grin came from knowing that miniature sterling silver outhouses, each with a hinged door opening on a minuscule man seated and reading a book, hung from my earlobes—a bon voyage present from a zany friend.) I took a long breath and visualized my spinal cord attached to the center of the earth, something that helps to calm me. Then, with searing lights blinding me to all but the first two rows of audience, I carefully pronounced "good afternoon" in five languages.

I talked about my mother, who died at 92—how if she had known that I'd flown half way around the world to address 800 people on the topic of shit, she would have crumpled to the floor.

(She also would have revived and asked me to sign several more copies of my book for her friends.)

I talked about wilderness and preserving it on the individual level of bodily functions. I spoke of the growing hordes of people trotting up mountainsides and flailing down rivers, and of the many with the burgeoning desire to dish out fortunes for lavishly catered excursions into "exotic" backcountry. Caroming off Uno, I talked about how the world's swelling population—in its answering of a soul's desperate need to breathe wild grandeur—is rendering remote places less and less remote.

I talked about digging environmentally sound *one-sit* holes and about *stirring*, the practice of loosening dirt on the sides of the hole to mix with your deposit, all to the purpose of speeding decomposition. In resounding support of Junko's Antarctica experience, I dived into the subject of packing-it-out: the toting of fecal matter out of the woods. I shared the history of the practice, how it first began in the Grand Canyon in the early 1970s—born of necessity from heavy group visitation on limited beaches in a steep-walled canyon. How today the U.S. Forest Service straps portable toilets onto mules that accompany trail crews into the high country. In graphic detail, I described the features of an array of new portable potties.

Then I proceeded to the *individual* packing-it-out, how this is necessary in sensitive ecosystems and high-use areas: for sea kayakers, for instance, repeatedly camped on the same small islands; for spelunkers exploring the almost static environs of caves; for hikers above timberline where burial is not possible; for rock climbers who have traditionally let it—bombs away!—fly; for cross-country skiers traversing the same terrain as spring hikers; and for park visitors on heavily trafficked trails, particularly in places of wilderness designation where regulations restrict the building of permanent structures, like outhouses.

In the manner of a grade schooler with show-and-tell, I unveiled a Canadian prototype of a biodegradable bag, the Personal Disposable Wilderness Toilet, conveniently shaped to position, with the assistance of handles, between your legs. From a red ditty bag, I pulled a ten-inch aluminum tube, another individual pack-it-out container, successfully tested in the western U.S.

As I spoke, from the far back reaches of the room, a singular, stout laugh floated almost rhythmically to the stage. I recognized it as erupting from someone with an English-speaking sense of humor. The rest of the audience seemed inert. My young interpreters had to be doing a fine job of filtering, I thought, expertly turning my speech into acceptably stale tortillas. Or perhaps I had stunned everyone into silence? Or the room had dulled to a fossilized stoicism?

After my talk, I received multiple compliments, though they all might have fallen into the range of inexplicit to polite, and I was to leave Japan a week later with a lingering uncertainty as to how my words were taken. Reassurance finally would arrive a month later in the form of a letter: an invitation to the next International Toilet Symposium!

My stay in Toyama drew to a close. The symposium's farewell party was a raucous, stand-up affair, flowing with sake and *biru* around long tables set with platters piled with elegantly presented morsels, among which were my favorites: sushi (raw fish atop pressed sweet rice) and sashimi (sliced raw fish), accompanied by paper-thin-pink-pickled ginger and dabs of green wasabi (a paste of horseradish). The large hall buzzed with a busy heat: the balancing of small plates and glasses, and quick dashes to the buffet table; the exchanging of token good-bye presents brought from home; the trading of business cards (a Japanese ritual); and the shuffling and reshuffling of newly made friends in front of flashing pocket cameras. There were speeches delivered and interpreted. Glasses raised. Hugs of good-bye and people still meeting.

At some prearranged cue, a member of the toilet association, a distinguished woman professor from a Tokyo women's college, hopped onto the stage—a wide wooden platform with a backdrop of shoji screens painted with the Japan Alps. Microphone in hand, she began singing a cappella—what I, in my cultural naïveté, perceived as off-key opera in Japanese, a grotesque baritone droning. Curiously, it swiftly grew on me. After the Malaysians, the French, the Australians, it was my turn for this unaccompanied karaoke. By far the tallest person in the room and dressed for the gala in a flowing leopard-skin-print tunic, a Navajo fetish necklace of ebony bears, and silk pants stuffed into spanking new, knee-high shit kickers, there I stood, shoulder-to-shoulder with the past president of the Minnesota-based Portable Sanitation Association International, singing for the honor of our country. "Old Macdonald Had a Farm!" Among the goats and the pigs and the cows, and thinking *How weird my life does get,* I couldn't help momentarily losing the greater global picture.

Then in looking out across the sea of toilet convention goers, at the varied ethnic faces so attentive to us, my heart thumped, and I was struck by an odd, inner thought: there were properties of shit I had never dreamed of—those of drawing peoples of the world into a grand and empathetic circle, a circle that had every chance of widening.

Thanks to the Japan Toilet Association.

*Kathleen Meyer is the author of the international best-selling outdoor guide* How to Shit in the Woods: An Environmentally Sound Approach to a Lost Art, *with more than 1.5 million copies in print in seven languages. Her Montana memoir,* Barefoot Hearted: A Wild Life Among Wildlife, *was published in 2001. She lives in the Bitterroot Valley of western Montana.*

DIANNE PARTIE LANGE

# The Moment of Truth

*A Thai child adopts an*
*American woman.*

I COULDN'T REMEMBER EVER FEELING WORSE. THREE DAYS AFTER I had moved out of the beautiful, four-bedroom, Pacific-view home I'd shared with my husband of more than twenty years to the three-room walk-up that was to be my postdivorce transition apartment, the pipes burst, expending the flow of hot water. The thought of taking cold showers indefinitely reduced me to tears. Then, from the far edges of my memory flashed an image of a shower I had taken six months earlier in a jungle lodge in southern Thailand.

I had worked hard to be in good shape for the physical challenges of the tour, consisting of hill trekking in the north and sea canoeing in the south, not realizing that it was my emotions rather than my body that would be put to the greatest test. That sixteen-day trip would also teach me lessons about my perception, including the relative value of a cold shower.

As I stood wondering how I was going to manage my suddenly single life and its diminished resources, the memory of that Thai shower magically broke my free fall into self-pity. After all, I joked to myself, I had paid $3,000 for the privilege of throwing cold rainwater over myself in Thailand and now, right here in Santa Monica, California, I could do it for free. Quickly, before the image

220

of that jungle lodge and its orchid-laden garden faded, I jumped into the tub, grabbed the half-inch-wide tube that connected to the faucet and let the icy liquid flow over my head. I was in the jungles of Thailand again, smiling for the first time in weeks.

Before going to Thailand, I had rarely wandered off the beaten track. Now my opportunity had arrived. My twenty-one-year-old son Jordan was studying in Chiang Mai, a city in northern Thailand; but he planned to take a semester off to surf in Indonesia. I suggested to my husband that we meet Jordan at one of the beach towns in southern Thailand. I added that I could go ahead of time to take an adventure travel tour similar to one a friend had taken the year before.

In retrospect, I realize I had another motive: I was setting myself up for an emotional pinch test. For more than a year, the pressure of finishing a book on cancer had absorbed my attention, allowing me to ignore the emotional impact of other aspects of my reality: turning fifty, my son's flight from the nest, and my husband's relentless business travel schedule. I had been in some kind of numbed state of denial, and it was time to wake up.

The day the colorful brochure arrived, I studied the various tours and settled on the Thailand trip. The itinerary informed me that most of the time would be spent in areas accessible only on foot or by river raft and far from conveniences such as running water, telephones, and electricity. After meeting in Bangkok, our group would fly to the 700-year-old city of Chiang Mai, the departure point for trekking in the northern mountains.

Following several days of traveling from one tribal village to another, we would head south to the busy town of Surat Thani and the nearby tropical rain forest. From the lush virgin forests, dramatic limestone cliffs, and fairy-tale landscape of Khao Sok National Park, we would go farther south to the resort island of Phuket. There we would embark on a support boat and, using it as our base, paddle sea canoes among the limestone islands (karsts) that pepper Phra Nang Bay.

I would travel by plane, overnight train, four-wheel drive truck, bamboo raft, long-tail boat, and elephant, as well as on foot. I would sleep surrounded by silk and teak in a traditional Thai home in Thon Buri, spend several nights in tribal village homes, make my bed in a jungle tree house and a floating raft house, and lie under the stars on pristine, deserted beaches surrounded by four-story cliffs covered by hanging forests.

In preparation for the physical challenges, I worked out with free weights three times a week and increased my cardio schedule. At least once a week, I hiked up and down a steep, two-mile trail. Two or three times a week, I ran three miles along the beach. My worst fear was that I wouldn't keep up with my group. As it turned out, the four of us—women ranging in age from thirty-to sixty-something and of varying levels of fitness—were perfectly matched. For all my conditioning, I never lifted anything heavier than a day pack; porters carried our sleeping bags, food, and water. The longest single day's trek was about seven miles, which included a few steep descents that were best navigated wearing hiking boots. Most uphill climbs were relatively gentle.

However, all those biceps curls were not in vain. Indeed, strong arms can save your life if you ever take a ride on an elephant. In the two hours I spent on the back of one of those hulking creatures, there were moments (which felt like aeons at the time) when my survival depended on my ability to lock my forearms around the three-inch-high ledge that ran along the sides and back of the flat wooden platform on which I sat. After one particularly scary and exhausting downhill segment, during which the mahout (elephant driver) was totally deaf to my shrieks of protest, I learned another lesson that can be applied to many of life's hairy ups and downs: sometimes it's best just to be quiet, use every ounce of strength to hold on, and not look back—or down!

Traveling without luggage was another challenge, and it injected a simplicity into my life that I would never have accomplished voluntarily. Although I had brought all the accoutrements I thought I couldn't be without—notebook, computer, blow-dryer, satchel filled with books and maps, clothes for every occasion—I was forced to leave most of it behind in a guest house for days at a time. The necessity of reducing my needs to what I could pack in a 12-inch-square army surplus rucksack completely changed my definition of luxury. Variety in clothes, CDs, and even books and magazines was not as essential as I thought. What really mattered was comfort, and nothing was more comforting than having fresh underwear. (Don't skimp on underwear unless you invest in the fast-drying kind and aren't embarrassed to hang them from your backpack.)

One thing I've learned when traveling is that there is always an unexpected moment of truth that crystallizes the clash between the postcard scenario and real life. On my last day in the hills north of Chiang Mai, that moment of truth was sparked by a two-year-old.

Our group's flotilla of four bamboo rafts had pulled up to the riverbank of a Lahu village, the final stop on our hill-tribe tour. As we trooped up the path to a cluster of huts, a small band of women and children came to greet us. We had seen many children in the Hmong, Lisu, Akha, and Karen villages we visited, but I kept my distance, despite my affinity for kids. Perhaps it was a defense against the losses I feared I was facing: my book, my son, my husband. I didn't want to share myself. My tour mates would draw pictures, offer gifts, and look at books with the children, but I was preoccupied with my inward journey. I felt more comfortable as an observer.

The Lahu children were different. They were not going to let me get away with hiding behind my camera. As I stepped onto the riverbank, a smiling toddler seized my hand immediately and looked up at me as if to say, What took you so long? Maybe it was a random grasp. Our tour guide told us that the Lahu people were the most outgoing that we would meet. Then again, maybe I was simply ready to be approached. Whatever it was, there was no escaping this child's tiny grip. Later, when she climbed onto my lap like she owned it, I noticed for the first time that her naked body was spotted with sores that looked like tiny volcano craters.

During the short time we spent in the Lahu village, the little girl rarely left my side. She stood next to me as we ate lunch prepared by our porters, and when two women gave me a Thai massage, she pressed her little hands into my arm, imitating the squeezing movements.

As she splashed with her friends in the river, I daydreamed about taking her home with me. I saw myself taking her to the doctor to have her sores treated, pushing her on a swing at the playground, and reading her a bedtime story before tucking her in between clean white sheets. The mothering fantasies became more and more elaborate as I watched her play at the river's edge in the natural swimming hole bordered by our rafts.

> ——— ☽ ———
>
> That second, my heart breaks open. I ask: am I worthy of the trust of a starving child who notices when a single grain of rice falls? Do we, both men and women, dare open our hearts to all human beings? There is no greater aspiration, no greater journey.
>
> ◆
>
> —Cherilyn Parsons, "Mother to the World," *A Mother's World: Journeys of the Heart*

Casually I asked our guide, who was British but had lived in Thailand most of his life and adopted three Thai children, what was involved in the process. "It's easy if you don't leave Thailand," he said. He explained that like many other children in this village, the little girl with whom I had so readily bonded was an orphan. Her mother had died of AIDS. She was looked after by the village, and while they cared for her, he said, they would happily give her to me. The problem was that I couldn't take her home. Without the proper papers, which were nearly impossible to arrange, I could be arrested for kidnapping.

After saying our good-byes, we settled ourselves in the center of our flat, narrow rafts. As we eased into the current that would carry us downstream, I saw the Lahu child turn away and leap playfully into the river. No one was watching her, I noticed, feeling a moment's panic. No one would save her if she cried for help. As our boatmen pressed their poles down into the muddy river bottom for the final push-off, I saw her tiny body emerge from the river and watched as she climbed onto the shore, becoming even smaller. It is an image that shadows me still.

Now, nearly a year later, when I look at a photograph of the Lahu girl smiling with delight to be wearing one of my tour mate's sunglasses, I know that it wasn't her I dreamed of saving. It was me.

I have thanked myself many times for taking that trip to Thailand. Experiencing the beauty of the country and the people certainly enriched my life. The accommodations I was forced to make along the way have changed my notion of life's basic necessities. I now appreciate that drinkable water and a light to see my way to a simple, squat toilet can be true luxuries. Certainly, simplifying my life has become a lot easier since I used a sarong purchased in Chiang Mai's bustling night market for a bathrobe, a best dress, and a sleep sheet.

I'm most grateful, though, for the little flashbacks from the journey—those moments of truth that keep coming to my rescue when I am feeling sad, frightened, angry, or just lost. Memories of floating past an open-air Buddha foundry on the Chao Phraya River and among mangrove forests in primeval lagoons in Phra Nang Bay soothe my mind. Remembrances of sharing an ice-cold Singha beer with our guide after a postjungle-hike leech inspection and sipping tea while listening to our guide Poon Chi recite Burmese myths on the candlelit porch of a village hut have become a refuge. These memories are like the small jasmine blossoms that Thai women thread on a string to make garlands for their spirit houses. One marble-sized bud doesn't look like much, but string enough of them together, and you can protect yourself from all sorts of evils.

*Dianne Partie Lange is a contributing editor for* Allure *magazine and coauthor of* Informed Decisions: The American Cancer Society's Guide to Cancer Detection and Treatment. *She lives in Lake Tahoe, California.*

ANN MACKINTOSH

\* \* \*

# An English Girl
# in Suez

*Cultures clash.*

THE PLANE TOUCHED DOWN AT CAIRO AIRPORT AT JUST BEFORE midnight, and we said *adiós y gracias* to the Spanish crew before stepping onto Egyptian ground, the unknown and mysterious. A sea of brown faces greeted us, and then Karim, our son-in-law, emerged from among them and gave us a warm welcome. Several men grabbed our various pieces of luggage, running ahead and out of sight. But the presence of Karim reassured us that our cases weren't disappearing forever, and eventually everything was piled into the boot of a car, and we set off at a rattling pace through the darkness. We raced over bumps and holes at what felt like a high speed, the roar of the engine mingling with the loud chanting of the Koran on a tape in the car. I decided to leave my fate to Allah, and curled up in the back to doze.

Two hours later, we arrived amongst tall, shadowy, concrete blocks of flats, stopping outside one with Arabic writing on the wall. Two floors up, we were met at the door by a sleepy but welcoming Beth, our youngest daughter, who hugged us and sat us down on cushions on the floor. We were in a high-ceilinged, windowless room, with grey concrete walls, a bare bulb hanging above, but colourful rugs, reminiscent of Spain where we live, covered the floor, brightening and softening the atmosphere. Beth was wearing the long blue dress we had sent her and looked peaceful and well, though pale.

She brought in an enormous, round brass-coloured tray, laid with fresh fruit, pita bread, tahini, and dates. We ate and talked, before going to look at the three sleeping angels, Zahra, Miriam, and Fatima. Zahra and Miriam were in a little bed next to their parents, with whom baby Fatima slept. We then fell into our bed thankfully, on a foam mattress in a corner of the room next door. Our bedroom was spacious, with the same concrete walls and bare bulb as the sitting room, but also with the redeeming cheerful rugs and a small shuttered window which, the following morning, filtered the strong Egyptian sunlight.

We were awakened at 5 A.M. by loudspeakers, calling the faithful to the mosque, filling the night air with sound. We dozed after this, waking late. Our first sight was of two huge brown eyes looking shyly at us round the curtain. It was Zahra, and she quickly responded to our "Come in!" and started talking to us, hardly stopping, bless her, till we left.

Meals were always eaten from a tray on the floor, and our breakfast that first morning was pita bread with tomatoes, tahini, and boiled eggs. We sat round in a circle with the children, the Koran playing on a tape in the background. Zahra at four and a half, was beautiful, large liquid eyes in a pale olive face, but a little thin and wan. She nibbled desultorily, talking volubly. Miriam, two years old, with chestnut curls and bright brown eyes, ate well and kept her counsel. Baby Fatima sat on Beth's lap with her own milk supply. I looked at the three lovely children, and thought how blessed we all were.

After breakfast, we gave Miriam her finger-paints and Zahra her more grown-up palette. Zahra started to change into her painting trousers, stopped suddenly, and asked her mother: "Is it all right for my grandparents to see my legs?" "Yes," said Beth. I remembered my other small grandchildren who often liked to run naked around the house. The children set to with great enthusiasm to finger-paint the doors of the toy cupboard, and mixed colours happily, till a sludge brown emerged; then, with the handle of a spoon, they drew creative patterns in the paint. Meanwhile, Fatima sat like a little doll, her large round eyes following the activities of her two sisters, and Beth made her ablutions prior to praying, veiling her head and going into the bedroom to pray.

After a tasty lunch that Beth prepared of lentil soup, followed by rice with sesame seeds and courgettes, Alex and I decided on a reconnoiter outside. We descended the dusty, concrete stairs, and walked through the rubbish lying in the roadside: we were surrounded by tall tower blocks that stretched in all directions as far as the eye could see, in between a wilderness of unpaved roads and building sites. A mountain range could just be discerned in the distance. "Recognize our washing," Beth had told us, "to find your way back." A few shrouded figures walked the streets, smiling at us. Two menacing-looking soldiers in camouflage and with rifles had wide grins on their faces as we neared, and said: "Welcome to Egypt!" At a kiosk, three young women in white veils, their lovely brown faces lighting up with smiles, sold us some sweet bread rolls and chocolate bars. Walking back, the rubbish blew around us in the cold wind that whirled between the buildings—it was March and still cool. An old man stood silhouetted in a doorway, in long charcoal-grey robes and a dark purple turban—a picture.

We came home to the electric-light brightness of the flat, the sound of the Koran still chanting, and the children sorting coloured circles of wood. Zahra told me, as I sat down with her on the floor, that the game they were play-

> *I*n the Arab quarter of the Old City, a shopkeeper showed me slippers that I ended up not buying. He then invited me to have tea. I said, "No thanks." He said, "When you don't buy my slippers, you are expressing a preference, but when you refuse my tea you are insulting me." I drank his tea and also took in his lesson in civility.
>
> ◆
>
> —Edith Pearlman, "My Junior Year Abroad"

ing had had dice, but Baba (Karim) had told them that using dice was like holding your hand in pig's blood... "and pig's blood is the most horrible thing there is, isn't it, Nana? It is because gambling is very wicked." She paused. "I did have to get used to the idea of not using dice," Zahra added, wistfully, I thought.

Later that evening, I mentioned to Beth that I would like to practice some yoga in our bedroom, with my tape on low, so as not to interfere with the playing of the Koran. "Does it have music?" she asked. "Only a little," I told her. She looked doubtful, so I put it on very quietly; but she came in to say the sound penetrated the curtain, and that music was forbidden in Islam. So I turned it off. Beth used to practise yoga, but said she now only does exercises that please Allah. Zahra was fascinated and came in to watch and copy me. But her mother called her away explaining that what I was doing wasn't Sunna, so she mustn't look. When Miriam peeped 'round the curtain, I felt like a subversive element, as Zahra repeated: "Nana's exercises aren't Sunna, Miriam, it isn't Islam, and we mustn't watch." I heard Miriam murmuring: "Nana Nana Nana..." but she didn't look through again, and soon after, I emerged guiltily, but refreshed. So ended our first day.

The following morning, Karim told us that we had to register our arrival in Suez. Before we left, Beth showed us the enveloping black robes she now wears to go out, and the two gauzelike black veils that hide her face from view, though she can see out. "It's much more comfortable than the veil that only covers your nose," she assured us, "and more people are veiling completely." Kissing little Fatima and with an Arabic blessing from Beth, we set off with Karim and the two girls, and quickly caught a van that serves as a minibus. As we entered Suez, we saw donkeys pulling carts piled high with oranges, a turbaned man, and often a child, sitting up behind. Battered bicycles wove in and out between the traffic, a rider sometimes miraculously balancing a big tray of pita bread on his head. The women were mostly veiled, often in a silky white material worn over long dresses. They looked colourful and pretty.

In the office, as Karim organized our registration, I noticed Zahra looking through a glass partition at a young man sitting there.

She was making a face, and I asked her what was the matter? "I don't like that man being there, because I'm not allowed to look at men. Are you allowed to look at him?" "Well…I may, if we have something to say to each other." "But are you allowed?" "Well, yes, I am." Confusing for her.

In the afternoon, we gave the children the two animal books we had brought them, carefully devoid of pigs, an animal that some Muslims abhor the sight of. Karim always checks our presents to the children, and had approved the books. Zahra's depicted exotic animals and birds. We hadn't realised—and Karim hadn't noticed—that occasionally the author indulged in fantasy. As Zahra and I looked at it together, I was glad she couldn't yet read and was unaware of: "This brightly coloured amphibian occasionally enjoys a glass of port!" Beth, seeing my crestfallen face, looked over my shoulder and sighed disapprovingly. I said we would obliterate the offending words. Miriam's book, of kittens, rabbits, puppies, and even a baby crocodile in life-size colour photographs, was fortunately free of sinful text, and the children happily traced their fingers over images that looked as though they might walk off the pages. I also gave Beth and Karim the patchwork quilt for their bed that I had been working on since they married, and they spread it over the bed and said they liked it very much.

Karim went out to the mosque, and Alex and I sat with Beth and the children, playing games and cuddling Fatima. Then Beth and Alex went into the kitchen to make tea, and I heard them discussing the Prophet Mohammed. He asked her about his childhood, and she told him that Mohammed had been an orphan. "Oh, so that accounts for it!" said Alex. "Accounts for what?" asked Beth. "His looking for security and creating a religion that gave him that!" Beth, sounding upset, told her father that the Prophet had heard the word of God direct, his experiences as a child having no bearing on the Muslim religion. She said she was unhappy to hear him speak disrespectfully of Mohammed, peace be upon him.

Our third day was spent entirely in the flat, and Alex was beginning to feel claustrophobic as the grey walls closed us in, and the Koran chanted ceaselessly. Karim took the two older girls to his mother's, and Alex took to his bed as the only comfortable place for him to be. I sat on the floor with Beth and Fatima in their bedroom, where Beth was finishing a shirt she was making for Karim. I was given some little socks to darn while she mastered the intricacies of button-holing on the sewing machine, with Fatima in her lap so she could see what was going on.

As I helped cook supper, Beth commented on how fulfilled and happy she felt, so blessed by Allah, with three beautiful children, a roof over their heads and enough to eat—more than millions of other people in the world. She surprised herself by her acceptance of the ugliness of their surroundings, no longer feeling the need for land to grow organic fruit and vegetables as she used to do with such enthusiasm. Desires seemed to have left her, she was the picture of contentment in what seemed to us a prison. Later, we wanted to take some photos of the children, previously an unclear issue with Beth and Karim. I saw that Fatima was dressed in the frock given her by her great-grandmother, and so we asked. But Beth was very adamant that we shouldn't take pictures or look at family photographs, so my photos stayed in my case and the camera went unused.

It was early evening when something went wrong with their tape recorder, and the sound of the Koran was distorted and squeaky. I asked Beth if the volume could be turned down but Karim refused, saying that he was trying to decipher the words. This annoyed Alex, who also asked. He said that as we were

> When I lived among the women of Islam, I became part of a world that is still, in the last decade of the twentieth century, an intensely private one. In public, most women move like shadows, constrained physically by their *hijab* or mentally by codes of conduct that inhibit them. It is only behind the high walls and the closed doors that women are ever really free.
>
> ◆
>
> —Geraldine Brooks, *Nine Parts of Desire: The Hidden World of Islamic Women*

all having to live together for this short period, we should try and consider each other's feelings. Karim then turned off the tape and went quietly out of the flat.

When he came back, he gathered his family into the bedroom, and all we could hear was the murmur of his voice. After half an hour, Zahra came out and announced: "Baba says it's the very last time unbelievers come into this house!" Alex looked at me. "It seems we aren't welcome...." Karim disappeared to the mosque and Beth prepared herself for prayer. When she had prayed, we sat down to an uneasy supper together, and she explained that it was a Muslim's sacred duty to listen to the Koran. The children went to bed, and I heard Beth chanting and talking softly to them. I had mentioned how much I'd like to read them a story, and she said I would have to learn some Muslim stories. After Zahra and Miriam were asleep, the three of us sat with Fatima and talked about tolerance and the lack of it. "I'm ready to admit to being intolerant," Beth said, "but the trouble is that you two won't admit it!" We conceded that often we had not felt very forbearing, although we had tried very hard to be accepting. But now the lid was off the cauldron, and up bubbled a soup of contention—we talked about the prohibitions in art and music and the separation of the sexes. Vegetarianism and the *fatwa* on Salman Rushdie, elicited our concepts of compassion. Emotions unexpressed rose to the surface. Beth accused us of ignorance, and Alex said Karim was a bigot. At this, Beth jumped up in anger and left the room. So we went with heavy hearts to pack our cases.

The next morning, Beth was specially solicitous, preparing an extra-nice breakfast of strawberries, pita bread, tahini, and baby cucumbers. We ate on our own, while Karim went to fetch a car for us. I kissed the silent children, telling them I loved them, kissed and hugged Beth, who gave me an Arabic blessing, and we carried our bags to the car. Karim accompanied us, wearing headphones as there was no Koran in the taxi, as far as the center of Suez, where he saw us wordlessly into a large van of about twelve people, destination Cairo.

✻

*Ann Mackintosh was born in London and lived there until her marriage to a Spaniard in Madrid. Widowed at a young age, she studied to be a schoolteacher, then married an artist with three young children whom she helped raise in a tiny village in England.*

JENNIFER L. LEO

# Chinese Like Me

*It's in the genes.*

FOR THE FIRST TIME IN MY LIFE I WAS ATTRACTED TO ASIAN MEN. IT happened on my first trip overseas, to be exact—in Hong Kong, 34 hours before Great Britain ceremoniously handed its Crown Colony back to China. Journalists were all over the island, schedules in hand, looking for anything newsworthy. The world was watching, waiting for change.

I was in the press lobby on the twenty-sixth floor of the Wanchai Towers, 6,900 miles from home in San Francisco. My friend Alison was somewhere down the hall trying to finagle last-minute press credentials, and I sat by the front desk wide-eyed and overwhelmed while reporters from around the globe rushed by to check in.

I've been attracted to men of all ages, five years my younger to twenty years my senior. I've run my fingers through the locks of brown hair, blond hair, red hair, black hair—and over the heads of some men with not much hair at all. I've loved Caucasian men, admired African-American men, fantasized about Latino men, but never have I once seen an Asian man that I cared to give the time of day. Some women might feel the same, but probably none of them are Chinese like me.

I've been half-Chinese all my life. My father's family is originally from Canton. My mother's family is Caucasian—a mix of English, Dutch, maybe even some Scottish. I'm what they call HAPA, from the Hawaiian term meaning half Asian, half white. However, growing up fourth-generation American-born in a white, middle-class, Southern California suburb, I always thought that I was not just half, but all white. Just like my friends.

At a young age, I formed my own assumptions and ideals about the men I wanted to be with. Men should be good-hearted, intelligent, hardworking, taller than me, wearing a nice smile, and musically talented. Adventuresome, a definite plus. I liked them white, and I preferred them Jewish. Or so I thought, until I went to Hong Kong and *they* walked in. The Chinese journalists, that is.

I couldn't take my eyes off them. One at a time, sometimes two, they walked up to the front desk. But they didn't just walk in, they entered. They arrived at the desk with a purpose. I was transfixed by their smart designer black and gray suits. Every inch of them was polished from their no-nonsense haircuts to their expensive Italian shoes. Their briefcases were unscuffed and their cell phones were kept professionally out of view. They, as almost all men in Hong Kong, wore silver oval glasses. Maybe they needed the prescriptions, and maybe they didn't. They looked intellectual. Distinguished. Complete. I didn't know their names, their dialects, or their business. All I knew was that they were tall, dark, handsome...and Asian.

I just sat and stared as they signed their papers, every move crisp and confident. Unlike any other journalist in the room, they knew where to go and what to do. My gaze followed them down the hall to the left, where they disappeared into unmarked rooms, official government attendants close behind.

Suddenly I noticed that my brow had tightened. A confusing paralysis overcame me, and I hid in my guidebook. I didn't want to think about how I looked to them. My grandparents never taught me the Cantonese word for wet monsoon rat. I was wearing gray cotton leggings with a red poncho tied around my waist. My hair was a mess and covered with a baseball cap. My feet hurt, and I didn't feel like being seen. My soggy umbrella fell off the couch, and I pushed it under my backpack. I felt like Cathy, that awkward, pathetic, comic-strip girl who never seems to have anything put together.

Then I heard American voices. My eyes lifted to three Caucasian guys, on the right, sauntering down the hall. A comfortable smile revealed itself on my face. They wore jeans and khaki photographer's vests. Their tripods, gigantic camcorders, and fuzzy microphones were slung over their shoulders. I knew their names were Jake, Mike, and Jack. Had to be. Rugged names, for rugged individuals. I wanted to go with them. I wanted to be them, roving Hong Kong for the perfect shot, the perfect story, fantasizing about a hostile Tiananmen-like outbreak that would bring home the Pulitzer. I imagined them pushing through crowds to get to Prince Charles, a shot of Governor Patten, a meeting with Martin Lee wouldn't phase them because they did it last week and probably would tomorrow too. Running and sweating and then drinking a cold beer with the boys at the end of the day.

The Chinese men came back, standing across from the Americans, both before me. A subtle quake quivered and shook along my spine. My head was shaken and my cranium seemed to crack. I looked from one to the other. Chinese composure. American ease. Chinese integrity. American enthusiasm. Why now, when never before had I admired a tailored suit? A cell phone? A briefcase? An Asian? I put my guidebook back in my pack and sat up straight. The quake continued, but my heart was still. I was separating, body and mind. I was opening up. Suddenly my blood was a river flowing through me. A thousand creeks flowing in and around my body, encircling the island of my heart. The Chinese were proud. The Americans were comfortable. Now my body was flooding, and I stood on my heart, the only solid ground.

I looked back and forth at them one more time, the Asians and the Caucasians. They didn't look at me. They didn't have to, they were me. I closed my eyes. When I opened them, they were gone. I had been lost in a mirror.

Alison was coming down the hall, without a pass, but ready for the street. Hong Kong awaited. The next day the British were going to return their last colony to the Chinese. We had come for the handover, but now I knew…I had come to take back me.

*Jennifer L. Leo is the editor of* Whose Panties Are These? More Misadventures from Funny Women on the Road; Sand in My Bra and Other Misadventures: Funny Women Write from the Road; *and co-editor of* A Woman's Path: True Stories of Adventure and Connection. *Her web site, WrittenRoad.com, is an online resource for travel writers.*

✦ ✦ ✦

# Jump

*A lonely college student struggles*
*to feel at home in a*
*strange country.*

ONLY A WEEK INTO MY STUDY-ABROAD PROGRAM IN BARCELONA, and there I was, sitting on the edge of a toilet in the Joan Miró Museum, crying uncontrollably. The tears had been triggered by a large lunch bill I'd just paid in the museum café. That's what started it, but really I was just bone-deep sad. I was homesick, I didn't speak the language, and my fellow students from America had already formed a foreign students club that didn't include me. At lunch they'd laughed, planned, chatted, and then went on their way without me. Worse, my awkward advances to be part of their club had only alienated me more.

I let myself cry until the tears slowed, then ventured out to the stainless steel sink, turned on the faucet, and scooped up water to give my red and swollen eyes a bath. I thought of my grandmother. Every night before going to bed, she'd tip her head back with a jerk while holding her special cobalt-blue eyecup to one eye, then the other. That's one of the few memories I have of her, that and her powdery-clean smell. She died when I was five.

Looking in the mirror, I wanted to cry again. This was not the face of someone having the time of her life in another country. I couldn't stay in the bathroom forever, so donning my sunglasses, I braved the exit, hoping I wouldn't run into any of my classmates.

Just outside the bathroom, of course, I bumped into one of my fellow students. But it was only Ruth; she wasn't a member of the club either. Ruth was about sixty-five years old, and her face was powdery smooth and serene. She saw that I was upset. I told her I was a bit homesick, and as I did, the tears struggled to escape again. She asked if I wanted company and if she could buy me a beer after browsing the museum. I took her up on the beer but said I wanted to roam the museum alone. We arranged to meet outside in an hour.

Feeling tragic, I wandered around the museum with little enthusiasm. I paused in front of one of Miró's larger pieces, a brightly colored wall-sculpture with fantastic shapes. I like Miró—usually his art puts a spring in my step. But that day his spirit wasn't getting through; the lightness and humor escaped me.

Wandering into a low-lit, quiet room, I came upon some black-and-white sketches that drew me into the worlds within them. I peered deep into detailed renditions of scenes from the Spanish Civil War. Gone were Miró's typical reds and yellows and blues, gone his lightness and humor. Here, barely kept alive in the dim light of this room, lived the victims of the war. My pace slowed as I went into each picture, one by one. I stayed with the images a while, meeting the mood of the room with the heaviness in my body.

As I exited the air-conditioned museum, the hot, moist Mediterranean air hit me like a blast furnace. My pores felt stuffed with anchovies and olive oil, and my spirit lacked fresh air. Ruth looked cool when she came out of the museum in her beige shorts and striped t-shirt. We rested on the grass awhile, and she showed me the postcards she'd just bought. Looking at the map, we chose a nearby neighborhood and decided to walk there. The walk was dreadful. There were no sidewalks, and the exhaust from cars and tour buses fuming up and down the steep and winding hill made the humid air thick and stinky.

At the bottom, we settled on an outdoor café. It was nothing special, just a few sooty tables sitting on the sidewalk near the street. The neighborhood seemed deserted. Perhaps it was more lively during the week, we remarked, but today, Saturday, there wasn't much life.

Ruth went in for the beers while I sank into a cool metal chair beneath a Cinzano umbrella. We settled down with our marginally cold *cervezas,* and Ruth asked me why I was so sad. I bounced all around in my answer—I was homesick, frustrated with the language, my boyfriend was back in Los Angeles, and though I wasn't sure that I was really in love with him, I missed him. I told her I wasn't exactly sure why I was feeling sad, I just was.

What I didn't tell her was that I felt fat, ugly; my hair was cut way too short; and I had just quit smoking. My insides didn't match the carefree person I felt I should be on this trip—as footloose as I imagined that my "members-only" fellow students were. They were happy, having fun. They were fun itself. Me? I was definitely NOT having fun.

Three teenage Spanish girls, full of life and exuding wide-open futures, skipped by our table arm in arm, singing a song. They wore midriff tops and baggy pants cinched with wide belts. They were stunningly beautiful. Since my arrival, the beauty of the girls and women in this city awed me; I couldn't hold a candle to them, I thought. And they all seemed to know each other so well. Beautiful, vibrant Barcelona youth were everywhere, it seemed, chatting gaily in cafés, calling out to each other on the streets, happy and full of life.

Tired of me, I asked Ruth about herself. Was she married, did she have kids? She jumped right into her story. She'd married young and had three children but wasn't happy. "My husband wasn't bad to me," she said, "but he wasn't supportive either." He broke her down, squashed her spirit. But she did what many women of her generation did: she stayed and raised her children. When the last child left home, so did she. She never wanted to marry again. To her marriage was a weight around her neck, a dampness on her soul. But, then there was John. She fell in love and married again. On their first date, he brought her flowers, and they dined and danced until two in the morning.

"We sat in his car outside my house and talked and necked until dawn. After that first date, I was hooked." Her cheeks reddened and brightened at the memory. "I was surprised that marriage could be so good," she said. "He was so supportive. He encouraged me to travel and do all the things I had always wanted to do. We didn't like all the same things, but we did have a mutual desire for each other's happiness." Ten years into their marriage, John got multiple sclerosis; in two years he was gone.

"He died five years ago," she said. "And my heart aches just as much as it did the day he died."

What courage, I thought. How can she carry that sadness? How can she visit a strange country and just jump back into life? I would want to hole up in my house and die.

As I marveled at the strength of the woman before me, a small child tentatively approached our table. She was alone. Her open face asked for an invitation into our circle. I wiped the tear sneaking down my cheek and said to the girl, *"Hola, niña."*

She gave a shy smile and stepped closer. *"¿Cómo te llamas?"* I said. What's your name?

"Sonia." She came to the table and climbed onto the chair next to mine, perfectly at home. She smiled.

I held out my hands to her. She immediately grabbed onto them with her little sausage fingers. *"Uno, dos, tres, ¡SALTE!"* I said. One, two, three, jump! She jumped off the chair, giggling as if we had played the game hundreds of times before. She climbed right back up on the chair and again I said, *"Uno, dos, tres, ¡SALTE!"* She jumped again and again, tireless and giggling. Ruth and I looked at each other and laughed.

After a few minutes of playing, I took out my camera. At the sight of it, the child grew pensive and serious, as if it might do her harm. Looking at her through the lens, I recognized her Moorish ancestry; her mysterious, dark eyes that evoked the fountains and the open-air architecture brought to Spain from the south. As soon as the camera was lowered, she again became a giggling four-year old with faded children prancing on the pockets of her yellow-and-white plaid dress. Each time she struggled to climb up on the chair, the glimpse of her stretched and yellowed underwear revealed her poverty.

*"Uno, dos, tres, ¡SALTE!"* Relentlessly, she climbed back up on the chair. *"Uno, dos, tres, ¡SALTE!"*

A woman came over and began speaking rapid-fire Spanish. She was clearly a laborer, with her dress worn, and her face more so. With my one semester of Spanish, I didn't at first understand what she was saying except that she was Sonia's mother. After she repeated herself several times, Ruth and I figured out that she wanted copies of the pictures I took of Sonia. Writing her address on the back of a scrap of paper, she told Sonia it was time to leave. Sonia's face clouded, but she obediently climbed down from the chair. Before following her mother, she climbed into my lap and gave me a big hug. It nearly broke my heart—or perhaps mended it.

It is better to be in chains with friends than in a garden with strangers.

—Persian proverb

After drinking another beer and sharing some lighter conversation, Ruth and I parted company, and I caught a bus. I felt sleepy from the alcohol. A residual sadness still lingered, but that seemed inevitable—usually melancholy remains until your dreams have a chance to massage it out. I thought about how disconnected I'd felt earlier that day; how separate from the world of friends and family. Yet, in my isolation, two generations of females—one older than I, one younger—helped me to once again find the thread. All at once, the open windows of the bus let in the soft Mediterranean afternoon breeze, and the passing city—so full of art and beauty and life—seemed familiar and within my reach.

Arriving at my lodgings, I unlocked the door with my wonderful large, ornate, and seemingly ancient key. I went to my small, clean room and lay on the single bed. I soon fell asleep with the wind and the passionate voice of José Carrera filtering into my room through the lace curtains. For once, my landlady's passion for high-volume opera played at all hours seemed more like a gift than an annoyance.

When I got back to California I couldn't find little Sonia's address; I'd misplaced the scrap of paper. At first I was fatalistic about getting the pictures to her mother. I didn't know the name of the café; I wasn't even sure which street it was on. My first reaction was to say, "Oh, well—that's that." But I just couldn't let it go.

Then I had an idea. I wrote to Jill, a friend still living in Barcelona. I sent her a photocopied map and circled the general area where Ruth and I had been that day. I sent her the pictures of Sonia and told her that her mission, should she choose to accept it, was to find Sonia and give her the pictures. Six weeks later, I received a postcard from Jill with a picture of one word written in sand: *"Sí."*

*Aleta Brown is a freelance writer who lives in Suisun City, California.*

RACHEL LOUISE SNYDER

# My Lai, Thirty Years After

*A scholar struggles with the past.*

THE SUN SCORCHES THROUGH THE METAL OF THE CAR, BAKING the black, vinyl seats. They feel pliable as new tar. Tank top and shorts—the uniform of choice—offers no respite and my bandanna is soaked in minutes. Sweat dribbles down my forehead, stings my eyes. The wind, through the car's open windows, feels like steady air from a torrid oven—relentless, constant, unbearable. This is Vietnam, mid-July.

I am on my way to visit the site of the 1968 My Lai Massacre during the Vietnam/American War. On that March day, soldiers from Charlie Company fired for four hours on the village of My Lai 4, near Pinkville in the Quang Ngai province. The result: 504 villagers dead, 6 survivors. I am an American traveling with an Australian couple three hours by car from Hoi An south to My Lai. I'd met them days before on a boat trip in Nha Trang and, as often happens with travelers, our paths had crossed again the night before in Hoi An. After telling them of my plans for the following day, they asked if they could split the cost and accompany me on my journey. We booked a car for 7 A.M. the following morning, hoping to drive before the worst of the midday heat began. We were assured an English-speaking driver.

"Hello," he said, when we climbed in the car. We'd arranged to be picked up outside of Hoi An, in an alley where authorities wouldn't see foreigners climbing in a car that wasn't government authorized. If caught, the driver would be heavily fined.

I greeted him, then asked how far it was to My Lai.

"Yes, My Lai," he said.

"How far?"

"Hello," he said.

I hadn't specified how many English words were required.

For three weeks, I had been in Vietnam—partly because I had wanderlust, but mostly because I had taught Vietnam War literature for nearly three years. I researched the topic in graduate school; the romance had appealed to me—innocent men following the orders of a wrong government, men losing their lives in a futile fight. But gradually, the romance slipped away, and my interest became academic. And personal. I wanted to experience a Vietnam outside of books. A Vietnam before capitalism changed the country's face entirely. Here was something, a war, our country couldn't seem to get past. I wanted to know why.

The mood in the car is somber; no one talks most of the way. Together, the Australians and I watch a motorbike buried under more than a hundred dead ducks tied together and slung behind, over top, and in front of the driver as he pulls beside, then passes our car. The ducks' eyes and beaks are open, flapping with the bumps in the road as if startled to be caught so suddenly by death. One of the Australians asks me how I feel.

"Hot," I tell her. "Sweaty. My water bottle is boiling."

This is not the answer she is looking for, I know. What does she want to hear? I feel guilty that American soldiers killed innocent Vietnamese? Remorse over the incident? Embarrassed by the actions of my country's citizens? A yearning to unravel the world and manipulate the past so that it wouldn't have happened?

I feel all these things.

I also feel nothing.

In March of 1968, when Charlie Company opened fire on the civilians of My Lai, I was barely even a fetus. When Lt. William

Calley was tried and found guilty, I was learning to wave good-bye. When he was released from house arrest, I was learning to count to three. I never protested. I never personally knew anyone who died in the war. I barely remember the tanks crashing through the gate at Saigon in 1975. The Vietnam veterans I have happened to meet are middle-aged men now, some bitter, some angry, some indifferent, and all with other lives. Why does any of this matter to me?

"How do Americans feel about England now?" one of the Australians asks me.

England? I am silent for a moment, wondering if I've missed some important news event, some skirmish between the U.S. and Great Britain.

"You know," she says, "the war?"

"The Revolutionary War?"

"Yes."

"I don't think Americans think of it at all." I am amazed to be asked this question; I nearly burst out laughing. Does anyone have the Revolutionary War even in the farthest recesses of his conscious mind? England? I think fish and chips, dark beer, castles, and scandalous royalty. It occurs to me she is looking for a connection to My Lai. It also occurs to me that 100 years from now the Vietnam/American War will be little more than a tiny phase of history taught in progressive colleges throughout the U.S. It's almost there now.

I explain to her that the circumstances between the two wars are different, not comparable, though I know her question stems from never having heard anything of My Lai until last night when I told her the story. I ask about the connection she's attempting to make, and she mumbles vaguely about imperialism and war. She has seen too much propaganda, I think. In Vietnam, Americans are referred to as the Imperialist Aggressors.

We are close to My Lai, and I feel my stomach muscles start to tighten. What will I find there? Will I be cursed? Hated? Spit on? Will I face what many U.S. soldiers faced upon their arrival home? Or am I blanketed by time, gender, age? The Australians in back have begun to lather themselves with suntan lotion—here, the sun can blister through sunblock in minutes. I am hoping the couple does not hate me by the end of the day.

Am I to blame?

Of course not. I was barely alive. But should future generations not strive to eradicate the mistakes of the past? Certainly. But the My Lai Massacre, to be seen objectively, must be seen in the context of war. That war, in particular. But 500 innocent people are dead. And I am a citizen from the country that killed them.

The car pulls in to a long driveway and parks under the shade of a tree. We are charged 20,000 dong each to enter the My Lai monument site—just under two dollars. To say that the Vietnamese have learned to market the American war sounds cynical and defensive. But you can buy Zippo lighters and flak jackets at Saigon's war surplus market. You can buy helicopter and B-52 bomber replicas made of bullets at the War Remnants Museum. You can buy compasses and rusting dog tags in every town along the coast from Ho Chi Minh City to Hanoi. The trick is not thinking about where they've come from.

——— ☽ ———

"*B*efore, I VeeCee!" he said in pidgin Vietnamese, loud enough to include several rows of openly eavesdropping passengers. "I kill two Americans in war. Bang bang!" He laughed, cocked an imaginary trigger, and fired twice. Before I could react, he reached into a plastic bag, pulled out a fresh baguette, and tore it in half. "Different now," he said, handing me a piece, "Welcome back!"

◆

—Karin Muller,
*Hitchhiking Vietnam*

"I wait," our driver says, urging us forward. A long sidewalk leads into an enormous concrete sculpture, though it is so far away I can't quite make it out. I look away, unprepared to discover exactly what it is yet. My palms are clammy and I know heat is not the cause. I grin stupidly at the Australians, feel like my skin is too loose for my bones. They are waiting for me to proceed. I am the expert here. I'd planned on coming here alone, but last night they'd insisted, and sharing the cost was a bonus for me. Now, I waver between elation and embarrassment, glad they are here and wishing them gone, all at once.

To my left is the grave of Mrs. Thong, her children, and two relatives. The marker is etched in stone. I read and reread the names, calculate each age of the victims had they lived, compare them to my own twenty-nine years. We walk forward. How long should one look at a stranger's grave? There is a fine line between remorse and obsession. I am all jumbled up; a curious mixture of emotion and numbness. Several stone statues line up along the sidewalk. These sculptures were done by a group of artists in Hanoi—all but the huge one in the distance.

One stone woman falls forward, her hand clutching her stomach—a replica of the photo by Ronald Herberle. Another woman kneels, her hair blowing in the wind as she falls sideways, one arm outstretched. Opposite her, down a thin sidewalk bordered by yellow wildflowers, is the temporary museum. A woman leans in the doorway, arms crossed, waiting for us. She wears long brown pants, a pink long-sleeved blouse. I am amazed at how the Vietnamese withstand the heat. Women ride bicycles covered head to toe, saving their skin from the sun, complete in elbow-high gloves and hats. In the mountains of Da Lat, where it may get down to seventy-eight degrees Fahrenheit at night, people wear winter coats, sweaters, scarves, knit caps.

The woman greets us in flawless English. Like most Vietnamese, she speaks quietly, gently. She welcomes us to My Lai, tells us she is a guide and will show us around. No other visitors are here, and the silence is loud, oppressive as the heat. The museum is maybe ten by twenty feet. She asks where we are from.

"Australia," my companions say together, maybe a little proudly.

"America," I say, shifting my weight, "the States."

She smiles at us, looks at me a second longer than the Australians, though this may be my imagination. First she explains that we need to look at a map of the area to understand how the Americans planned the attack.

"Planned?" I ask her.

She nods. "Yes, the massacre was planned."

I hear the Australians gasp, slightly, under their breath. The woman continues to smile.

Planned? How could it have been planned? A recon patrol, perhaps, was planned, maybe even a search-and-destroy mission; burn the hamlets, interrogate the villagers, and all that. But a full-scale massacre? Strategies are planned. Brutalities just happen. My heart is thumping. She shows us how My Lai is actually a series of villages: My Lai 1, 2, 3, 4, 5, 6. She points to the hill near My Lai 4 where the Americans were based. She explains how the Americans knew the people of My Lai 4, how the soldiers would come down and play with the children.

"So you can see," she says softly, "how this wasn't an accident."

No, I want to tell her, I don't see. I don't see what you see at all. I see men who obeyed the leaders of their country, then lost themselves. The Australians are nodding, horrified. Clearly, they believe her. I want to tell them she is wrong, that this wasn't planned, but I cannot be sure, and anyway, the three of them have moved on to other displays. I stumble, follow, stand behind them.

The woman walks us around the room. On the walls there are pictures of people: Lieutenant Calley, who was the First Platoon leader, Captain Ernest Medina, the company commander, Oran Henderson, the brigade commander. Of them all, soldiers and commanders, Calley was the sole man tried and found guilty. He served three years house arrest. There are others, Ron Ridenhour, the soldier whose letters spurred the initial investigation in Washington, Ron Herberle, the American photographer whose photos told the story of My Lai 4, and two South Vietnamese interpreters who testified to the massacre in 1978. You see, the pictures seem to suggest, how even many Americans knew what had happened was wrong? The people at this museum have done their homework. They do not blame all Americans, I think; they blame one group of American soldiers. Perhaps it is not in the Vietnamese where we will find our forgiveness.

There are pictures of helicopters landing, soldiers walking with guns drawn or M16s blasting away, hamlets burning to the ground. The black-and-white photos have been blown up so that the details are blurry, everything a little less focused like the world that day was trapped in shadow.

Glass cases hold items from the villagers: one woman's conical hat and betel nut spittoon, a young girl's shoe, a bullet-riddled cooking pot, marbles, and a little boy's school notebooks. There are the 1978 testimonies from the ARVN interpreters encased, along with blown-up news clips from papers all over the world. The woman points to the photo of a wounded American soldier after he'd shot himself in the foot because he refused to participate.

"He killed himself a few years ago," the woman tells us, then adds, "he was unable to live with the memories of the massacre."

Does she know how many men and women are unable to live with the memories? Or how many are forced to? Does she know how many men were following orders that day, and how few were giving them? Yes, men from my country did a horrible thing; they were wrong. But men from my country also brought this horrible thing to light. Men from my country fed Vietnamese citizens, played with Vietnamese children, were led to believe they fought for something worthwhile.

It occurs to me that the nationality—American—doesn't matter, not to this woman, anyway. What matters is that innocent people from her village were lost. The monument is not put here simply to remember American sins, it is put here to honor lost lives.

Our guide shows us the graves of entire families killed. Next to each grave is the foundation that was once the family's hamlet. Though they were all burned down, the foundations remain, a foot higher than ground level and covered with grass, weeds, flowers. There are two replicas of bomb shelters, which we crawl inside; the darkness is remarkably cool. There is a monument next to an irrigation ditch where over 100 bodies were found. There is a wall of tiny colored tiles constructed to depict the horror and suffering of that day. Flames shoot up and around people running, falling, screaming. It is mostly red. There is a heated stillness to everything here. Not a sound. Not even the construction on the new museum is audible, like the horror of that day was the final voice, the village now enshrined in silence.

The woman leads us to a tiny room next to the temporary museum where we are offered hot tea and given a large, red book to record our thoughts and feelings. She leaves for a few minutes then returns, places a box on the table for donations. I do not remind her that we already paid entrance fees. The Australians and I leave the box untouched. I am glad to see, on this small measure, they feel as I do.

The guest book is passed to me, and I suddenly feel the pressure to write something profound and remorseful. I thumb through the hundreds of entries. A few from U.S. soldiers catch my eye; they all write their rank and years for their tours of duty. Many apologize. There are foreigners: Germans, Australians, Dutch, Japanese. Some write about war in general, how wrong and evil it is. Others are more personal. "The Americans should pay retribution," one German writes, ironically. "How can the Americans commit such atrocities?" a Japanese woman questions.

I write something general in the book, something about wanting better actions in the future, something about learning from our mistakes, about learning to have the character to admit our blunders. What I really want to write, though, is how strangely proud I am, at that moment, for that one hour, and on that one day in the relentless heat of a wounded village, to be an American confronting her nation's ugly past, to see how no one, no history, no country, is free from its dark moments, and it is this human frailty, in these imperfections that we can find unity, that we can build a future where My Lai 4s will never happen again.

*Rachel Louise Snyder is a Chicago-based writer specializing in foreign issues. Together with photojournalist Ann Maxwell, she has traveled to more than 40 countries and has written for* Ms., Mademoiselle, Salon, Seventeen, *the* Chicago Tribune, Hemispheres, *and* Country America.

PART FOUR

# IN THE SHADOWS

CLAIRE TRISTRAM

# Why I Have Never Seen the Mona Lisa Smile

*A forgotten umbrella leads
to a night of terror.*

APRIL IN PARIS. IT RAINED. I STOOD UNDER AN AWNING SOMEWHERE on the Champs d'Elysees. A black-haired man walked up to me and handed me his umbrella. And so I found myself at the vortex of several Gene Kelly movies at once. How charming, I thought. So many charming things will happen when you travel, if you only open yourself to the experience. He offered to walk me back to my hotel, insisting I keep the umbrella while he, head bare, walked in the rain. I could return his umbrella after I was safely home, he said. But would I mind a short detour, for another umbrella, since we were going by his apartment anyway? Of course not. Once there, four flights up an old building that appeared abandoned except for his apartment, he closed the door behind us, and another kind of movie began.

Sit down, he said, not unkindly. There was only one place to sit, a straight-backed wooden chair, painted dirty blue. I preferred to stand, I told him. Sit down, he said again, and pushed me forward. More a nudge, really. I must not exaggerate. I reached around him for the doorknob, shaking my head and smiling my regrets, and he hit me, hard, with the back of his hand. I sat on the chair. He locked the door, really locked it. Four deadbolts, two slide bolts, and a latch at the top. It would take thirty seconds to open that door. He took two steps to the refrigerator and hot plate and shelf along the back wall that was his kitchen. A single step was all it would take me to reach the door. But all those locks. I'd never make it. Then he was back, sitting across from me, on the bed. With a knife. A cook's knife, suitable for chopping onions or carrots. Not a proper rapist's knife at all. The room was so small that our knees touched.

He spoke to me then. I listened. I still believe it wasn't fear that kept me sitting there, quietly, feeling the heat of his knees against mine. Not fear. Not that. More this: for the first time in my life I was completely, baldly awake. I could see everything clearly. I felt in balance. Something was going to happen. But just now, we were at rest. Just now, he was only talking to me.

He told me the coffee in Paris was too expensive. He told me that his mother was a virgin, that there were strange circumstances surrounding his birth that were only now being revealed to him. He told me that his girlfriend had died in a car accident, and that he'd been despairing ever since, that people followed him, mysterious, sinister people, that all he wanted from me really was a hug, that my lips

*Nothing to fear but fear itself? Like most women I understand the philosophical concept, but less how to send fear running to its damp, dark closet. And I know I am not alone in this. At some forever-to-be-remembered point in the lives of all women they will lock arms with fear and dance a deadly tango. And it will not be just ordinary fear they pair with, but fear that can undo lives and lay barren the core of the self. Call it the enemy. Some women will size it up. Some will try to deny it. Some will take it dead on. And it will not be a matter of strength or weakness who is victorious, but who in its grip surrenders fastest, and in that moment of surrender glimpses the barest fragment of the thing fear fears most—faith.*

◆

—Jessica Maxwell,
*Femme d'Adventure*

were so beautiful. He told me I must really go to Lourdes while I was visiting France, that miracles really do happen there. Now and then he touched my hair, my lips, my leg with the hand that didn't hold the knife. He told me his best friend had stolen money from him. He told me no one had remembered his birthday that year. Then, his voice overflowing with desperate, mad grief, he told me that he was going to kill me, and he rested the knife, blade flat and cool, against the side of my face that he hadn't struck.

Somehow, deeply, even then, I felt as if I were protected by a special grace. I would get through this. Only later did I begin to believe that all murder victims must feel this same grace, and this incredulity, deeper than fear, that anything bad would never really happen to them. I waited, so still, so calm. I could see the tip of the knife below my left eye. My posture was very good.

He took the knife away and reached under the bed with a manic swiftness, pulling out a photo album and smiling at me, brightly, as if he'd suddenly remembered why he had invited me. We looked at the photos together, one by one. His trip to Egypt last autumn. Page after page of him standing alone, sullen and squinting, in front of the ruins. Now that the knife had been withdrawn, I was afraid again. Ask questions, I thought. Keep him happy. I was filled with the understanding that as long as the pictures lasted, so would the knife remain next to him on the bed instead of resting on my face or buried in my eye.

A cat jumped on his lap. Where was the cat before? Somewhere. It startled us both. He dropped the photo album and grabbed his precious knife again, glaring at me as if I had somehow betrayed him. He held the point of the knife under the cat's neck. I am going to kill this cat, he told me, in a petulant whisper, as if I had forced him to this outcome. His words filled me with relief. I leapt immediately to the fragile hope that only one blood sacrifice would be required that night. Kill the damn cat, I thought.

He sighed and pushed the cat off his lap. Will you lie down here with me a while, he asked, just until morning? I told him I didn't think so. Lie down with me or I'll kill you, he said. So I did. He nestled close to me, like a child, his head resting on my shoulder. It's possible that he slept, except that his grip never loosened either on the knife or on my hair, which he clenched in the other hand. I lay there with him, until dawn. He seemed then to let go of me a little. I moved the knife-arm to one side and slid away from him, standing up. I waited by the window. It seemed terribly important to not leave before he released me. I was afraid that he would hear all of those bolts turning and wake up, wild-eyed, and stab me after all. I looked out. It had begun to snow. Four flights down, an old woman was sweeping the courtyard with a push broom. He opened his eyes.

"I'll let you go if you promise to send me a postcard," he said.

I nodded. He stood, delighted, and began searching for paper, at last finding an old catalog on top of the refrigerator. He tore off the edge of one page and printed his name and address in tiny, perfect block letters, borrowing my pen. He handed the paper to me on the point of his knife, a dramatic flourish to assure me he'd meant no harm. Then he opened the door. He unlocked all of those locks. And I walked out into the morning.

I sent him a postcard, right from the train station, after collecting my bags and checking out of Paris a week early. "Be well," I wrote, and meant it. Then I threw his address away and rode the train to Madrid. I went to the Prado, where I stood for hours in front of *Saturn Devouring One of His Children*. Saturn's eyes in that painting were filled with sadness beyond knowing, as if he were mourning his children even as he killed and ate them. I knew those eyes very well. And after a while, standing there, it occurred that Goya had known that I was coming, and had painted those eyes just for me.

*Claire Tristram is a freelance journalist, travel writer, and past contributor to Travelers' Tales. Her short fiction has appeared in numerous literary journals and anthologies. Her first novel,* After, *was published in May 2004, and she has written about politics, science, and culture for Salon.com,* Wired, *and* The New York Times. *It took her twenty years to write about her trip to Paris, not because she felt so traumatized by it, but because she hated to admit to anyone that she could be so stupid.*

PAMELA CONLEY

# Souvenirs from Belize

*She left only footprints but brought
home more than pictures.*

ADVENTURES SOMETIMES DON'T STOP WHEN THE VACATION ENDS
and the suitcases have been unpacked. For me, the unbelievable
adventure began after my return and lasted for two long months.
My husband and I had spent two high-romance, adventure-packed
weeks in Belize, climbing the Mayan pyramids, birding the Jaguar
Preserve rain forests, and snorkeling the second-longest reef in the
world. One month later, the trip behind us, we were back to the rat
race and work when I discovered I had brought back some unexpected souvenirs.

It began on an overcast, cool day in the Jaguar Preserve. The
roads were muddy and almost impassable from the rain the night
before. There were a few times I thought our rented Suzuki would
not make it. The birds were active and noisy, and I was extremely
excited as I continued jumping out of the car and raising the binoculars to my eyes. I ripped my hat off my head impatiently and
tossed it in the backseat; a mistake that I would later never forget. I
could smell the dampness. I heard the alarm calls of the white-
crowned parrots as they flew over, and the constant hum of mosquitoes nearby my head. I remembered seeing shades of green that

I didn't know existed before. Vines reached for big dark leaves emanating energy so fast that I thought I could see them grow. My husband and I were bursting with excitement as we compared the scarlet-rumped and crimson-collared tanagers sitting next to each other in the same tree. An explosion of wing beats took off from a nearby tree, causing me to jump in alarm. I loved the thrill of the hunt to add these feathered jewels to my treasure list.

Several days later at Lamanai, we were standing on one of the highest Mayan pyramids we had ever climbed in Central America. We could see many other mounds around us, all covered with trees and vines, all waiting to be discovered as the one we were standing on. I remembered the thrill of coming down that pyramid and hearing the brazen bark explode from the howler monkeys above us. Through my binoculars, I saw the big male puff himself up to appear even more immense. A mother with a baby on her back took a daring leap from a swinging vine and landed on a branch of a nearby tree. Again, the jungle exploded in a raucous, rowdy roar as the group of monkeys raged overhead.

We completed our trip with a stay at Ramons Reef on Ambergris Cay, enjoying the warm tropical sun and snorkeling the second-largest barrier reef in the world. We floated gently and quietly on top, as we watched a school of squid swimming smoothly underneath us. I memorized the sensation as I dove down and became one with a bright school of fish. Frigate birds sailed in the warm breeze above us.

One month later, I was not feeling well. I found three oozy sores, close together on the back of my head. My lymph glands swelled up like balloons, and I was running a low fever off and on. I went to a doctor who examined me and said that these sores on my head looked like infected bites. He sent me home with some antibiotics. Another two weeks went by and two of the sores became larger. I also started to suffer from what I called sharp zingers. These were needlelike pains in my head that lasted only a few seconds and were sporadic. Clearly, the antibiotics were not working.

My husband scheduled an appointment with his dermatologist

for me. She examined my head and finally with a doctor's routine composure said, "This is unlike anything I have ever seen. I'm going to send you to surgery and have them open up these sores and see what is going on."

A slow, creeping sensation of dread began to trickle through me. Sometimes, when fear takes over, we are able to mask our panic with a protective layer of calmness. I responded with a fake self-assured smile, "Whatever you think, doctor."

"Lets call surgery and make an appointment now," she said.

I left feeling numb. I sat staring out the window when I returned home pondering in silence what was happening to me. Did I get bit by a spider while I was in Belize? Where did it happen? Did it happen at Lamanai or at the Jaguar Preserve?

One long week later, I was finally on my way to the surgery. My husband went with me as support, but I suspected more out of curiosity. I explained to the surgeon what he was suppose to do. He looked at me with blatant disbelief. Let me see if I'm getting this right? You want me to open up these sores and see what is inside? I was moved into a larger room, and the surgeon went off looking for the dermatologist who had scheduled my appointment. When he returned, he appeared even more unsure. What little confidence I had was gone now. Trusting this doctor with a knife to my head was almost as bad as the proposition of continuing to live in this frightening condition.

There I was lying on my stomach face down when the doctor put a needle to my head and inserted lanocaine near one of the bumps. I heard the doctor exclaim, "Oh my God, its coming up."

My husband yelled, "Oh, honey, you won't believe this. He's got a long neck and little sensory projections." I felt as though I had just given birth to an alien. Apparently, this exotic creature did not like the lanocaine and had come directly up to the surface.

The surgeon removed the second one from my head in much the same way he did the first one. My head was stitched up, and I lost some hair but at least the ordeal was over. Or so I thought.

These strange animals were white and approximately ⅜ inches long with a crown of sensory organs on the head. We stood staring at these creatures in amazement. The nurse appeared pale and in a quiet voice said, May I leave now, doctor? My husband and I asked the surgeon if we could keep one of these freeloading transients. We were now going to begin investigating to find out just who these aliens were.

My husband returned that night with a big text in his hands which he slammed down on the table with a loud, decisive thump and said, "Here he is." His scientific name was *Dermatobia hominus,* but to most of the natives of Belize, he is known as the dreaded botfly.

The life cycle began when a mosquito was seized by a botfly who laid its eggs on the stomach of the mosquito. The mosquito was released and flew away to look for a furry host. As the mosquito fed, the blood temperature of the host caused the eggs to hatch within seconds and the larvae crawled into the hole made by the mosquito proboscis or a hair follicle. They then began to grow and incubate for five to eighteen weeks. After that period, if they had been allowed to complete their full life cycle, they would have fallen out to pupate in the soil for another few weeks before they turned into an adult fly and flew away. The zingers I had been experiencing were when they decided to do their aerobics. We also discovered, that I had picked them up at the Jaguar Preserve. These botflies were found only to live in highland rain forests.

One month went by and I was having lunch at work when I felt another zinger doing the Watusi in my head. I thought, *no, it's not possible.* I asked my coworker and friend, who had a strong stomach, to look and see if there was another large bump on my head.

She said, "Oh, yes, I can see the air bubble go up and down when it breathes." On that afternoon, I called and got an appointment with a doctor immediately.

The doctor (another one), said he was glad to meet the Botfly Lady.

The first surgeon, had taken the botfly specimen all over the hospital and grossed everybody out. I had instant fame at the hospital. After removing the last of the freeloading transients from my head, he said, "Congratulations, you have given birth to your third botfly."

★

What continued to amaze me about this experience was the way other people reacted. My husband and I are great naturalists and interested in all life cycles. Through this intimate involvement of being chosen to be a host for *Dermatobia hominus*, I actually felt empathy for them.

Most people registered anything from fear to repulsion, and some were afraid that they might get it. Other than fear in the beginning when I didn't know what it was, the horrid zingers, having my head cut into three times, and three bald spots on the back of my head, I wouldn't have missed this experience of rejection and revulsion by all my friends for anything.

Am I ready to go back to Belize? In a minute. But the next time I go to the Jaguar Preserve, I plan to wear my hat and lots of mosquito repellent.

*Pamela Conley was an international flight attendant for eighteen years and an international travel consultant for a major insurance company for eight years. She is now a freelance writer and still traveling and bird-watching when not in her redwood garden in Northern California. She writes a weekly nature and birding column for the* Bodega Bay Navigator.

# Where Is the Girl Who Speaks English?

*In many parts of the world,*
*education is for boys only.*

"Do you paint your hair?" a small boy asks me in English. It's midmorning at 10,000 feet in northwest Nepal. The boy and his friends have skipped school to check us out.

"How old are you?" queries another boy. "Where is your husband?" asks a third.

I sit in a Himalayan field in Simikot with a dozen trekkers. About twenty schoolboys have found us. "Where are your sisters?" I ask them. "Where is a girl who speaks English?"

The boys shrug and ask, "Camera?" I let them look through my telephoto lens. I make the camera pull a mountain, then a grazing horse, then one of their friends toward us. The boys shriek and laugh.

Our group starts hiking up into the Himalayas, toward Tibet. It will take us a week on this steep mountain path, an old and active trade route that follows the Karnali River.

Nearby, girls sing in harmony while they cultivate the wheat and barley sprouts in the terraced fields. This region is newly opened to Westerners, open provided they buy the expensive trekking permits.

At Kermi village we rent a tiny schoolyard, a pocket of rare flat land etched in the side of the ravine. Eight schoolboys scramble onto the little school roof, where they perch to watch the pitching of our yellow tents.

When the boys come down to look at us more closely, I dig out a phrase book. I try, *"Tapaaiko naam ke ho?"* (What is your name?). Then I venture, *"Kati janaa didibahini?"* (How many sisters do you have?). They giggle and chatter and don't understand.

The English teacher arrives. "The school is just for boys," he explains. As men so often tell us on this trip, he says that girls only want to work in the fields and help at home. We hear once again that the girls don't want to go to school and that their families don't want them to go to school.

Two days later we visit another school, a monastery. The young apprentice monks shine in their clean maroon robes and saffron undershirts. They are beginning twenty-three years of education. "How much education do the nuns get?" we ask. None at all, we are told.

It goes like this for a whole week as we climb to the prayer flags and painted skulls and snowy mountains of Tibet. We are scheduled to visit Tibet for three weeks, and we begin by walking around the great pilgrimage mountain Kailas.

> $\mathcal{I}$n today's world, two-thirds of the children who never finished school are girls. Two-thirds of the one billion people who remain illiterate are women.
>
> ◆
>
> —MBB & PM

But after eleven days the Chinese cancel our visas and escort us out. They won't let us take our trucks to Lhasa. They force us to an unexpected extra one-week hike, through the Himalayas, down into Nepal.

When we finally reach Simikot, we are greeted by local children—all boys. They play Frisbee and soccer with us.

I have still not found a girl who speaks English. We will fly out first thing tomorrow.

By late afternoon most of my friends are in their tents. Some nap.

Others write in their journals. I look for an elusive pair of clean underwear. Suddenly I hear a little girl's voice. A tiny face smiles at my open tent door.

"Elbow," she says firmly, and whacks one of hers.

"Head," she says, and bops herself on the side of her head.

"I've been looking for you," I say.

"Mouth," she says, and slaps hers.

"Here you are," I say, getting out the pens and paper I brought for her. "Here you are at last."

*Joan Zimmerman was born in Britain and now lives in California. She earned her doctorate in physics from Oxford University in 1971. Her travel articles on Tibet and Nepal have appeared nationally, most recently in* Travelers' Tales Nepal. *She has also published poems in* Quarry West, Writing for Our Lives, *and* Coast Lines, *and she is a past winner of the Mary Lonnberg Smith Poetry Award. Her day job is a software designer, and she is immensely grateful to her writing friends for their frequent reminders that "writers write."*

JO ANN BEARD

⋆ ⋆ ⋆

# Out There

*Where are Thelma and Louise*
*when you need them?*

IT ISN'T EVEN 8 A.M. AND I'M HOT. MY REAR END IS WELDED to the seat just like it was yesterday. I'm fifty miles from the motel and about a thousand and a half from home, in a little white Mazda with 140,000 miles on it and no rust. I'm all alone in Alabama, with only a cooler and a tape deck for company. It's already in the high 80s. Yesterday, coming up from the Keys through Florida, I had a day-long anxiety attack that I decided last night was really heat prostration. I was a cinder with a brain; I was actually whimpering. I kept thinking I saw alligators at the edge of the highway.

There were about 400 exploded armadillos, too, but I got used to them. They were real, and real dead. The alligators weren't real or dead, but they may have been after me. I'm running away from running away from home.

I bolted four weeks ago, leaving my husband to tend the dogs and tool around town on his bicycle. He doesn't love me anymore, it's both trite and true. He does love himself, though. He's begun wearing cologne and staring into the mirror for long minutes, trying out smiles. He's become a politician. After thirteen years he came to realize that the more successful he got, the less he loved me. That's how he put it, late one night. He won that

267

screaming match. He said, gently and sadly. "I feel sort of embarrassed of you."

I said, "Of what? The way I look? The way I act?"

And he said, softly, "Everything, sort of."

And it was true. Well, I decided to take a trip to Florida. I sat on my haunches in Key West for four weeks, writing and seething and striking up conversations with strangers. I had my thirty-fifth birthday there, weeping into a basket of shrimp. I drank beer and had long involved dreams about cigarettes; I wrote nearly fifty pages on my novel. It's in my trunk at this very moment, dead and decomposing. Boy, do I need a cup of coffee.

There's not much happening this early in the morning. The highway looks interminable again. So far, no alligators. I have a box of seashells in my backseat, and I reach back and get a fluted one, pale gray with a pearly interior, to put on the dashboard. I can do everything while I'm driving. At the end of this trip, I will have driven 3,999 miles all alone, me and the windshield, me and the radio, me and the creepy alligators. Don't ask me why I didn't get that last mile in, driving around the block a few times or getting a tiny bit lost once. I didn't though, and there you have it. Four thousand sounds like a lot more than 3,999 does; I feel sort of embarrassed for myself.

My window is broken, the crank fell off in Tallahassee on the way down. In order to roll it up or down, I have to put the crank back on and turn it slowly and carefully, using one hand to push up the glass. So, mostly I leave it down. I baked like a biscuit yesterday, my left arm is so brown it looks like a branch. Today I'm wearing a long-sleeved white shirt to protect myself. I compromised on wearing long sleeves by going naked underneath. It's actually cooler this way, compared to yesterday when I drove in my swimming suit top with my hair stuck up like a fountain on top of my head. Plus, I'm having a nervous breakdown. I've got that wild-eyed look.

A little four-lane blacktop running through the Alabama countryside, that's what I'm on. It's pretty, too, better than Florida, which was billboards and condos built on old dump sites. This is like driving between rolling emerald carpets. You can't see the two lanes going in the opposite direction because there's a screen of trees. I'm starting to get in a good mood again. The best was Georgia, coming down. Willow trees and red dirt and snakes stretched out alongside the road. I kept thinking, that looks like a *rope*, and then it would be a huge snake. A few miles later I would think, that looks like a *snake*, and it would be some snarl of something dropped off a truck.

Little convenience store, stuck out in the middle of nothing, a stain on the carpet. I'm gassing it up, getting some coffee. My white shirt is gaping open, and I have nothing on underneath it, but who cares, I'll never see these people again. What do I care what Alabama thinks about me. This is a new and unusual attitude for me. I'm practicing being snotty, in anticipation of being dumped by my husband when I get back to Iowa.

I swagger from the gas pump to the store, I don't even care if my boobs are roaming around inside my shirt, if my hair is a freaky snarl, if I look defiant and uppity. There's nothing to be embarrassed of. I bring my coffee cup along and fill it at the counter. Various men, oldish and grungy, sit at tables eating eggs with wadded-up toast. They stare at me carefully while they chew. I ignore them and pay the woman at the counter. She's smoking a cigarette, so I envy her.

"Great day, huh?" I ask her. She counts out my change.

"It is, honey," she says. She reaches for her cigarette and takes a puff, blows it up above my head. "Wish I wudn't in *here*."

"Well, it's getting hotter by the minute," I tell her. I've adopted an accent in just four weeks, an intermittent drawl that makes me think I'm not who everyone thinks I am.

"Y'all think this's hot?" she says idly. "*This* ain't hot."

When I leave, the men are still staring at me in a sullen way. I get in, rearrange all my junk so I have everything handy that I need, choose a Neil Young tape and pop it in the deck, fasten the belt, and then move back out on the highway. Back to the emerald carpet and the road home. Iowa is creeping toward me like a panther.

All I do is sing when I drive. Sing and drink: coffee, Coke, water, juice, coffee. And think. I sing and drink and think. On the way down I would sing, drink, think, and weep uncontrollably, but I'm past that now. Now I suffer bouts of free-floating hostility, which is much better. I plan to use it when I get home.

A car swings up alongside me so I pause in my singing until it goes past. People who sing in their cars always cheer me up, but I'd rather not be caught doing it. On the road, we're all singing, picking our noses, embarrassing ourselves wildly; it gets tiresome. I pause and hum, but the car sticks alongside me so I glance over. It's a guy. He grins and makes a lewd gesture with his mouth. I don't even want to say what it is, it's that disgusting. Tongue darting in and out, quickly. A python testing its food.

I hate this kind of thing. Who do they think they are, these men? I've had my fill of it. I give him the finger, slowly and deliberately. He picked the wrong day to mess with me, I think to myself. I take a sip of coffee.

He's still there.

I glance over briefly and he's making the gesture with his tongue again. I can't believe this. He's from the convenience store, I realize. He has on a fishing hat with lures stuck in it. I saw him back there, but I can't remember if he was sitting with the other men or by himself. He's big, overweight, and dirty, wearing a thin, unbuttoned shirt and the terrible fishing hat. His passenger-side window in down. He begins screaming at me.

He followed me from that convenience store. The road is end-

> *I*t is not easy to move through the world alone, and it is never easy for a woman. You must keep your wits about you. You mustn't get yourself into dark places you can't get out of. Keep money you can get to, an exit behind you, and some language at your fingertips. You should know how to strike a proud pose, curse like a sailor, kick like a mule, and scream out your brother's name, though he may be 3,000 miles away.
>
> ◆
>
> —Mary Morris,
> *Nothing to Declare: Memoirs of a Woman Traveling Alone*

less, in front there is nothing, no cars, no anything, behind is the same. Just road and grass and trees. The other two lanes are still invisible behind their screen of trees. I'm all alone out here. With him. He's screaming and screaming at me, reaching out his right arm like he's throttling me. I speed up. He speeds up, too, next to me. We're only a few feet apart, my window won't roll up.

He's got slobber on his face, and there's no one in either direction. I slam on my brakes and for an instant he's ahead of me, I can breathe, then he slams on his brakes, and we're next to each other again. I can't even repeat what he's screaming at me. He's telling me, amid the hot wind and poor Neil Young, what he wants to do to me. He wants to kill me. He's screaming and screaming, I can't look over.

I stare straight ahead through the windshield, hands at ten and two. The front end of his car moving into my lane. He's saying he'll cut me with a knife, how he'll do it, all that. I can't listen. The front end of his Impala is about four inches from my white Mazda, my little car. This is really my husband's car, my beloved's. My Volkswagen died a lingering death a few months ago. There is no husband, there is no Volkswagen, there is nothing. There isn't even a Jo Ann right now. Whatever I am is sitting here, clenched hands on the wheel, I've stopped being her, now I'm something else. I'm absolutely terrified. He won't stop screaming it, over and over, what he's going to do.

I refuse to give him an inch. I will not move one inch over. If I do he'll have me off the road in an instant. I will not move. I speed up, he speeds up, I slow down, he slows down, I can see him out of the corner of my eye, driving with one hand, reaching like he's grabbing me with the other. "You whore," he screams at me. "I'll *kill* you, I'll *kill* you, I'll *kill* you…."

He'll kill me.

If I give him an inch, he'll shove me off the road and get his hands on me, then the end will begin in some unimaginable, unspeakable style that will be all his. I'll be an actor in his drama. We're going too fast, I've got the pedal pressed up to 80, and it's wobbling, his old Impala can probably do 140 on a straightaway like this. There will be blood; he won't want me to die quickly.

I will not lose control, I will ride it out, I cannot let him push me over onto the gravel. His car noses less than two inches from mine; I'm getting rattled. My God, he can almost reach me through his window, he's moved over in his seat, driving just with the left hand, the right is grabbing the hot air. I move over to the edge of my seat, toward the center of the car, carefully, without swerving.

In the rearview mirror a speck appears. Don't look, watch your front end. I glance up again; it's a truck. He can't get me. It's a trucker. Without looking at him, I jerk my thumb backward to show him. He screams and screams and screams. He's not leaving. Suddenly a road appears on the right, a dirty and rutted thing leading off into the trees. He hits the brakes, drops behind, and takes it. In my rearview mirror, I see that the license plate on the front of his car is buried in dried mud. That road is where he was hoping to push me. He wanted to push my car off the highway and get me on that road. He was hoping to kill me. He was hoping to do what maniacs, furious men, do to women alongside roads, in woods. I can't stop pressing too hard on the gas pedal. I'm at 85 now, and my leg is shaking uncontrollably, coffee is spilled all over the passenger seat, the atlas is wet, Neil Young is still howling on the tape deck. By force of will, I slow down to 65, eject the tape, and wait for the truck to overtake me. When it does, when it comes up along beside me, I don't look over at all, I keep my eyes straight ahead. As it moves in front of me, I speed up enough to stay two car lengths behind it. It says *England* on the back, ornate red letters, outlines in black. England.

That guy chased me on purpose, he *hated* me, with more passion than anyone has ever felt for me. Ever. Out there are all those decomposing bodies, all those disappeared daughters, discovered by joggers and hunters, their bodies long abandoned, the memory of final desperate moments lingering on the leaves, the trees, the mindless stumps and mushrooms. Images taped to tollbooth windows, faces pressed into the dirt alongside a path somewhere.

I want out of Alabama, I want to be in England. The air is still a blast furnace. I want to roll my window up, but I'd have to stop and get the crank out and lift it by hand. I'm too scared. He's out there still, waiting behind the screen of trees. I have to follow England until I'm out of Alabama. Green car, old Impala, unreadable license plate, lots of rust. Seat covers made out of that spongy stuff, something standing on the dashboard, a coffee cup or a sad Jesus. The fishing hat with a sweat ring around it right above the brim. Lures with feathers and barbs. I've never been so close to so much hatred in my whole life. He *wanted* to *kill* me. Think of England, with its white cows and broken-toothed farmers and dark-green pastures. Think of the Beatles. I'm hugging the truck so closely now I'm almost under it. Me, of all people, he wanted to kill. Me. Everywhere I go I'm finding out new things about myself. Each way I turn, there it is. It's Jo Ann he wanted to kill.

By noon I want to kill him. I took a right somewhere and got onto the interstate, had the nerve to pee in a rest area, adrenaline running like an engine inside me, my keys threaded through my fingers in case anyone tried anything. I didn't do anything to earn it, I realize. His anger. I didn't do anything. Unless you count giving him the finger, which I don't. He earned it.

As it turned out, my husband couldn't bring himself to leave me when I got back to Iowa, so I waited awhile, and watched, then disentangled myself. History: we each got ten photo albums and six trays of slides. We took a lot of pictures in thirteen years. In the early years, he looks stoned and contented, distant; in the later years, he looks straight and slightly worried. In that last year he only appears by chance, near the edges, a blur of suffering, almost out of frame.

Just before we split, when we were driving somewhere, I told him about the guy in the green car. "Wow," he said. Then he turned up the radio, checked his image in the rearview mirror, and smiled sincerely at the passing landscape.

*Jo Ann Beard won a 1997 Whiting Foundation Award for her book,* The Boys of My Youth, *in which this story appears. Her work also has appeared in* The New Yorker *and* Story *magazines, among other publications. She attended the nonfiction writing program at the University of Iowa, and now lives with her dog in Ithaca, New York.*

JENNIFER DUFFY

# Fever

*Down and out in Rajasthan.*

THE ARUN HOTEL IN JODHPUR WAS A NARROW, THREE-STORY building near the bus terminal. My guidebook described it as "good, clean, and handy." Its own business card claimed "hygenic self contained comfortable Rooms. Best Arrangement for Auspicious Occasions." They gave me a room without windows and a ceiling fan that didn't work.

The hotel clerk leaned against the door while he chewed his betel, swung his keys, and eyed me with a look of unabashed salaciousness.

"Madam," he addressed me, staring at my breasts, "Where is your husband?"

I considered lying. "I don't have one."

"You are American?"

"Yes." He smiled. I should have lied.

"In America you have free love."

"No we don't have free love."

"Yes, you do!"

I ignored him while I cased the dingy room—no visible roaches and a door I could padlock from the inside. Being in no mood to look for something better, I threw my backpack down on the mattress. I had plans to catch a train to Jaisalmer the next day and only needed a place to sleep.

In what remained of the afternoon, I walked aimlessly through the old section of Jodhpur. There is not a more colorful sight in India than the streets of a Rajasthani city as the sun sets. Women wearing mirrored skirts of brilliant reds and yellows catch darts of fleeting light as they gracefully maneuver great brass jugs of water above them through the crowds. The shadows of cows and camels, rickshaws and bicycles seem less hurried against the white walls of homes and temples, and children selling marigolds and artichokes squint in the sunlight as you pass. I sat on the marble steps of a deserted bathing ghat and enjoyed a blissful moment of solitude before a group of children spotted me and clamored for baksheesh. I was feeling a little dizzy, and on my way back to the Arun I bought several bottles of drinking water and a roll of coarse toilet paper.

Sleep that night was murky with fever. I got up every few hours, slipped on my rubber thongs, and shuffled down the hallway hoping to purge the sickness from my system. With each trip, a shoe-shine man, who must have regularly roamed the halls of the Arun in the middle of the night, greeted me at my door with his monotonal offer: "Shine?" Droning his service, he followed me down the hall to the toilet, eyes fixed on my shoes. Patiently he stood outside and proceeded with the litany: "Shiiiine. Shiiiine. Shiiiine," while I squatted in misery. Then together, again and again, we shuffled back to my room to the dull beat of his offer.

I awoke to angry voices in the hallway. My head was spinning and my body ached. I looked at my watch: four more hours until the train. I took some Nuprin and resigned myself to spending the morning in bed.

The room smelled like a sweaty night of agitated sleep and disturbing dreams. The only light came from a narrow opening over the door. I stared at the torn screen that covered it and realized the opening was big enough for someone to crawl through. Commotion resonated from everywhere in the Arun. Men argued loudly just outside my door. I needed to get to the toilet, but I didn't want anyone to know I was in there alone.

I closed my eyes and tried to relax. Everything hurt. I drank more water and checked my watch. My eyes burned. I kicked the sheet off and pulled it up again. Suddenly it was time to leave, and I was getting hotter and hotter.

I panicked when I saw I had a temperature of 106.

Calmly, very calmly, I packed my bag and went downstairs.

"I'm sick and I need to see a doctor." There was no response from either of the two men behind the Arun reception desk, eyes intent on a small black-and-white television—a cricket game. I could hear the announcer's comments and the shrieks of the crowd from TVs all over the hotel.

"Excuse me." Louder, "Hello!"

"Yes, madam," in his best brusque and intimidating manner, "What is it?"

"I'm sick and I need to see a doctor. Do you…"

"Sick. Why are you sick?"—demanding, three-quarters of an ear to the television set.

"I don't know. I…"

India scored. Or won. Or did something worthy of utter bedlam in the office and in the stairwell behind me. People rushed excitedly up and down the steps, swinging wide arcs with their bodies as they rounded the landing. I was having a hard time standing up.

The man did a double take in the midst of his celebrating, remembering I was there: "I don't know any doctor. Why don't you rest," and I was dismissed with a wave of the hand.

I went outside, smacked by the heat and dust of the day, and crossed the street to where several autorickshaw drivers were drinking *chai* and heatedly discussing something—probably cricket. They scattered to their vehicles like children racing to be the first in line when they saw me coming.

I climbed into the nearest rickshaw. "I'm sick and I need to see a doctor." The driver's face registered complete incomprehension.

Let me finish my tea, he said in that universal language of gesture, smile, nod, and muttering of native tongue.

I might die right here if we don't go now, I said in the same language. He put down his glass and hopped into the driver's seat, glancing back at me with a troubled look.

"Doctor," I said. Nothing happened. "Hospital?" He just stared at me. I stuck my finger down my throat and pretended to vomit— A flash of understanding and a roar of the motor.

The next thing I remember is screeching to a halt in front of the local tourist hotel. I'm sure I paid the driver, but I don't recall haggling the price. I don't remember anything about the lobby of the hotel either. I do remember saying "I'm sick" to Rajiv, who was at work behind the reception desk, and collapsing into a heap.

Rajiv was a man of average stature, probably in his late twenties, with shiny black hair and soft, but distinguished, features. He had a full mustache and was wearing a white shirt and brown pants. I don't believe I ever saw him wear anything different. He brought me tea and I sat up a little to drink it. I was in an institutional green room adjacent to the hotel office, stretched out on a dark-green vinyl couch. The blinds were drawn.

"How do you feel now, madam?" Rajiv said in a measured, even tone. There was nothing of the chaos of India in this room.

"Not very good. Do you know a doctor?"

He came back shortly and said a doctor would be there in a few hours. I could stay on the couch. "Just rest. You can sleep." He sounded so calm. He asked me questions in his soft, steady voice; questions with nice one-word answers. His calmness was a bit disquieting; he must want something, I thought. Everyone in India wanted something. How could he be so calm?

I put my arm over my eyes. My head started to scream. I was getting hotter and hotter until I thought I would burst. The couch spun. I needed to breathe.

Then suddenly it became very amusing. I was much calmer. It seemed absurd to be there. In that room. Me. In India. In the desert. Dying! On vinyl furniture. How funny. I fell asleep.

The doctor was a big, ugly man with bulging eyes and betel-stained teeth. He barged into the room carrying a black doctor's bag, set it down, yanked out a stethoscope, and put it to my chest. In a most decisive manner, he said something I couldn't understand.

"What?" He still hadn't looked at me.

"Malaria."

"What!" I was not too far gone to know I did not have malaria.

"Bugs," he said, opening and closing the fingers and thumbs of both hands fiercely in front of my face like the jaws of giant mosquitoes with big bulging eyes and betel-stained teeth.

"But I couldn't have malaria; I…"

"This is Malaria!" He snapped together the jaws of his black bag, loudly. "Take this with the juice of a lemon." Something was scribbled on a crumpled piece of yellow paper.

"What is this?"

"It is for The Malaria!" his right arm swinging. And he took his fifty rupees and ran.

I sobbed. Actually, I tried to sob. Calm, steady, smiling Rajiv came in and sat down.

"Malaria," I said.

Rajiv bobbed his head and planted his forefingers together in front of his lips.

"I don't have malaria."

Rajiv just looked at me.

"Look, I should go to the hospital."

"Madam," and he paused, as if to impress on me the gravity of the situation, "This is India."

I tried to sit up. Hysteria was rising again. I was reaching the end of my rope. Rajiv sat erect in his chair, his fingers in front of his lips, and didn't say a word. I closed my eyes and tried to sleep.

Suddenly I had to get out of there. "Can I call Delhi? The Embassy?"

It was a terrible connection. The angry voice at the other end shrilled distantly through the archaic phone receiver. "You people," she said, "get yourself into…static…We're just…static…and think we…static…static…responsible. If you were my child, I…static… two aspirin and go to bed."

All I had wanted was the name of a doctor.

I couldn't lie on the couch forever. I offered Rajiv a tip, which was perfectly logical, and figured I would…I don't know what I thought I would do. I couldn't very well go back to the Arun; I couldn't even sit up. Puzzled and a little insulted, Rajiv refused the money. I vaguely remember swallowing three Nuprin and getting into a bed at the hotel.

Rajiv stopped by my room that evening, and I asked him to call another doctor. The following morning a doctor with a greasy forehead and thick lips knocked at the door. He waddled his large polyester-covered belly into the room, dragged a chair to my bedside, sat down hard, and spread his legs wide. "Hi," I said weakly, eyeing him with careful disgust, "I have this fever." He grunted and looked at me leisurely before his short, hairy fingers touched my hot skin, measured my pulse, poked at my abdomen, and cautiously slid between my legs.

"Get out of here," I said.

And he did.

I decided to get better. I simply had no choice. Dawns came misty and pink, and nights were always a disappointment. I lay in one of the twin beds and studied the dingy, blank walls. The room was a deluxe. It had a door to a balcony and a hot-water tap. Once I went out on the balcony to look but there was nothing to see.

I was miserably alone. Rajiv came for an hour during his break and sometimes for a few minutes in the evening. Once he even came on his day off. I looked forward to his visits with apprehension and uncertainty. I had been cheated, leered at, grabbed and harassed in India. I had learned to walk the streets with my arms across my chest, bargain with gritted teeth, and sleep with my money belted to my body. What was I doing letting a stranger into my room? I stashed my valuables under the mattress and dragged myself to the door when he knocked.

Rajiv brought tea, bottled water, bananas, toast, and often an egg when he came. He accepted no payment and shrugged thanks. He was my link to life outside, but he brought me no news of events, only timeless conversation. He sat in the chair at the end of the bed, and in his steady, soothing voice, told me tales of Rajasthan. I listened with my eyes closed and envisioned the glorious events he described atop the hill in Jodhpur where an ancient fort stood. I remember few details, only the calming sound of his voice and tranquil images.

Rajiv believed I was going to get better. He asked me no questions—nothing of family, where I was from, or what I was doing alone in Jodhpur—and never attempted to give me advice or make a decision on my behalf. Slowly and cautiously, I began to trust him.

Then late one night, I lay still on my back basking in the moonlight and cool breeze that streamed in through the locked screen door. I stared, entranced, at the full moon, which showed itself exactly in the two-foot gap between the overhang of the roof and the top of the balcony wall. Suddenly there was blackness in the space above the wall, and the room became dark. Very, very slowly a silent figure, crouched on the edge of the slim wall, swung his legs around and gingerly lowered himself to the floor of my balcony. Moonlight poured into the room again, and the silhouette turned and reached for the door. "What are you doing!" I sat up and shrieked. The figure disappeared over the wall in an instant, and with a burst of adrenaline I ran to the door and slammed it shut.

The man had looked exactly like Rajiv. When he knocked the next day and the next, I didn't answer.

In daylight, the prowler seemed tragic and ridiculous. When night came, my eyes were transfixed on the door. Now the room was hot and still. I thrashed around in bed. The fever went up and down but would not break. My stomach twisted with pain and I cried hot, useless tears.

I pored over the grim descriptions of symptoms of diseases of insanitation in my guidebook. I seemed to have almost everything: "Fatal if untreated"; "Feels like imminent death." I had to go home. I was not the sort of person who just died in a hotel room in India. The book said an Indian Airlines desk was in the hotel lobby. When I tried to go buy a ticket to Delhi, I fainted.

The ceiling was filthy and the curtains were ugly. The sheets stank. Sleep came easily and I awoke in a sweat. I would send a telegram. Who would come get me? In the afternoon, a band of women marched under my window banging on pots and pans: a demonstration against killing widows.

I crawled to the door and waited for someone to walk down the hall. The linoleum floor was cool and dirty. After a long time, a man from Jaipur passed and agreed to bring me fruit and water from the market. I ate the bananas and finished the water. Rajiv knocked the following day and I let him in.

The third doctor was short and round, with a balding head and a pleasant demeanor. He wore loose white cotton garments and shuffled his feet when he walked. He examined me and smiled and patted my arm and told me I had typhoid.

"What's typhoid?"

"It is holes in the intestine."

"How can you say I have typhoid without even taking any tests?" That afternoon someone came to my room to draw blood. I watched as he unwrapped the sterile packaging, wiped the crease of my elbow, and dropped the needle on the floor. I didn't have the energy to protest when he picked it up and stuck it in my arm.

The doctor gave me great pink pills to take three times a day and told me I could not eat solid food. He held my hand and said "Will you be my friend?" over and over. I lived on tea and pineapple juice, which Rajiv brought from the market in rusty cans.

In three days the fever broke, and the doctor patted my arm and triumphantly proclaimed it must not have been typhoid. I sat on the floor of the shower with my eyes shut tight and let the tepid water cascade over my body.

My ribs were sticking out and my skin was gray. I stood in front of the mirror and decided I looked too sick to go home. Besides, I hadn't finished my trip.

Rajiv stretched his smile and said, of course, you're getting better. He showed me to a rooftop terrace just down the hall and helped me stand for a minute in the sunshine. Below us taxis and rickshaws, camels and people jostled noisily for position in a chaotic intersection. The markets, houses, and glistening marble temples of the city extended for hazy miles of desert and haphazard development. In the distance, the fort I had imagined from his stories rose on a stark hill, surrounded by the narrow alleys and brilliant-white dwellings of old Jodhpur. Everything looked remarkably sharp and beautiful to me.

I expected Rajiv to visit, but I never saw him again. As soon as I was strong enough to lift my pack, I went to the train station and bought a ticket out of town.

The hotel bill was expensive, but I didn't care. I tried not to step in cow dung as I worked my way through the crowds to the station. People were aggressively hawking tea and sweets to passengers through the train windows while the families who lived on blankets on the platform covered their faces and slept. I asked a man with a suitcase which train was going to Jaisalmer. "Follow me," he said.

*One day Jennifer Duffy set off for Asia, where she lived, worked, and traveled for most of the next ten years. She is now a writer and ceramic artist, and lives in Peterborough, New Hampshire.*

PART FIVE

# THE LAST WORD

SUSAN SPANO

# My Mother's Boots

*Following in her mother's footsteps, a daughter*
*finds the world at her feet.*

TEN YEARS AGO I SPENT A WEEK WALKING THE CHALK DOWNS OF Wiltshire, a county about 75 miles west of London. It was May, and the paths I tramped were sloppy. But I was prepared, because I'd packed a pair of thirty-year-old boots my mother had produced from the bottom of a closet before I left and bestowed on me, her youngest daughter. They served me well in England, led me past ruins of Iron Age forts, took me up the mossy steps of medieval churches, and finally came home encrusted with gray Wiltshire clay.

I had no reason to summon my mother's boots to duty again until a year or so later, when I was assembling my gear for a Kentucky spelunking adventure. At the time, I was just starting to really travel, which is why that trip became an exercise in taking risks and testing my limits. On it I did a lot of things I probably shouldn't have, like climbing into caves without a flashlight and hiking alone on trails known to be sunbathing spots for poisonous snakes. I still like to get a rise out of my mother, so when I got home I told her about my adventures. She has been a worrywart for as long as I've known her, but she just smiled and said that a person can strike out in boots like hers without fear of snakebite.

After many excursions in my mother's boots, I've begun to suspect that they are magic. I never wear them without seeing inspiring sights, experiencing life and nature more deeply, and coming home changed. I can rarely say how, but more and more this is the whole reason I travel.

My mother's boots are chestnut tan, Boy Scout standard issue, purchased about the time she bought a virtually identical pair for my brother, while suiting him up to win a chestful of merit badges. They are lined with wrinkles now, familiar to a certain Italian shoe repairman in the West Village of New York, who told me to throw them away two springs ago before I went for a hike along the Brittany coast. But I insisted that he sew the tongues back in, flew to France, and set off—at first barefoot in the sand north of Saint-Malo, and then trustingly shod all the way to Mont Saint-Michel. I do know how that walk changed me. I realized that there is no good reason to be cynical, eating oysters in Cancale and lying in clover above the Atlantic Ocean at the Pointe de la Varda. The world is still beautiful, if you have boots to see it from.

Back home, I called my mother and told her so. But she wanted to know something more mundane. "Are the bindings of the boots coming out? The bindings were coming out the year I didn't climb Longs."

For nearly ten summers during my childhood, my family spent two weeks at a YMCA camp just outside the Rocky Mountain National Park in Colorado. My mother broke in her boots while hiking over the Front Range. Whenever I lace them up, that place comes back to me, especially 14,256-foot Longs Peak, the patriarch of the Front Range.

"Why didn't you make Longs?" I prod. "Dad and Johnnie did."

"Because of you," she says, and then I recall the trial and tribulation I was to her when she took me for a climb. I remember crying all the way up Deer Mountain—puny by anyone's estimation, except mine, at ten.

My mother loved the mountains and cut a dashing figure among them, a red bandanna around her neck, her hair blowing free—so unlike the woman who, back home, cooked dinners, ironed, and spent every Saturday morning at the beauty parlor. When she tried to leave me at the Y's children's program, I cried and screamed, in effect, holding her prisoner while my father and brother conquered Longs.

We talk about this, she without rancor. "I'd rather be a mother than a mountain climber," she says. But then, "I know I could have made Longs."

Indeed, she could have. She has been to places I may never see, sunk her feet in the sand around the Pyramids and touched Alaskan glaciers. A social studies teacher, she saw travel as a way of learning. Because of her, my vacations are never vacant. Places mean something, and it's up to me to find out what it is—that's my mother's mandate. Besides being magical, her boots symbolize this.

But as a symbol, they're complex. When I climb mountains in them, I feel as if, by rights, my mother should be there, even though she's too old to do much walking now. I never could imagine making the kinds of sacrifices she made for her children, which is partly why I never had any. And she never pushed me.

I've wondered, though, what I'm missing. Could it be that life is really more about making sacrifices than reaching mountain summits? Is this what I'm to take from my mom—a woman who, in all respects, seems to me successful? Then why did she give me her boots, if not to urge me to climb on?

"We think back through our mothers if we are women," Virginia Woolf wrote.

On my fortieth birthday I climbed Longs, in my mother's boots, of course. I had a fellow hiker record my ascent with a camera, mostly for the benefit of my doubtful father and brother. When I got my pictures back, I stood in the camera shop amazed, because in the picture of me at the top, I looked so oddly like my mother. Oddly, because I'm the image of my dad. But on the top of Longs I looked like her.

My mother's boots are one legacy I guess I won't pass on. So, maybe they are more a link than a legacy, between mother and daughter, two travelers on the same journey.

*

*Susan Spano writes the "Her World" column and cover stories for the travel section of the* Los Angeles Times. *Her work has appeared in numerous books and magazines, she is a past winner of a Lowell Thomas Award, and she originated "The Frugal Traveler" column for* The New York Times' *travel section.*

# Recommended Reading

Allende, Isabel. *Aphrodite: A Memoir of the Senses*. New York: HarperPerennial, 1999.

Arvigo, Rosita. *Sastun: My Apprenticeship with a Maya Healer*. San Francisco: HarperCollins, 1995.

Baranay, Inez. *Rascal Rain: A Year in Papua New Guinea*. Sydney, Australia: Angus & Robertson, 1994; New York: HarperCollins, 1995.

Beard, Jo Ann. *The Boys of My Youth*. New York: Little, Brown and Company, 1998.

Bond, Marybeth, and Pamela Michael, eds. *A Mother's World: Journeys of the Heart*. San Francisco: Travelers' Tales, 1998.

Brooks, Geraldine. *Nine Parts of Desire: The Hidden World of Islamic Women*. New York: Anchor Books, 1995.

Bruns, Rebecca, et al. *Hidden Mexico*. Berkeley: Ulysses Press, 1992.

Bumiller, Elisabeth. *May You Be the Mother of a Hundred Sons: A Journey Among the Women of India*. New York: Random House, 1990.

Cain, Chelsea. *Dharma Girl: A Road Trip Across the American Generations*. Seattle, Seal Press, 1996.

Campbell, SueEllen. *Bringing the Mountain Home*. Tuscon: University of Arizona Press, 1996.

Carpenter, Dana, and Woody Winfree, eds. *I Am Beautiful: A Celebration of Women in their Own Words*. Bridgeport, Conn.: Rose Communications, 1996.

Connelly, Karen. *Touch the Dragon*. Winnipeg, Canada: Turnstone Press, 1992.

Cox, Lynn. *Swimming to Antarctica: Tales of a Long-Distance Swimmer.* New York: Knopf, 2004.

Ehrlich, Gretel. *Islands, The Universe, Home.* New York: Viking Penguin, 1991.

Erdrich, Louise. *Books and Islands in Ojibwe Country.* Washington, D.C.: National Geographic, 2003.

Fraser, Laura. *An Italian Affair.* New York: Vintage, 2002.

Gelman, Riga Golden. *Tales of a Female Nomad: Living at Large in the World.* New York: Three Rivers Press, 2002.

Gough, Laurie. *Kite Strings of the Southern Cross: A Woman's Travel Odyssey.* San Francisco: Travelers' Tales, 1999; Toronto: Turnstone Press, 1998.

Guillermoprieto, Alma. *Samba.* New York: Vintage Books, 1990.

Halliday, Ayun. *No Touch Monkey: And Other Travel Lessons Learned Too Late.* Seattle: Seal Press, 2003.

Hogan, Linda. *Dwellings: A Spiritual History of the Living World.* New York: W. W. Norton & Company, 1995.

James, Kelly. *Dancing with the Witchdoctor: One Woman's Stories of Mystery and Adventure in Africa.* New York: Perennial, 2002.

Jung, Anees. *Unveiling India: A Woman's Journey.* New Delhi: Penguin India, 1987.

Kizlos, Katherine. *The Olive Grove: Travels in Greece.* Hawthorn, Australia: Lonely Planet, 1997.

Maxwell, Jessica. *Femme d'Adventure: Travel Tales from Inner Montana to Outer Mongolia.* Seattle: Seal Press, 1997.

Mayes, Frances. *Bella Tuscany: The Sweet Life in Italy.* New York: Broadway, 1999.

Moore, Kathleen Dean. *Riverwalking: Reflections on Moving Water.* New York: Lyons & Burford Publishers, 1995.

Morris, Mary. *Nothing to Declare: Memoirs of a Woman Traveling Alone.* New York: Picador, 1998.

Nye, Naomi Shihab. *Never in a Hurry: Essays on People and Places.* Columbia: University of South Carolina, 1996.

Nzenza–Shand, Sekai. *Songs to an African Sunset: A Zimbabwean Story.* Oakland: Lonely Planet, 1997.

Peterson, Brenda. *Living by Water: True Stories of Nature and Spirit.* New York: Fulcrum, 2002.

Rees, Lucy. *The Maze: A Desert Journey.* New York: The Countryman Press, 1996.

Rogers, Susan Fox, ed. *Solo: On Her Own Adventure.* Seattle: Seal Press, 1996.

Scot, Barbara J. *The Violet Shyness of Their Eyes: Notes from Nepal.* Corvallis, Oreg.: Calyx Books, 1993.

Shaffer, Tanya. *Somebody's Heart is Burning: A Woman Wanderer in Africa.* New York: Vintage, 2003.

Sheldon, Dyan. *Dream Catching: On the Road Reluctantly.* London, Abacus, 1995.

Simon, Kate. *Mexico: Places and Pleasures.* New York: HarperCollins Publishers, 1984.

Solnit, Rebecca. *Savage Dreams: A Journey into the Hidden Wars of the American West.* Berkeley: University of California Press, 1999.

Steinbach, Alice. *Without Reservations: The Travels of an Independent Woman.* New York: Random House, 2002.

Stewart, Lucretia. *The Weather Prophet: A Caribbean Journey.* London, Vintage Books, 1996.

Vega, Janine Pommy. *Tracking the Serpent: Journeys to Four Continents.* San Francisco: City Lights Books, 1997.

Wakefield, Celia. *Under the Tabachin Tree: A New Home in Mexico.* Berkeley: Creative Arts Book Company, 1997.

# Index of Contributors

# Acknowledgments

We have been inspired, advised, encouraged, and comforted by each other. We would like to thank each other for mutual support and being cheerleaders for each others' lives and careers.

We would also like to give our heartfelt thanks to Tanya Pearlman for her tireless research, enthusiasm, and wonderful way with words.

A special thanks to Larry Habegger, James O'Reilly, Susan Brady, Deborah Greco and the entire Travelers' Tales family for their invaluable help. And especially to Lisa Bach for her enthusiasm, keen editorial sensibilities, and her fierce devotion to women's literature and travel.

Pamela would like to give special thanks to her dear friend Arthur Schmidt for his good ear and warm heart.

Marybeth would like to thank her supportive, encouraging husband who has tolerated and understood her absences in mind and body while working on this book.

"Looking for Abdelati" by Tanya Shaffer first appeared in *SALON*.com at http://www.salon.com. Copyright © 1999 by Tanya Shaffer. Reprinted by permission of the author.

"The Spanish Church" by Catherine Watson published with permission from the author. Copyright © 1999 by Catherine Watson.

"Special Delivery" by Lindsy van Gelder first appeared in *SALON*.com at http://www.salon.com. An online version remains in the *Salon* archives. Reprinted with permission.

"The Boatman's Gift" by Pamela Michael published with permission from the author. Copyright © 1999 by Pamela Michael.

"Mysteries of Life" by Anne Lamott first appeared as "Mysteries of Life: How My Boy was Saved by the Seals" in *SALON*.com at http://www.salon.com. Copyright © 1996 by Anne Lamott. Reprinted by permission of the author.

"L'Air du Temps" by Marilyn McFarlane published with permission from the author. Copyright © 1999 by Marilyn McFarlane.

"Light on a Moonless Night" by Laurie Gough excerpted from *Kite Strings of the Southern Cross: A Woman's Travel Odyssey* by Laurie Gough. Copyright © 1998, 1999 by Laurie Gough. Reprinted by permission of Travelers' Tales Inc. and Turnstone Press

"On Italian Time" by Mary Morris reprinted from the August 1995 issue of *Travel & Leisure*. Reprinted by permission of Ellen Levine Literary Agency, Inc. Copyright © 1995 by Mary Morris.

"Unpaved Roads" by Virginia Barton Brownback reprinted from the May/June 1996 issue of *Modern Maturity*. Copyright © 1996 by Virginia Barton Brownback. Reprinted by permission of the author.

"Following the Tracks Back" by Sekai Nzenza-Shand excerpted from *Songs to an African Sunset: A Zimbabwean Story* by Sekai Nzenza-Shand. Copyright © 1997 by Sekai Nzenza-Shand. Reproduced by permission of Lonely Planet Publications.

"Guardians of the Dark" by Marybeth Bond published with permission from the author. Copyright © 1999 by Marybeth Bond.

"And Miles to Go" by Letty Cottin Pogrebin. Copyright © 1996 by Letty Cottin Pogrebin. Originally appeared in the April 21, 1996 issue of *The New York Times*. No part of this material may be reproduced in whole or part without the express written permission of the author or her agent.

"Kenya on Horseback" by Ann Jones reprinted from the August 1994 issue of *Town & Country*. Copyright © 1994 by Ann Jones. Reprinted by permission of the author.

"Sex, Yams, and the Kula Ring" by Lynn Ferrin reprinted from the March 16, 1986 issue of *Great Escapes*. Copyright © 1986 by Lynn Ferrin. Reprinted by permission of the author.

"River of Life" by Leila Philip published with permission from the author. Copyright © 1999 by Leila Philip.

"Venice" by Frances Mayes excerpted from *Bella Tuscany: The Sweet Life in Italy* by Frances Mayes. Copyright © 1999 by Frances Mayes. Used by permission of Broadway Books, a division of Random House, Inc., and Transworld Publishers. All rights reserved.

"Winter Walk" by Deborah Johansen published with permission from the author. Copyright © 1999 by Deborah Johansen.

"Extended Family" by Alison DaRosa reprinted from the October 19, 1997 issue of *The San Diego Union-Tribune*. Copyright © 1997 by Alison DaRosa. Reprinted by permission of the author.

"The Center of Nowhere" by Barbara Ras published with permission from the author. Copyright © 1999 by Barbara Ras.

"Ndume" by Rosalind Aveling published with permission from the author. Copyright © 1999 by Rosalind Aveling.

"Girl Kayak Guides of Juneau" by Candace Dempsey published with permission from the author and *UnderWire*.msn.com. Copyright © 1999 by Candace Dempsey.

"Scorpion Hunting" by Diane Rigda published with permission from the author. Copyright © 1999 by Diane Rigda.

"Bathing Suit Anxiety" by Marilyn Lutzker published with permission from the author. Copyright © 1999 by Marilyn Lutzker.

"The Stowaway" by Celia Wakefield originally appeared as "Nineteen Kids and No Pencil" excerpted from *Under the Tabachin Tree: A New Home in Mexico* by

**Additional Credits (Arranged alphabetically by title)**

Selection from *Aphrodite: A Memoir of the Senses* by Isabel Allende copyright
© 1998 by Isabel Allende. Reprinted by permission of HarperCollins
Publishers, Inc.

Selection from *Bringing the Mountain Home* by SueEllen Campbell copyright
© 1996 by SueEllen Campbell. Reprinted by permission of the University of
Arizona Press.

Selection by Amy Greimann Carlson published with permission from the author.
Copyright © 1999 by Amy Greimann Carlson.

Selection from "Escapes Artists" by Gina Hyams published with permission
from the author. Copyright © 1999 by Gina Hyams.

Selections from *Femme d'Adventure: Travel Tales from Inner Montana to Outer Mongolia*
by Jessica Maxwell copyright © 1997 by Jessica Maxwell. Reprinted by permission of Seal Press.

Selection by Judy Wade excerpted from *Gutsy Women: Travel Tips and Wisdom for
the Road* by Marybeth Bond and Pamela Michael. Copyright © 1996 by Judy
Wade. Reprinted by permission of Judy Wade.

Selection from "A Heart to Heart Workout" copyright © by Letty Cottin
Pogrebin. Originally appeared in *The New York Times*. No part of this material
may be reproduced in whole or part without the express written permission
of the author or her agent.

Selection from *Hidden Mexico* by Rebecca Bruns, reprinted by permission of
Ulysses Press and the Rebecca L. Bruns Trust. Copyright © 1992 by Ray
Riegert.

Selection by Sarah excerpted from *I Am Beautiful* edited by Dana Carpenter and
Woody Winfree. Reprinted by permission of Rose Communications, L.L.C.

Selection from "Imbrication" by Rebecca Lawton published with permission from
the author. Copyright © 1999 Rebecca Lawton.

Selection from "Island Life" by Marguerite Rigoglioso published with permission
from the author. Copyright © 1999 by Marguerite Rigoglioso.

Selection from *Islands, The Universe, Home* by Gretel Ehrlich copyright © 1991 by
Gretel Ehrlich. Used by permission of Viking Penguin, a division of Penguin
Books USA, Inc., and Darhansoff & Verrill Literary Agency.

Selection from "The Kill Hole" by Linda Hogan excerpted from *Dwellings: A
Spiritual History of the Living World* by Linda Hogan. Copyright © 1995 by
Linda Hogan. Reprinted by permission of W. W. Norton and Company.

Selection from "The Lakshman Rekha" by Shana Sippy published with permission from the author. Copyright © 1999 by Shana Sippy.

Selection from *May You Be the Mother of a Hundred Sons: A Journey Among the
Women of India* by Elisabeth Bumiller published by Random House, Inc.
Copyright © 1990 by Elisabeth Bumiller.

Selection from *The Maze: A Desert Journey* by Lucy Rees copyright © 1996 by
Lucy Rees. Reprinted by permission of W. W. Norton and Company.

Selection from *Mexico: Places and Pleasures* by Kate Simon copyright © 1988 by
Kate Simon. Reprinted by permission of HarperCollins Publishers, Inc. and
International Creative Management, Inc.

# *About the Editors*

Marybeth Bond is well known in the world of travel. She is the award-winning author/editor of five women's travel books in the Travelers' Tales series, was the travel expert for CBS Evening Magazine, and was also a featured guest on *The Oprah Winfrey Show*. Her travel articles have been published worldwide in magazines such as *Islands* and *Shape*, and newspapers such as the *San Francisco Examiner* and *Kuala Lumpur Star*. She is also the travel columnist for a Northern California newspaper. She has appeared on more than 250 television and radio shows and her Travelers' Tales book, *Gutsy Women: Travel Tips and Wisdom for the Road*, was featured on the *Today* show and *The Oprah Winfrey Show*.

She has been a marketing executive for Xerox and Honeywell, spokesperson for Fortune 500 companies, travel editor/expert for ivillage.com and Outside Radio, consultant for international tour operators, and frequent guest on CNN, Oxygen, NPR, and "Ask the Experts" (*Reader's Digest*).

Marybeth has hiked, cycled, climbed, dived, and kayaked her way through six continents and more than seventy countries around the world, from the depths of the Flores Sea to the summit of Mt. Kilimanjaro. She has trekked in the Himalayas and ridden camels across the Thar and Sahara Deserts. At age thirty, she left her corporate job in the computer industry, put all her possessions in storage, bought a one-way ticket to Bangkok, and took off. She continued to travel for two years around the world solo, and on that journey met her future husband in Kathmandu. In the past two decades she has traveled with her daughters and husband from Lombok to Luxor, Zanzibar to Killarny.

Marybeth is a member of the Society of American Travel Writers and was an advisor for Northwestern University's Medill School of Journalism. She lives in Northern California with her husband, two children, and a dog.

Pamela Michael has been a freelance writer for over twenty years. In the 1980's she wrote for technical audio journals and later began doing curriculum development for the Discovery Channel. While director of the United Nations'-sponsored International Task Force on Media and Education, she edited a groundbreaking book on media's role in education called *The Whole World is Watching* (UNESCO 1992).

In her youth, Pam crossed the U.S. several times, by thumb, rail, bus, and car, sometimes with her infant son in tow (and often her Irish wolfhound as well). She didn't leave the continent until she was over forty, but has made up for lost time, visiting over thirty countries in the last decade. In 1997, she won the British Airways/Book Passage Travel Writing Grand Prize for her story, *The Khan Men of Agra*. In 2003, the anthology she edited with her writing group, *Wild Writing Women: Stories of World Travel* won the National Association of Travel Journalists Award for Best Travel Book of 2002. Her most recent book, *River of Words: Images and Poetry in Praise of Water*, won the 2004 Skipping Stones Award for "best book on ecology or nature."

Pam has written numerous articles on education, community, media, and travel for a variety of magazines and newspapers, including the *San Francisco Examiner, Resurgence, Odyssey,* Salon.com, *Shape, Orion Afield, Maiden Voyages,* and others. Her Travelers' Tales books include, in addition to *A Woman's Passion for Travel, A Mother's World: Journeys of the Heart* (also with Marybeth Bond), and *The Gift of Rivers.*

Michael is the co-founder (with former U.S. Poet Laureate Robert Hass) of River of Words, an international non-profit organization that fosters environmental and art education in affiliation with The Library of Congress. River of Words operates one of the first art galleries in the country devoted to children's art, Young at Art, in Berkeley, California.

Also a longtime radio journalist, Pamela is the travel editor of KPFA-fm in the San Francisco Bay Area. Her earlier radio work includes writing and producing a four-part series on Buddhism in the United States, narrated by Richard Gere. Pamela lives on the "morning side" of Mt. Diablo in Northern California.

# TRAVELERS' TALES

T H E   P O W E R   O F   A   G O O D   S T O R Y

## New Releases

**THE BEST**                 **$16.95**
**TRAVELERS' TALES 2004**
**True Stories from Around the World**
*Edited by James O'Reilly, Larry Habegger & Sean O'Reilly*
The launch of a new annual collection presenting fresh, lively storytelling and
compelling narrative to make the reader laugh, weep, and buy a plane ticket.

**INDIA**                 **$18.95**
**True Stories**
*Edited by James O'Reilly & Larry Habegger*
"*Travelers' Tales India* is ravishing in the texture and variety of tales."
                          —*Foreign Service Journal*

**A WOMAN'S EUROPE**          **$17.95**
**True Stories**
*Edited by Marybeth Bond*
An exhilarating collection of inspirational, adventurous, and entertaining stories
by women exploring the romantic continent of Europe. From the bestselling
author Marybeth Bond.

**WOMEN IN THE WILD**        **$17.95**
**True Stories of Adventure and Connection**
*Edited by Lucy McCauley*
"A spiritual, moving, and totally female book to take you around the world and
back."                               —*Mademoiselle*

**CHINA**                 **$18.95**
**True Stories**
*Edited by James O'Reilly, Larry Habegger & Sean O'Reilly*
A must for any traveler to China, for anyone wanting to learn more
about the Middle Kingdom, offering a breadth and depth of experience
from both new and well-known authors; helps make the China
experience unforgettable and transforming.

**BRAZIL**                 **$17.95**
**True Stories**
*Edited by Annette Haddad & Scott Doggett*
*Introduction by Alex Shoumatoff*
"Only the lowest wattage dim bulb would visit Brazil without reading this
book."            —Tim Cahill, author of *Pass the Butterworms*

**THE PENNY PINCHER'S PASSPORT TO**    **$14.95**
**LUXURY TRAVEL (2ND EDITION)**
**The Art of Cultivating Preferred Customer Status**
*By Joel L. Widzer*
Completely updated and revised, this 2nd edition of the popular guide to travel-
ing like the rich and famous without being either describes, both philosophically
and in practical terms, how to obtain luxurious travel benefits by building rela-
tionships with airlines and other travel companies.

# Women's Travel

## A WOMAN'S EUROPE $17.95
**True Stories**
*Edited by Marybeth Bond*
An exhilarating collection of inspirational, adventurous, and entertaining stories by women exploring the romantic continent of Europe. From the bestselling author Marybeth Bond.

## WOMEN IN THE WILD $17.95
**True Stories of Adventure and Connection**
*Edited by Lucy McCauley*
"A spiritual, moving, and totally female book to take you around the world and back."
— *Mademoiselle*

## A MOTHER'S WORLD $14.95
**Journeys of the Heart**
*Edited by Marybeth Bond & Pamela Michael*
"These stories remind us that motherhood is one of the great unifying forces in the world"
— *San Francisco Examiner*

## A WOMAN'S WORLD $18.95
**True Stories of Life on the Road**
*Edited by Marybeth Bond*
*Introduction by Dervla Murphy*

— ★ ★ ★ —
*Lowell Thomas Award*
*—Best Travel Book*

## A WOMAN'S PASSION FOR TRAVEL $17.95
**More True Stories from A Woman's World**
*Edited by Marybeth Bond & Pamela Michael*
"A diverse and gripping series of stories!"
—Arlene Blum, author of
*Annapurna: A Woman's Place*

# Food

## ADVENTURES IN WINE $17.95
**True Stories of Vineyards and Vintages around the World**
*Edited by Thom Elkjer*
Humanity, community, and brotherhood comprise the marvelous virtues of the wine world. This collection toasts the warmth and wonders of this large extended family in stories by travelers who are wine novices and experts alike.

## HER FORK IN THE ROAD $16.95
**Women Celebrate Food and Travel**
*Edited by Lisa Bach*
A savory sampling of stories by the best writers in and out of the food and travel fields.

## FOOD $18.95
**A Taste of the Road**
*Edited by Richard Sterling*
*Introduction by Margo True*

— ★ ★ ★ —
*Silver Medal Winner of the*
*Lowell Thomas Award*
*—Best Travel Book*

## THE ADVENTURE OF FOOD $17.95
**True Stories of Eating Everything**
*Edited by Richard Sterling*
"Bound to whet appetites for more than food."
— *Publishers Weekly*

## THE FEARLESS DINER $7.95
**Travel Tips and Wisdom for Eating around the World**
*By Richard Sterling*
Combines practical advice on foodstuffs, habits, and etiquette, with hilarious accounts of others' eating adventures.

# Travel Humor

**SAND IN MY BRA AND**    $14.95
**OTHER MISADVENTURES**
**Funny Women Write from the Road**
*Edited by Jennifer L. Leo*
"A collection of ridiculous and sublime travel
experiences."
       —*San Francisco Chronicle*

**HYENAS LAUGHED AT ME**   $14.95
**AND NOW I KNOW WHY**
**The Best of Travel Humor and Misadventure**
*Edited by Sean O'Reilly, Larry Habegger, and James
O'Reilly*
Hilarious, outrageous and reluctant voyagers indulge
us with the best misadventures around the world.

**LAST TROUT IN VENICE**    $14.95
**The Far-Flung Escapades of an
Accidental Adventurer**
*By Doug Lansky*
"Traveling with Doug Lansky might result in
a considerably shortened life expectancy…but
what a way to go."
     —Tony Wheeler, Lonely Planet Publications

**NOT SO FUNNY WHEN**    $12.95
**IT HAPPENED**
**The Best of Travel Humor and
Misadventure**
*Edited by Tim Cahill*
Laugh with Bill Bryson, Dave Barry, Anne
Lamott, Adair Lara, and many more.

**THERE'S NO TOILET PAPER…ON THE ROAD LESS TRAVELED**      $12.95
**The Best of Travel Humor and Misadventure**
*Edited by Doug Lansky*

——— ★ ✦ ★ ———

*Humor Book of the Year*
*—Independent Publisher's Book
Award*

——— ★ ✦ ★ ———

*ForeWord Gold Medal
Winner—Humor
Book of the Year*

# Travelers' Tales Classics

**COAST TO COAST**    $16.95
**A Journey Across 1950s America**
*By Jan Morris*
After reporting on the first Everest ascent in
1953, Morris spent a year journeying across
the United States. In brilliant prose, Morris
records with exuberance and curiosity a time
of innocence in the U.S.

**TRADER HORN**    $16.95
**A Young Man's Astounding Adventures
in 19th Century Equatorial Africa**
*By Alfred Aloysius Horn*
Here is the stuff of legends—thrills and
danger, wild beasts, serpents, and savages.
An unforgettable and vivid portrait of a
vanished Africa.

**THE ROYAL ROAD**    $14.95
**TO ROMANCE**
*By Richard Halliburton*
"Laughing at hardships, dreaming of beauty,
ardent for adventure, Halliburton has managed
to sing into the pages of this glorious book his
own exultant spirit of youth and freedom."
     —*Chicago Post*

**UNBEATEN TRACKS**    $14.95
**IN JAPAN**
*By Isabella L. Bird*
Isabella Bird was one of the most adventurous
women travelers of the 19th century with
journeys to Tibet, Canada, Korea, Turkey,
Hawaii, and Japan. A fascinating read.

**THE RIVERS RAN EAST**      $16.95
*By Leonard Clark*
Clark is the original Indiana Jones, telling the breathtaking story of his search for the legendary El
Dorado gold in the Amazon.

# Spiritual Travel

### THE SPIRITUAL GIFTS OF TRAVEL $16.95
**The Best of Travelers' Tales**
*Edited by James O'Reilly and Sean O'Reilly*
Favorite stories of transformation on the road that shows the myriad ways travel indelibly alters our inner landscapes.

### PILGRIMAGE $16.95
**Adventures of the Spirit**
*Edited by Sean O'Reilly & James O'Reilly*
*Introduction by Phil Cousineau*

*ForeWord Silver Medal Winner*
*— Travel Book of the Year*

### THE ROAD WITHIN $18.95
**True Stories of Transformation and the Soul**
*Edited by Sean O'Reilly, James O'Reilly & Tim O'Reilly*

*Independent Publisher's Book Award*
*—Best Travel Book*

### THE WAY OF THE WANDERER $14.95
**Discover Your True Self Through Travel**
*By David Yeadon*
Experience transformation through travel with this delightful, illustrated collection by award-winning author David Yeadon.

### A WOMAN'S PATH $16.95
**Women's Best Spiritual Travel Writing**
*Edited by Lucy McCauley, Amy G. Carlson & Jennifer Leo*
"A sensitive exploration of women's lives that have been unexpectedly and spiritually touched by travel experiences.… Highly recommended."
*— Library Journal*

### THE ULTIMATE JOURNEY $17.95
**Inspiring Stories of Living and Dying**
*James O'Reilly, Sean O'Reilly & Richard Sterling*
"A glorious collection of writings about the ultimate adventure. A book to keep by one's bedside—and close to one's heart."
—Philip Zaleski, editor,
*The Best Spiritual Writing series*

# Special Interest

### THE BEST TRAVELERS' TALES 2004 $16.95
**True Stories from Around the World**
*Edited by James O'Reilly, Larry Habegger & Sean O'Reilly*
The launch of a new annual collection presenting fresh, lively storytelling and compelling narrative to make the reader laugh, weep, and buy a plane ticket.

### TESTOSTERONE PLANET $17.95
**True Stories from a Man's World**
*Edited by Sean O'Reilly, Larry Habegger & James O'Reilly*
Thrills and laughter with some of today's best writers: Sebastian Junger, Tim Cahill, Bill Bryson, and Jon Krakauer.

### THE GIFT OF TRAVEL $14.95
**The Best of Travelers' Tales**
*Edited by Larry Habegger, James O'Reilly & Sean O'Reilly*
"Like gourmet chefs in a French market, the editors of Travelers' Tales pick, sift, and prod their way through the weighty shelves of contemporary travel writing, creaming off the very best."
—William Dalrymple, author of *City of Djinns*

### DANGER! $17.95
**True Stories of Trouble and Survival**
*Edited by James O'Reilly, Larry Habegger & Sean O'Reilly*
"Exciting…for those who enjoy living on the edge or prefer to read the survival stories of others, this is a good pick."
*— Library Journal*

### 365 TRAVEL $14.95
**A Daily Book of Journeys, Meditations, and Adventures**
*Edited by Lisa Bach*
An illuminating collection of travel wisdom and adventures that reminds us all of the lessons we learn while on the road.

### FAMILY TRAVEL $17.95
**The Farther You Go, the Closer You Get**
*Edited by Laura Manske*
"This is family travel at its finest."
—*Working Mother*

### THE GIFT OF BIRDS $17.95
**True Encounters with Avian Spirits**
*Edited by Larry Habegger & Amy G. Carlson*
"These are all wonderful, entertaining stories offering a *bird's-eye view!* of our avian friends."
—*Booklist*

### THE GIFT OF RIVERS $14.95
**True Stories of Life on the Water**
*Edited by Pamela Michael*
*Introduction by Robert Hass*
...a soulful compendium of wonderful stories that illuminate, educate, inspire, and delight."
—David Brower, Chairman of Earth Island Institute

### LOVE & ROMANCE $17.95
**True Stories of Passion on the Road**
*Edited by Judith Babcock Wylie*
"A wonderful book to read by a crackling fire." —*Romantic Traveling*

### A DOG'S WORLD $12.95
**True Stories of Man's Best Friend on the Road**
*Edited by Christine Hunsicker*
*Introduction by Maria Goodavage*

# Travel Advice

### THE PENNY PINCHER'S PASSPORT TO LUXURY TRAVEL $14.95
### (2ND EDITION)
**The Art of Cultivating Preferred Customer Status**
*By Joel L. Widzer*
Completely updated and revised, this 2nd edition of the popular guide to traveling like the rich and famous without being either describes, both philosophically and in practical terms, how to obtain luxurious travel benefits by building relationships with airlines and other travel companies.

### SAFETY AND SECURITY $12.95
### FOR WOMEN WHO TRAVEL
*By Sheila Swan & Peter Laufer*
"An engaging book, with plenty of first-person stories about strategies women have used while traveling to feel safe but still find their way into a culture."
—*Chicago Herald*

### SHITTING PRETTY $12.95
**How to Stay Clean and Healthy While Traveling**
*By Dr. Jane Wilson-Howarth*
A light-hearted book about a serious subject for millions of travelers— staying healthy on the road—written by international health expert, Dr. Jane Wilson-Howarth.

### THE FEARLESS SHOPPER $14.95
**How to Get the Best Deals on the Planet**
*By Kathy Borrus*
"Anyone who reads *The Fearless Shopper* will come away a smarter, more responsible shopper and a more curious, culturally attuned traveler."
—Jo Mancuso, *The Shopologist*

### GUTSY WOMEN $12.95
**More Travel Tips and Wisdom for the Road**
*By Marybeth Bond*
Second Edition
Packed with funny, instructive, and inspiring advice for women heading out to see the world.

### GUTSY MAMAS $7.95
**Travel Tips and Wisdom for Mothers on the Road**
*By Marybeth Bond*
A delightful guide for mothers traveling with their children—or without them!

# Destination Titles

**ALASKA**     $18.95
*Edited by Bill Sherwonit, Andromeda Romano-Lax, & Ellen Bielawski*

**AMERICA**     $19.95
*Edited by Fred Setterberg*

**AMERICAN SOUTHWEST**     $17.95
*Edited by Sean O'Reilly & James O'Reilly*

**AUSTRALIA**     $17.95
*Edited by Larry Habegger*

**BRAZIL**     $17.95
*Edited by Annette Haddad & Scott Doggett*
*Introduction by Alex Shoumatoff*

**CENTRAL AMERICA**     $17.95
*Edited by Larry Habegger & Natanya Pearlman*

**CHINA**     $18.95
*Edited by James O'Reilly, Larry Habegger & Sean O'Reilly*

**CUBA**     $17.95
*Edited by Tom Miller*

**FRANCE**     $18.95
*Edited by James O'Reilly, Larry Habegger & Sean O'Reilly*

**GRAND CANYON**     $17.95
*Edited by Sean O'Reilly, James O'Reilly & Larry Habegger*

**GREECE**     $18.95
*Edited by Larry Habegger, Sean O'Reilly & Brian Alexander*

**HAWAI'I**     $17.95
*Edited by Rick & Marcie Carroll*

**HONG KONG**     $17.95
*Edited by James O'Reilly, Larry Habegger & Sean O'Reilly*

**INDIA**     $18.95
*Edited by James O'Reilly & Larry Habegger*

**IRELAND**     $18.95
*Edited by James O'Reilly, Larry Habegger & Sean O'Reilly*

**ITALY**       $18.95
*Edited by Anne Calcagno*
*Introduction by Jan Morris*

**JAPAN**       $17.95
*Edited by Donald W. George & Amy G. Carlson*

**MEXICO**       $17.95
*Edited by James O'Reilly & Larry Habegger*

**NEPAL**       $17.95
*Edited by Rajendra S. Khadka*

**PARIS**       $18.95
*Edited by James O'Reilly, Larry Habegger & Sean O'Reilly*

**PROVENCE**       $16.95
*Edited by James O'Reilly & Tara Austen Weaver*

**SAN FRANCISCO**       $18.95
*Edited by James O'Reilly, Larry Habegger & Sean O'Reilly*

**SPAIN**       $19.95
*Edited by Lucy McCauley*

**THAILAND**       $18.95
*Edited by James O'Reilly & Larry Habegger*

**TIBET**       $18.95
*Edited by James O'Reilly & Larry Habegger*

**TURKEY**       $18.95
*Edited by James Villers Jr.*

**TUSCANY**       $16.95
*Edited by James O'Reilly & Tara Austen Weaver*
*Introduction by Anne Calcagno*

# Footsteps Series

### THE FIRE NEVER DIES
$14.95
**One Man's Raucous Romp Down the Road of Food,
Passion, and Adventure**
*By Richard Sterling*
"Sterling's writing is like spitfire, foursquare and jazzy with
crackle...."                                    —*Kirkus Reviews*

### ONE YEAR OFF
$14.95
**Leaving It All Behind for a Round-the-World Journey
with Our Children**
*By David Elliot Cohen*
A once-in-a-lifetime adventure generously shared, from the
author/editor of *America 24/7* and *A Day in the Life of Africa*

### THE WAY OF THE WANDERER
$14.95
**Discover Your True Self Through Travel**
*By David Yeadon*
Experience transformation through travel with this delightful,
illustrated collection by award-winning author David Yeadon.

### TAKE ME WITH YOU
$24.00
**A Round-the-World Journey to Invite a Stranger Home**
*By Brad Newsham*
"Newsham is an ideal guide. His journey, at heart, is into
humanity."                    —Pico Iyer, author of *The Global Soul*

### KITE STRINGS OF THE SOUTHERN CROSS
$14.95
**A Woman's Travel Odyssey**
*By Laurie Gough*
Short-listed for the prestigious Thomas Cook Award, this is an
exquisite rendering of a young woman's search for meaning.

*ForeWord Silver Medal Winner*
*— Travel Book of the Year*

—— ★ ★ ★ ——

### THE SWORD OF HEAVEN
$24.00
**A Five Continent Odyssey to Save the World**
*By Mikkel Aaland*
"Few books capture the soul of the road like The *Sword of
Heaven,* a sharp-edged, beautifully rendered memoir that will
inspire anyone."
            —Phil Cousineau, author of *The Art of Pilgrimage*

### STORM
$24.00
**A Motorcycle Journey of Love, Endurance,
and Transformation**
*By Allen Noren*
"Beautiful, tumultuous, deeply engaging and very satisfying.
Anyone who looks for truth in travel will find it here."
            —Ted Simon, author of Jupiter's Travels

*ForeWord Gold Medal Winner*
*— Travel Book of the Year*

—— ★ ★ ★ ——